Governance of Food Security Policies in India

Governance of Food Security Policies in India

Ch. Bala Ramulu
National Fellow, ICSSR

KALPAZ

ISBN: 978-93-5128-203-7

Price: ₹ 650

First Published, 2016

Published by

Kalpaz Publications
C-30, Satyawati Nagar,
Delhi – 110052
E-mail: kalpaz@hotmail.com
Ph.: 9212142040

Printed at: G. Print Process, Delhi

Cataloging in Publication Data—DK
Courtesy: D.K. Agencies (P) Ltd. <docinfo@dkagencies.com>

Balaramulu, Ch., author.
Governance of food security policies in India : a study in Andhra Pradesh / Professor Ch. Bala Ramulu.
pages cm
"Submitted to the Indian Council of Social Science Research, New Delhi, 2014."
Includes bibliographical references.
ISBN 9789351282037 (hardback)

1. Food supply—Government policy—India—Andhra Pradesh. 2. Food security—Government policy—India—Andhra Pradesh. 3. Agriculture and state—India—Andhra Pradesh. I. Indian Council of Social Science Research. II. Title.

HD9016.I43A53 2016 DDC 363.856095485 23

Contents

Acknowledgements

The present book is an outcome of the research project supported by Indian Council of Social Science Research, New Delhi. I am deeply indebted to the Council for awarding National Fellowship and granting financial support for undertaking the research project "Governance of Food Security Policies in India." I am grateful to the Council and the authorities, particularly Chairman, Professor Sukhadeo Thorat and Dr Sanchita Dutta, Deputy Director, for the support. I am grateful to the Centre for Economic and Social Studies, Hyderabad for giving affiliation and providing necessary environment to pursue my research. I am thankful to Professor Manoj Panda, Former Director, Professor S. Galab, Director and Professor M. Gopinath Reddy for their support and encouragement in the completion of the project work. Professor Samba Murthy, Senior Fellow, ICSSR, Sri, Venkataiah, Programme Coordinator and the Library staff have helped me at various stages of my work. The Administrative staff always extended cooperation in providing necessary environment in carrying out my project work. I am most indebted to them. Further, I acknowledge the services of Sri G. Edaiah, Dr P. Steeven and Sri. V. Sreenivas for their support and keen interest in the completion of this task.

Professor G. Hara Gopal, my teacher, guide and National Fellow, Indian Council of Social Science Research, New Delhi, has been a constant source of encouragement and inspiration in all my academic pursuits. Professor V.S. Prasad, my teacher and former Director of NACC, Bangalore gave me valuable guidance and encouragement to pursue this project. I am beholden to them. I would like to express my sincere thanks to Professor G. Sudharshanam, Head, Department of Political Science, University of Hyderabad for his unstinted support and encouragement in all my academic activities and his warmth and affection towards me. I express my thanks to Prof. P. Narashima Rao, Kaktiya University for his support at every stage of this work. I thank the Director, Gyan Publishing House and Kalpaz Publications for undertaking the publication of this work.

I am beholden to Kakatiya University, Warangal, Telangana State, which gave me an opportunity to serve as member of Faculty in the Department of Public Administration for more than three decades and enrich my academic insights.

Ch. Bala Ramulu

Abbreviation

AoA	: Agreement on Agriculture
ADM	: Archer Daniels Midland
AMCs	: Agricultural Marketing Committees
AP	: Andhra Pradesh
APL	: Above Poverty Line
APSCSCL	: Andhra Pradesh State Civil Supplies Corporation Limited
BPL	: Below Poverty Line
CSS	: Centrally Sponsored Scheme
CWFS	: Committee on World Food Security
DCP	: Decentralised Procurement
DPC	: District Planning Committees
FAC	: Food Advisory Committee
FCI	: Food Corporation of India
FICCI	: Federation of Indian Chamber of Commerce and Industry
FS	: Food Security
FAO	: Food and Agriculture Organisation
FCCI	: Federation of Chamber of Commerce and Industry
FPS	: Fair Price Shop
GCC	: Girijan Cooperative Corporation
GAIN	: Global Alliance for Improved Nutrition
GoI	: Government of India
GO	: Government Order
GR	: Green Revolution
HH	: Household
IBH	: Indian Business House
ICDS	: Integrated Child Development Service
IGOs	: International Governmental Organisations
IFPRI	: International Food Policy and Research Institute

IMF	: International Monetary Fund
ITDA	: Integrated Tribal Development Agency
KSY	: Kishore Sakti Yojana
MLA	: Member of Legislative Assembly
MLS	: Mandal Level Stock
MNC	: Multinational Corporation
MTs	: Metric Tonnes
NDA	: National Democratic Alliance
NFSA	: National Food Security Act
NFSM	: National Food Security Mission
NGOs	: Non-Governmental Organisations
NHRM	: National Health Rural Mission
NRLM	: National Rural Livelihood Mission
NNP	: National Nutrition Policy
NPAG	: Nutrition Programme for Adolescent Girls
NPM	: New Public Management
OF	: Operation Flood
PDS	: Public Distribution System
PESA	: Panchyat Extension Scheduled Act
PRI	: Panchayat Raj Institutions
PPP	: Public-Private Partnership
SERP	: Society for Elimination of Rural Poverty
SFDA	: Small Farmers Development Agency
SNP	: Supplementary Nutrition Programme
SRS	: Subsidized Rice Scheme
TDP	: Telugu Desam Party
TPDS	: Targeted Public Distribution System
TFAoA	: Trade Facilitation Agreement on Agriculture
UNDP	: United Nations Development Programme
UPA	: United Progressive Alliance
USDA	: United States Department of Agriculture
US PL	: United States Public Law
WB	: World Bank
WEF	: World Employment Programme
WFO	: World Food Programme
WHO	: World Health Organisation
WTO	: World Trade Organisation

Chapter–I

Introduction

Background of the Study

Food Security (FS) to the people has attracted the international and national attention and a matter of concern of governments the world over, in the recent past. Over the last few decades, International Governmental Organisations (IGOs), National Governments and the Non-Governmental Organisations (NGOs) are contributing substantially to the debates on what constitutes food and food security, the policies and governance system and making efforts to bring consensus among the governments and other stakeholders how food security can be ensured at global, national, state, household and individual levels?

The United Nations recognised the food security as one of the challenges of the modern government. The World Food Programme (WFP) - a branch of the United Nations and the world's largest organisation has unique network with national governments, UN partners and NGOs since 1961, in addressing hunger, malnutrition, child mortality, HIV and AIDS. The World Food Conference of 1974 recognised that world food security was a common responsibility of all the nations and that international approaches was needed to achieve improved world food security (Sarris and Taylor, 1976). The Committee on World Food Security (CWFS) established in 1974 as an intergovernmental body to serve as a forum in the Nations System for reviewing and follow-up of policies concerning world food security including production and physical and economic access to food.

The purpose of the CWFS is to improve coordination and guide synchronised action by a wide range of stakeholders in support of global, regional and country-led actions to prevent future food crises, eliminate hunger and ensure food security and nutrition for all human beings. The CWSF offers guidelines and recommendations for coherent action at the global, regional and country levels by the full range of stakeholders, while emphasising the central role of country ownership of programmes to combat food insecurity and malnutrition.

Several other institutions have been organising conferences on food security related concerns and highlighted subject at length. They include; The Conference on Environment and Development held in Rio de Janeiro in 1992 emphasised the need to ensure food security at all levels, within the framework of sustainable development. The joint FAO/WHO conference on nutrition, held in Rome in 1992, declared, "Hunger and malnutrition are unacceptable in a world that has both knowledge and resources to end this human catastrophe" and recognised that, "access to nutritionally adequate and safe food is a right of each individual." The World Conference on Human Rights (Vienna, 1993) emphasised the need to ensure that everyone enjoy a right to food. The International Conference on Population and Development (Cairo, 1994) highlighted the linkage between population growth and food production and the need to evolve global measures to satisfy the ever-growing food needs.

The World Summit on Social Development (Copenhagen, 1995) made a strong commitment to the campaign against hunger through its emphasis on poverty eradication. The fourth World Conference on Women (Beijing, 1995) drew the attention of the international community to the key role played by women in food production. The Habitat II Conference (Istanbul, 1996) specified the need to establish healthy linkages between rural and urban areas and emphasised the role of cities in ensuring proper food distribution and drinking water supply.

The 'G 33' group of developing countries (which now comprises 46 nations) has been calling for a revision of the Agreement on Agriculture (AoA) to enable it to address their national food security concerns, but have not had much success. Frustrated, the WTO's trade facilitation agreement is being made provisionally subject to progress on revision of the AoA. Since the AoA took effect in 1995, most exorbitant subsidies that wealthy countries give their farmers and agribusinesses are classified as non-distorting measures, described as 'green box' subsidies. These include direct income support to farmers, as well as financial support for environmental protection and regional development. Conversely, a majority of indebted developing countries, including India, are simply unable to provide adequate subsidies to their farmers because of fiscal constraints on their governments. These countries are also under simultaneous pressure from multilateral lenders such as the IMF and the World Bank, which also call for the removal of all kinds of subsidies.

As malnutrition is the dire concern of the developing countries, the private institutions/ associations are setting the agenda for nutrition in different countries, including India. These institutions establish role and legitimacy by associating themselves with key institutions and people. For instance, the GAIN (Global Alliance for Improved Nutrition) with 40 global companies is the significant player that maintains rapport with the governments and Nations Organisation bodies to scale up nutrition business network. The Lancet recently published 2013 series on maternal and child nutrition emphasising the consumption of nutrition food (Gupta *et.al,* 2014).

The Ministerial Conference at Bali in December 2013, emphasised on the livelihoods and food security of millions of marginal and small farmers and others in the developing countries. However, the Bali Package formulated by the WTO in Indonesia in 2013, on Trade Facilitation Agreement on Agriculture (TFAoA), which is aimed to fast track any movement of goods among countries by cutting down bureaucratic obligations is a major setback to the food security programmes. The problem with (TFAoA) is a clause that says farm subsidies cannot be more than 10 per cent of the value of agricultural production. If the cap is breached, other members can challenge it and go on to impose trade sanctions on the country. The US and other developed countries have raised objections to India's recent expansion of its National Food Security Act, 2013 (NFSA, 2013) terming it a trade-distorting agricultural subsidy. India justifies state procurement of crops in order to feed its populace. Other developing countries, including Pakistan, which regulates wheat procurement, employ a similar rationale. Nevertheless trade facilitation and food security agreements, was saved when India accepted a 'peace clause' granting its public (food) stockpiling efforts a four-year grace period (2017) until a more permanent solution to the global dispute over food reserves was hammered out.

All the above factors indicate that the IGOs and Private agencies are directly or indirectly influencing the food security policies in the developing countries, including India. This would not only affect the autonomy of the governments in formulating the policies but also its implementation process, as they are not being formulated based on the ground realities.

Indian Situation

Today, in India, it has become political agenda of all the political parties and groups/agencies. Though the Indian Constitution does not explicitly mention the right to food as a fundamental right, it is implicitly enshrined in Article 21 of the Indian Constitution as the fundamental right to life of every Indian citizen (Supreme Court, 2001). According to the Article 38 it is the responsibility of the State to secure a social order for the promotion of welfare of the people. The article specify that "State shall strive to promote the welfare of the people by securing and protecting as effectively as it may a social order in which justice, social, economic and political, shall inform all the institutions of the national life. Article 38 (2) necessities the State shall, in particular, strive to minimise the inequalities in income, and endeavour to eliminate inequalities in status, facilities and opportunities, not only amongst individuals but also amongst groups of people residing in different areas or engaged in different vocations." Article 39 categorically states that the "State shall direct its policy toward securing; (a) that the citizens have the right to have adequate means of livelihood; (b) the ownership and control of the material resources of the community are so distributed as best to sub-serve the common good; and (c) that the operation of economic system does not result in the concentration of wealth and means or production to the common determent. Article 41 states that State shall within the limits of its economic capacity and development make effective provision to ensure Right to Work to every citizen. But the Article 47 of the

Indian Constitution more explicitly direct that 'The State shall regard the raising of the level of nutrition and standard of living of its people and the improvement of public health as among its primary duties and, in particular, the State shall endeavour to bring about prohibition of the consumption, expect for medical purpose, of intoxicating drinks and of drugs which are injurious to health'. In addition to these, Constitutional provisions, the continuous struggles of the poor and left political parties and efforts of the civil society bodies, donor agencies and intervention of the Judiciary and others have compelled the national, state and local governments to adopt a development strategy and suitable legislation that guarantees food to the people and make the "Right to Food as a Fundamental Right" and eliminate poverty.

Development Model for Poverty Alleviation

India, during late 1940's and early 1950's, adopted the Western model for development emphasising on the neutrality of bureaucracy and commitment to socio-economic change. The development experience in India of the last six and a half decades reveals that Central and State Governments have evolved and experimented different strategies – starting from 'Growth with Trickle Down' (1950s), 'Green Revolution'(1960s), 'Growth with Social Justice' (1969), 'Minimum Needs Programmes' (1975), 'Structural Adjustment Programmes' (1991), 'Governance and Development'(1992),'Millennium Development Goals' (2000) 'Reforms with Human Face' (2004), 'Inclusive Growth' (2007) to 'New Public Management/ Good Governance/ Public Private Partnership' (2007) or 'Least Government and Maximum Governance' (2014) model now. The experience with the developmental policies reveals that fruits of economic growth have not benefited everyone uniformly. Some are left behind and some others are not touched by the benefits of economic growth. Globally it is proved that the so-called trickledown effect does not work in all the societies and India is no exception to this.

One of the mistakes of the development models is adopting one economic model and governance for all the societies, where there is enormous diversity in socio-economic and cultural setting, particularly food habits. The critics argue that a move towards the localisation of essential production, trade, health, education and other services is eminently possible if civil society organisations and the governance sensitively assist communities. There are thousands of Indian initiatives of decentralised development models in the areas: water harvesting, biodiversity conservation, food grain production, education, health, energy generation (Agarwal, A and Narain, S, 1997; and several others).

The IGOs and NGOs/donor agencies have covertly or overtly influenced the developmental strategies. The strategies instead of correcting century old problems such as inequalities, they succumbed to local conditions and did not make any significant positive impact on the society. The non-government sector has benefited very significantly from taking on a service delivery role. The NGOs/SHGs/CBOs as representatives of Civil Society are gaining a powerful stronghold in development process. In the interest of sustainability, most donors require that NGOs demonstrate a relationship with governments. State Governments themselves are vulnerable because they lack strategic planning and vision. A nexus of NGOs, political bodies, commercial organisations and major donors/funders, making decisions that have short-term outputs but no long-term affect, therefore, sometimes tightly binds them. NGOs in India are under regulated, political, and recipients of large government and international donor funds. NGOs often take up responsibilities outside their skill ambit. Governments have no access to the number of projects or amount of funding received by these NGOs (Deborah Eade, 2005). Recent IB report of Government of India on Impact of NGOs Development revels that the NGOs are misusing the foreign funds and sometimes working against launching of development projects (Bala Ramulu, Ch & AVN Reddy, 2014).

There are various reasons for this uneven development in the society. Modern economy is technology driven and not labour-intensive. High volume of high quality goods and services are produced with fewer labour hands (Bala Ramulu, Ch, 2004). In short, the modern economy is not generating much employment and sometimes it displaces and replaces labour with machines and tools. The fruits of economic reform are not evenly distributed and some are even deprived of the benefits. Some of the social groups are unable to be part of the economic reform, as they do not have the mandatory capacity to participate in the economic development process. Such groups need government intervention to ensure that they are not left behind in the development process and deprived of the benefits. The Poverty Alleviation Programmes (PAP), including food and nutrition-based interventions has not ensured food security to the people. An assessment of food security policies reveals that there is wide gap between the promise and performance. This is mostly due to the failure of the policies and its governance to reach the poor (Bala Ramulu, Ch, 2013).

The Hon'ble Supreme Court of India, in a Writ Petition No. (C) 196 of 2001 passed an order constituting a Committee to be headed by Hon'ble Mr Justice D. P. Wadhwa, Former Judge, and Supreme Court of India to look into the maladies affecting the proper functioning of the public distribution system (PDS) and to suggest remedial measures. In particular, the Committee was directed to focus on: (a) the mode of appointment of dealers; (b) the ideal commission or the rates payable to the dealers; (c) modalities as to how the food committees already in place, can function better; and (d) modes as to how there can be transparency in allotment of the food stock to be sold at the shops. This indicates the relevance of launching and implementation of food security programmes in the country.

The above factors obliged the national and state governments to initiate measures for ensuring food security to the people. The Government of India, in 2009, has promised to its people that it will bring legislation on right to food, which would give food guarantees for infants and children maternal entitlements, and special guarantees for vulnerable groups -such as those living with starvation, the destitute, persons affected by natural and human made disasters and migrants. President of India announced that in the Joint Session of the Parliament on 21st February 2011, legislating a Right to Food Act was among the government's highest priorities. Accordingly, the Parliament passed the National Food Security Bill, in August 2013. The President of India gave his assent to the Bill on September 12th, 2013. The objective of the Act is "to provide for food and nutritional security in human life cycle approach, by ensuring access to adequate quantity of quality food at affordable prices to people (67 per cent of population) to live a life with dignity. Thus, the courts and peoples movement have shown the way for the right to food to become a judicial legal entitlement and binding on every government. The Central Government has directed the State Governments to change or modify the respective State Acts in accordance with the NFSA, 2013, within one year.

However, the present NDA government disowns the NFSA. The High Power Committee appointed by NDA under the Chairmanship of former Union Minister for Food Shanta Kumar recommended sweeping changes in the mode of operation of Food Corporation of India (FCI) and downsizing the NFSA. These include reducing the coverage of Public Distribution System (PDS) from 67 per cent to 40 per cent of population, raising the issue prices to half of the relevant Minimum Support Price (MSP) and a gradual transition to cash transfer. The crux of the Committee argument is that PDS leakages are unacceptably high and cash transfers would save money. The report disputes the view that the recent PDS reforms have led to reduced leakages. Further, the implementation of the NFSA is being held up in many states due to prolonged delays in the release of socio-economic and caste census data and others (Editorial, EPW, and Jan. 2015). These trends reveal that the food security to all the people and all the time is a doubtful proposition. Against this backdrop, this study seeks to examine the governance of food security policies to rural poor in India. In this chapter, an attempt is made to present the concept of food, definitions of food security; food sovereignty; food insecurity; and the development model for food security/ poverty alleviation, which would give us deeper insights on the phenomenon.

Food and its Dimensions

Food, along with water, is basic foundation to human society as a whole. It is both a basic need and a basic pleasure to the individual. In the life of an individual, it is primary recurrent want, while in the wider sphere of society it determines...the nature of social groups and the shape their activities. Food is carefully chosen and classified means of social communication and the object of a richly expressive and varied aesthetic. Its production, storage and distribution are a provider of work and livelihoods and source of legitimacy to the governments. It is also a subject of conflict within the household, between social groups, between nations. Food may be a cause of dependence and subordination (Harriss-White, 1995).

Food has several dimensions. However, most important of them are food as nutritional commodity, as an economic commodity and as political commodity. As Audrey Richards explains: 'nutrition is more fundamental than sex' (quoted in Mintz, 1985). People starve when their energy and protein intake is not sufficient over a period. Food is also a source of profit in exchange. Traders, brokers, commission agents and/or other intermediaries in trade are less concerned with the nutritional content and function of food for human well-being than with price. For them, food is primarily a source of profit, to be purchased as cheaply as possible and sold for a much higher price. The result of this profit orientation can be speculation, impoverishment of the producers, artificial scarcity, and inadequate access to food by some who lack sufficient purchasing power and famines even when food is available in the market (Amartya Sen, 1991).

Food is also a political commodity, as it is so essential for human survival food is a means of power. Those who have command over food can exercise power or influence political relations. Those whose access to food is insufficient and/or insecure are vulnerable and easy objects of control and domination exercised by others who control food. Food is the stake in many a political struggle: between nations, between governments and subjects, between traders, producers and consumers, within the households, and between male and female members, etc. For those in command of food, it is powerful resource that can be used to influence, manipulate or enforce one's will on others. For those less fortunate, food is not a resource in political struggles but an end in itself. This characterises the fundamental inequality: the means of some are the ends for others (Mooji, Jos, 1999).

The Definitions of the Food Security

The commonly used definitions of food security come from the World Bank, UN's Food and Agriculture Organisation (FAO), World Health Organisation (WHO) and the United States Department of Agriculture (USDA):

World Bank defines food security "as access by all people at all times to sufficient food for an active and healthy life." In other words, it can be considered as enough food to supply the energy needed to live healthy, active and productive life.

Food security exists when all people, at all times, have physical, social and economic access to sufficient, safe and nutritious food to meet their dietary needs and food preferences for an active and healthy life (FAO).[1]

The World Health Organisation defines food security as having three facets: food availability, food access, and food use. Food availability is having available sufficient quantities of food on a consistent basis. Food access is having sufficient resources, both economic and physical, to obtain appropriate foods for a nutritious diet. Food use is the appropriate use based on knowledge of basic nutrition and care, as well as adequate water and sanitation.

Statz defined food security as "ability to assure on a long-term basis, that the food system provides the total population access to a timely, reliable and nutritionally adequate supply of food."

United States Department of Agriculture (USDA) illustrates Food security for a household means access by all members at all times to enough food for an active, healthy life. Food security includes at a minimum (1) the ready availability of nutritionally adequate and safe foods, and (2) an assured ability to acquire acceptable foods in socially acceptable ways (that is, without resorting to emergency food supplies, scavenging, stealing, or other coping strategies).

The above notions/factors form part of a broader food security frame work, that includes policy issues relating to elimination of hunger and poverty; provision of subsidised cereals; availability of and access to sufficient, safe, nutritious food to maintain a healthy and active life to all the people and at all the times; availability of adequate and safe food and acquiring socially and cultural acceptable food; entitlements that guarantee good nutrition, child care, clean water, hygiene, basic healthcare; right to define own food and agriculture systems; implementation of genuine agrarian reform; sustainable agriculture and rural development; price stabilisation mechanisms; improved access and international trade. Thus, the meaning and concept of food security has varied dimensions and intensity.

The Concept of Food Sovereignty

The concept of food sovereignty has evolved over the years, worldwide. It is a result of years of tireless work of grassroots advocates.

In 1996, during the World Food Conference, grassroots advocates highlighted the food sovereignty, as a priority to policy change. Lawmakers, supported by the analysis of grassroots organisers, saw that the right to food could help to advance the implementation of the goals expressed in the UN Human Rights Declaration of 1946. In addition, in the same conference, the members discussed the concept of food sovereignty the newest expression of the peasant movement for land, water, seeds and food rights, advocated for the **rights of peasants to produce their own food,** and the rights of communities around the world to control their food production and consumption.

Food sovereignty is the right of people to have healthy and culturally appropriate food produced through sustainable methods and their right to define their own food and agriculture systems. It develops a model of small-scale sustainable production benefiting communities and their environment. It puts the aspirations, needs and livelihoods of those who produce distribute and consume food at the heart of food systems and policies rather than the demands of markets and corporations.

Food sovereignty prioritises local food production and consumption. It gives a country the right to protect its local producers from cheap imports and to control production. It ensures that the rights to use and manage lands, territories, water, seeds, livestock and biodiversity are in the hands of those who produce food and not of the corporate sector. Therefore, the implementation of genuine agrarian reform is one of the top priorities of the farmer's movement (Saulo Araujo, September 27th, 2012).

The Right to Food

The **right to food** signifies that every individual must have access to sufficient, nutritionally adequate and culturally acceptable food for an active and healthy life. The UN Rapporteur calls for **"food democracy**." Food security must be built around food systems that secure the ability of smallholders to thrive. National strategies on the right to food should be co-designed by relevant stakeholders, in particular the groups most affected by hunger and malnutrition, which include many smallholders. The UN Rapporteur, De Schutter underscores the importance of communities to thrive through production, consumption and redistribution of wealth. Solutions to hunger and food insecurity should be based on the real needs of the poor and the vulnerable, which include many smallholders. Producing food alone is not sufficient. In a sound global food system, production should focus on local and regional markets, provide job opportunities to the community, and generate tax income for covering the needs of the poor and the disadvantaged. These factors indicate that the State has moral, constitutional and legal responsibility to ensure food security to the people, particularly the poor and vulnerable households.

The Changing Concept of Food Security

The concept of food security is interpreted in a variety of ways. In practice, Food Security is generally equated with the absence of hunger; or at best provision of pre-determined number of calories at the household: a situation where everybody has sufficient and affordable food (Vas, 2000). However, the concept of food security has undergone major shifts in terms of its focus due to the efforts of international, national, and state governments and civil society organisations. Until the seventies **food availability, stability** and **control of food prices** were considered as the major components or synonymous to food security. The focus was to understand food security at the aggregate level.

During1980's this conventional approach to food security was shifted to the individual level following Amartya Sen's **food entitlement approach**. According to him, starvation is the characteristic of some people not having enough to eat. He clearly puts it that: availability of food is only one factor affecting food security or starvation. Food insecurity is not only caused by non-availability of food but also by entitlement failure. Entitlement failure refers to the inability of people to command food through the legal means available in the society, including the use of production possibilities, trade opportunities, entitlement vis-à-vis the state, and other methods of acquiring food (Sen, 1982). This approach stresses the importance of economic resources, which provide a person some **purchasing power to access food.**

In late 1980's the issue of giving **assurance of nutrition food** to the people gained prominence in the literature, with experts arguing that under-nutrition is caused not only by food shortage but also due to other social, demographic and health-related factors. Starting from the 1990's, the focus has totally shifted from the 'food first' perspective to **livelihood perspective**, where food and nutrition security are the subsets in the larger framework of livelihood security.

During the first decade of twenty first century, the emphasis is on **Right to Food.** It is a legal mechanism to protect local communities' access to food. As a law, the Right to Food enables communities as well as nations to demand their food rights. The Right to Food goes beyond the provision of subsidised cereals. It is about ensuring freedom from hunger, malnutrition and other deprivations associated with lack of food. Viewed from this manner, it is obvious that the public policies would, along with providing access to grain, have to create other entitlements that guarantee good nutrition. This requires not only nutritious food (including a balanced intake of calories, protein, fats and essential micronutrients) but also attention to child care, clean water, hygiene, basic healthcare and so on (Reetika Khera, 2009). Recently, the concept has become broader when the WFP pointed out that food security is a **multidimensional phenomenon** that relates to demographic, nutritional, economic and social causes (Misra, 2005). The Food Security is also linked to other notions of security i.e. **economic security** (related to employment, income and gender) **socio-political security** (related to inequality, governance and conflicts) and **environmental security** (related to natural resources) (International Food Policy and Research Institute, IFPRI, 2011).

The Review of Literature

After advent of independence the policy formulators in India, repeatedly, pronounced that the government would pay utmost attention to the problem of poverty, hunger, foodgrain crises, inequalities, etc. The food security has always been one the major development priorities of governments since inception of India's Five Year Planning process and several poverty alleviation programmes were launched since 1951. However, the experience with India's planned development process, during the past six and a half decades, unfolds that hunger, malnutrition, poverty, unemployment, inequalities, etc, persist across the country. The literature on the subject indicates that both the international and national institutions and scholars have highlighted the factors- internal and external- contributed for food insecurity and its intensity in India. The studies on the subject underscored the following concerns, which are useful for proper understanding of the food security subject.

Food Insecurity in India

The studies on poverty alleviation programmes, including food security policies and their impact on the living conditions of marginalised sections indicate that India's food security situation continues to rank as 'alarming' and its rank is 67 of the 81 countries of the world with the worst food security status and it is 'alarming' (IFPRI, GHI, 2011). The United Nations World Food Programme's report indicates that India, which is considered one of the fastest growing economies of the world and an emerging superpower- paradoxically, tops the global hunger chart with more than 27 per cent of the world's undernourished population. Notwithstanding India's self-sufficiency in food-grain production India remains a low-income, food deficit country in which as much as 35 per cent of the population consumes less than 80 per cent of its minimum human energy requirements; where nine out of ten pregnant women suffer from malnutrition and anaemia, and, in consequence, 47 per cent of children under the age of five are moderately to severely undernourished (World Food Programme 2008, www.wfp.org).

FAO observes that although the number of people, who are below the poverty line, has reduced significantly during 1993-1994 and 1999-2000, it is striking that the number of undernourished people has increased during the period between triennium1992 and triennium 1999. Further, the prices of most of the essential food items of daily life have doubled in the last two years (Rajamani, RC, 2012).

The London-based 'Action Aid' in its recent report (2010) found that nearly one-fourth of the poor in the world live in India. This organisation further highlights that our per capita income almost tripled during 1990-2005, but during the same period 5.3 crore more hungry people were added to our population. Commenting on hunger aspect, Gunnar Myrdal observed that the hidden hunger is due to low calorie intake and particularly the lack of protective nutrients gives rise to serious health risks and more generally, to lethargy and lack of initiative and drive (Gunnar Myrdal, 1970).

Undernourishment in the Rural India

The problem of undernourishment is more in the rural India. People in the rural areas still struggle for their basic necessities of life like food, drinking water, sanitation and education. In spite of some improvement of nutritional status at the national level, nearly half of the rural children are suffering from malnutrition. Vitamin- A deficiency, which leads to preventable blindness among the children, is found to be more prevalent among children from the rural households. Iron deficiency is quite rampant among the pregnant women residing in remote villages. On the other hand, micronutrient deficiency is equally common among the rural population and especially among the vulnerable groups such as women and children (Anupam Hazra, 2012).

Children are the most visible victims of under-nutrition. Children who are poorly nourished suffer upto 160 days of illness each year. Forty two per cent of our children below five years of age are affected by malnutrition- (i) protein-energy malnutrition (the lack of enough protein from meat and other sources); (ii) micronutrient deficiency (vitamin and mineral). Under-nutrition magnifies the effect of every disease, including measles and malaria. The estimated proportions of deaths in which under-nutrition is an underlying cause are roughly similar for diarrheal (61 per cent), malaria (57 per cent), pneumonia (52 per cent), and measles (45 per cent), (Black, 2003; Bryce, 2005). The National Family Health Survey in 2005-06 points out that in India 46 per cent of children below three are underweight, 33 per cent women and 28 per cent men have a below normal body mass index; 79 per cent of children aged 6-35 months, 56 per cent married women aged 15-49 years and 24 per cent similar men have anaemia. It is evident that food insecurity is a reality in India where every third adult has a low body mass index (BMI) at less than 18.5. Limiting body size as a way of adapting to low levels of energy (calories) adversely affects health in three ways: (i) premature failure of vital organs occurs during adulthood; (ii) stunted individuals suffer a far higher rate of disease and illness than those who have not undergone stunting; and (iii) severe malnutrition in early childhood often leads to defects in cognitive development. Despite the existence of PDS, reports of hunger and malnutrition have been pouring in from different parts of the country (Anupam Hazra, 2012).

Harish Mander, (2011) is of the opinion that the individual men women and children –and sometimes entire tribals or dalits communities and poor household members –are compelled to subsist for long periods without sufficient food. They cut back on their food intakes, sometimes reduced to eating one meal a day; or to beg for food; or to eat tubers, grasses and mango kernels that fill their stomach but provide no nutrition ; or sometimes just to drink the starch water left over after cooking rice, winch their neighbours give them in tight-fisted charity. On the other hand, the state granaries are full, grain rots, the economy is resurgent and many of the world's wealthiest people are Indians. Yet, the paradox persists that one in every two Indian children is unable to access enough food, her body and brain to develop to their full potential and two out of three women are anaemic, because even within families, women eat the least and only after all others have been fed.

Decline in Foodgrain Consumption and Rising Poverty during Economic Reform Phase

Patnaik's study reveals that the worsening nutritional situation and rising poverty are closely linked to the observed decline in the consumption of foodgrains per head. The food-spending share of total spending, in the recent past, is actually observed to fall, when people are getting worse off…since owing to greater monetisation of the economy and higher cost of utilities, they are forced to spend more on the bare minimum of non-food essentials (Usta Patnaik, 2005). The NSS data shows a clear decline in direct foodgrains consumption per head in physical terms, a trend that predates economic reforms and continues to the present. It is not only direct consumption alone; the use of grain for all purposes has been declining as well on a per capita basis, specifically during the period of reforms whereas it was rising during the pre-reforms period (Utsa patnaik, 2013).

With decline in per head, cereals consumed for all uses over the reform period, India at present registers at 175 kg, the lowest level of cereal consumption per capita for all purposes, below the average for sub-Saharan Africa and even below the figure for the least developed countries. Such a remarkable decline in total grain consumption per head in India is explicable only in terms of adverse shifts in income distribution (Patnaik, 2009, 2010c). The process of mass income deflation and rising unemployment through fiscal contraction under economic reforms, combined with fast rise in the real incomes of a minority means not merely that income inequalities have risen, but there is absolute decline of purchasing power and real consumption of the majority, which is swamping out the rising consumption per capita of the minority which has gained from reforms. Many poor households do not have the purchasing power and lack of access to food. The lack of access or lack of purchasing power has been forcefully brought out by Amartya Sen when he describes it as deprivation due to non-entitlement or "the inability of certain people to command food through the legal means available in the society, including the use of production possibilities, trade opportunities, entitlement in the State and other methods of acquiring food" (Amartya Sen, 1981).

Inflation Undermines Real Income

Inflation is sustained rise in prices. It is also, at bottom, a process of redistribution of real income- away from creditors (to whom money owed) and those whose compensation has a significant variable component of profits or capital income, which typically rise with inflation. Modern economies suffer constantly from inflation. When it affects the prices of food and essential items, it redistributes real incomes and wealth in the economy even faster.

Seen in this light, inflation in the prices of essential commodities and services is a market-ruled process of growing economic exclusion, though it is never recognised as such. At a time when bio fuel is displacing the cultivation of food in so many countries, driving up the world price of grain in the process, money becomes a universal weapon of mass discrimination. Prices in India cannot remain unaffected by world prices in a world of open economy agriculture. In a country like India in which hunger and malnutrition are so widespread and deep-rooted, rising prices of essential items like food, medicines or housing effectively exclude large numbers of people from the most elementary wherewithal of subsistence (Lester Brown, 2007).

Reduction in Food Subsidies

In 1997, in line with the requirement of reducing food subsidies in order to trim public expenditure (as stipulated by the IMF/World Bank conditions), a new, Targeted PDS was introduced. Under this, a distinction was made between households above and below poverty line (APL and BPL), with lower prices for the latter set of families. In a bid to cut the subsidy bill of the government, the issue price (at which is grain is sold) was raised several times over the years after 1997, for both categories of households accessing the PDS (expect certain states like Andhra Pradesh, which reduced the price of the grain to Re one per kg). This led to a sharp divergence between the procurement of foodgrains from farmers by the government and the off-take from the ration shops- as fewer and fewer people could afford the grain- the difference adding to the 'excess' food buffer stocks in the FCI's godowns. In the years from 1997 to 2004, this difference exceeded 100 million tonnes, half the annual production of the country for a year. It generated the shameful anomaly of India exporting large quantities of food (often contributing to cattle-feed in the EU), even as hundreds of millions of people went hungry within the country (Aseem Shrivastava and Ashish Kothari, 2012).

Studies also show that a significant proportion of deserving poor households were wrongly excluded from access to food. The inevitable result was a significant rise in malnutrition in many parts of the country, while the reduction of malnutrition slowed down in other regions- a high price to pay to reduce an item on the government budget, which usually takes up well under one per cent of the GDP (Upadhyay, V and Shakti Kak, 2005; Madhura Saminadhan and Neeta Mishra, 2001).

De facto Hoarder

The phenomenon of the government turning into a de facto hoarder repeated itself in 2010, for the same reasons as before but also because the storage and distribution facilities of the FCI seemed to have deteriorated even further. In August 2010, in the midst of double-digit inflation in food items, the FCI was sitting on a stock of 17 million tonnes of wheat, much of it rotting away or being consumed by rats. This could have fed 201 million hungry people in the country for a year (Erika Kinetz, 2010).

Meanwhile, inflation has been clawing into the standards of living of working poor around the country. According to the RBI, since March 2007, year-on-year consumer price inflation in food prices has ranged between 9 and 14 per cent for all categories of workers (including urban industrial workers and agricultural labourers), rising particularly sharply in the first half of 2008 when prices were rising globally. Between April 2007 and April 2008, for instance, the retail price of rice increased by over 20 per cent, tur dal (spilt pigeon pea) by over 15 per cent, mustered oil by 28 per cent (RBI, Annual Report, 2008-09).

Deregulation of Markets in Grain and Commodity

In addition to the above, the rise in the price of oil and increasing use of land for bio fuels, speculation in commodities, which has become a key area for financial investment in recent years, has contributed to food inflation. This has been prodded by governments around the world deregulating markets in grain and commodity futures-agreements between the two parties to transact at a predetermined price at a future date. In India, in April 2003, the NDA (National Democratic Alliance) government lifted the ban on the forward trading in fifty-four commodities, including several agricultural ones. Further market liberalisation has happened in the form of new instruments such as 'commodity derivatives' and 'options', all of which favour the speculative buyer, rather than the producer, of agricultural commodities.

Entry of Multinational Corporations in Agribusiness

The entry of Multinational Corporations (MNCs) in agribusiness in the commodity bazaar has given scope for the traders / companies to speculate the availability or non-availability of grains in the market. Importantly, the legal limit for grain that can be stored for private trading was quietly raised a few years back from 10,000 to 50,000 tonnes. The government has often upbraided small speculators. However, the global players, like Cargill or Archer Daniels Midland (ADM), have obliviously never been shown up in public. The amount of grain such hoarders may be holding at any point of time ought to be public information-but that would be to give the game away from the private traders' perspective, and they are protected by laws. The game is rooted in uncertainty and asymmetries of information. The annual profits of the food MNCs engaging in commodities trade have risen in recent years at annual rates of 30 to 90 per cent (Aseem Shrivastava and Ashish Kothari, 2012).

Poor Monsoon and the Uncertain Harvests

The rise of price of foodgrains is linked to failure of monsoon. The production of pulses, for instance, did fall a little short of demand in 2009. However, the imports of over two million tonnes should have made up for this. Why did prices continue to rise, is the main issue? The price of tur dal rose by as much as 33 per cent in just a month, rising to Rs 60-80 per kg in July 2009 in the four largest metros of the country. The price increase from 2008 was of the order of 50-90 per cent. It is possible that the expectation of rising prices led, once again, to hoarding and speculation. In states where the government raided hoarders and released supplies in the market prices fell (ibid). Another argument was sowing was reduced due to poor monsoon. The area under paddy- a kharif crop- shrank by over six million ha across the country in 2009. This, along with lower yields than normal, was expected to lead to a fall in annual rice production by 17 per cent. This announcement by the Minister of Agriculture was enough to drive up the price of rice to more than Rs 40 a kg. The story with respect to sugar was similar (Ravinder Bawa, 2009). In 2010, during one of the runway food inflation episodes, the Times of India reported:

> In Ahmadabad's Gokuldham settlement, Mona Rajput has had to make the painful decision to stop giving milk to her four-year old son so that her five month-old infant can get some. In a country in which half of all children are already malnourished, the seemingly unstoppable rise in food prices is threading to sow the seeds of a dangerously undernourishment future generation (Times of India, July 2010).

Poverty and Food Insecurity

Studies also highlight that many of the households have inadequate access of foodgrains and are food insecure. The root cause of such non-access or food in-security is poverty. The poor households, which, because of their poverty, are unable to effectively register their demand and purchase even the minimum quantity of foodgrains, required for the entire family's nutritional well-being. The National Nutrition Policy of India recognised that the adverse affect of poverty on nutritional status of people. "Widespread poverty resulting in chronic and persistent hunger is the single biggest curse of the developing world today. The physical expression of this continuously re-enacted tragedy is the condition of under-nutrition, which manifests itself among large section of the poor, particularly among the women and children. This condition of under nutrition, therefore, reduces work capacity and productivity amongst adults and enhances mortality and morbidity amongst children. Such reduced productivity translates into reduced earning capacity, leading to further poverty and the vicious cycle goes on" (The National Nutrition Policy NNP 1993). The vicious cycle of poverty make the individual; low earning capacity, low intake of nutritious food, under-nutrition and insults from nutrition-related diseases and infections, stunted development of children and growth faltering, small body size of adults, impaired productivity, etc.

Poverty and chronic food insecurity translates into high degree of vulnerability to famine and hunger. Rangarajan report 'on poverty' estimates that those spending (both food and non-food expenditure) below Rs 47 per day in cities and Rs 33 per day in rural areas are considered as poor. Based on this, the report stated that three out of ten people, in India, are poor. As per the report, poverty stood at 38.2 per cent in 2009-10 and came down 29.5 per cent in 2011-12, which suggests that 363 million people are still poor in the country (Indian Express, Hyderabad edition, 8th July 2014). Apart from all other considerations, the sheer number of persons living below poverty line speaks about the intensity of the problem of food insecurity and the need for evolving development strategies and governance models for poverty alleviation in the country.

The Changing Concept of Governance

The governance in general terms, may be referred to the action or manner of governing, administering, conducting public affairs, etc, of an organisation/society. The word *governance* derives from the Greek verb κυβερνάω [*kubernáo*] that means *to steer* and was used for the first time in a metaphorical sense by Plato. It then passed on to Latin and then on to many languages. A reasonable or rational purpose of governance might aim to assure that an organisation produces a worthwhile pattern of good results while avoiding an undesirable pattern of bad circumstances.

During the end of the twentieth century and in the early twenty first century, governance has gained the prominent attention of social scientists, civil society bodies, philanthropists, donor agencies the world over. Following the onset of New Economic Reforms/ Globalisation (downplaying the role of State and overvaluing the market in providing services to the people) the donor agencies, social scientists, especially the western scholars of Public Administration have labelled that the traditional bureaucratic or state-centric-model appears to have lost its significance in addressing the problems of the society both in the developed and developing countries. They advocated for Good Governance or New Public Management (NPM), which emphasis on a declining role of the nation-state; networking of formal institutions of government, the market and the private sector, and civil society bodies; creation of infrastructure on Public-Private Partnership (PPP) mode; outsourcing of public services; greater flexibility; accountability; etc, for executing the development policies, including the food security policies. The involvement or assistance (financial and technology) of non-state actors or multiple actors (civil society bodies, philanthropists, donor agencies) for development, obliged the developing countries to accept NPM model as universally applicable model of governance to arrest the arbitrary policy-making, abuse of power and corrupt practices in the administration. This has brought changes in the concept and meaning of governance of public affairs (Chakrabathy, Bidyut and Bhattacharya, M, 2008). The present NDA Government (2014) is emphasising on 'Least Government and Maximum Governance' for development in the society.

The International Governmental Organisations (IGOs) such as UNO WB, Department for International Development (DFID), Nations Development Programme (UNDP) and Scholars have defined the Governance, identified its key elements, and advocated them as universally applicable for development in any society. The UNDP defined the Governance as the rules of the political system to solve conflicts between actors and adopt decision (legality). It has also been used to describe the "proper functioning of institutions and their acceptance by the public", legitimacy to invoke the efficacy of government and the achievement of consensus by democratic means (participation).

The World Bank, have evolved dimensions of governance an internationally comparable measure. They include voice and accountability, political stability and lack of violence, government effectiveness, regulatory quality, rule of law, control of corruption. A new World Governance Index (WGI) specify that peace and security, rule of law, human rights and participation, sustainable development, and human development are the part of governance.

The World Bank, in 1993, defined the governance as 'the manner which the power is exercised in the management of a country's economic and social resources for development'. The Worldwide Governance indicators project of the World Bank defines governance as the traditions and institutions by which authority in a country is exercised. An alternate definition sees governance as the use of institutions, structures of authority and even collaboration to allocate resources and coordinate or control activity in society or the economy.

The WB, in 1996, advocated for good governance to overcome the administrative dysfunctionalities. "Good governance means the effective management of country's resources in a manner that is open, transparent, accountable, equitable and responsive to people's needs. The rule of law, transparency, accountability and effectiveness of public organisations are all essential components of good governance. According to the Bank, Good Governance (GG) entails sound public sector management (efficiency, economy and effectiveness) accountability, exchange and free flow of information (transparency) and a legal framework for development (justice, respect for human rights and liberties). Department for International Development (DFID) defines GG by focusing on four major components namely, legitimacy (government should have the consent of the governed); accountability (ensuring transparency, being answerable for actions and media freedom); competence (effective policy-making, implementation and service delivery); and respect for law and protection for human rights (ODA, 1993). The UNDP notes that GG is, among other things is participatory, consensus oriented, accountable, transparent, responsive, effective and efficient equitable and inclusive, and follows the rule of law; and the voices of the poorest and most vulnerable are heard in decision-making over the allocation of resources. World Development Report, 1997 identified the mechanisms for assuring GG have three key elements: internal rules and restraints (for example, internal accounting and auditing systems, independence of the judiciary and the central bank, civil service and budgeting rules); voice and partnership (for example, public-private deliberation councils and delivery, private partnership in infrastructure, alternative dispute resolution mechanisms) and outright privatisation of certain market driven activities. These factors have become universally applicable to all the development projects supported by IGOs in the developing countries, including India, and are the major challenges of governance.

Scenario in India

As India is one of the major recipient countries in getting financial aid and technical assistance from IGOs or donor agencies such as WB, FAO, DFID, UNICEF, UNDP, WFP, World Employment Programme, (WEP) etc, for development projects, like irrigation, power, roads, airports, communication, urban civic amenities, health, education, distribution of essential commodities, etc, it also opted for NPM for executing them, especially during the post-economic reform period (1991 onwards). The State is withdrawing from its socio-economic responsibilities and leaving them to private sector or assigning them to civil society bodies / non-governmental organisations. It is also according priority to undertake projects/ services on NPM mode. The Fifth Pay Commission (1996), Government of India outlined the managerial reforms package on lines of NPM that intended to transform the administration through appropriate measures that would cover accountability; transparency and openness; economy and economy and civil service performance and integrity.

The present model of development- New Economic Reforms Strategy-, though contributed for inflow of foreign capital, creation of infrastructural facilities, consumer goods, expansion of middle class, enhancing the GDP growth rate, etc, it widened the gap between the rich and poor and between better-endowed areas and backward areas. The reforms, instead of protecting the local capital and resources from the external capital, it is increasingly facilitating the global capital to penetrate in to the economy, which will have adverse impact on the living conditions of people, especially the marginalised sections. Further it is also adopting the New Public Management (NPM), which emphasis on a declining role of the nation-state; networking of formal institutions of government, the market and the private sector, and civil society bodies; creation of infrastructure on Public-Private Partnership (PPP) mode; for development.

The rise of neo-liberalism and so-called Washington consensus[2] have generated a powerful international ideology concerning what constitutes good governance, democratisation, and the proper rules of the State and civil society in advancing development. The IGOs, especially the members of the World Bank, have evolved dimensions of governance, an internationally comparable measure. They include: reforms in macro economy, reduction in fiscal deficiency, peace and security, political stability, government effectiveness, control of corruption, rule of law, protection of human rights, and respect for voice of people, transparency and accountability of institutions of governance, participation of people in the development process, sustainable development, and human development are the part of the governance. These trends affect both positively and negatively the growth of agricultural production and poverty alleviation programmes, including food security programmes and governance systems and mode of operations.

The analysis indicates that the concept of food security has undergone major shifts in terms of its focus due to the efforts of international agencies, national and state governments and NGOs and civil society bodies. Today, it has become multi-dimensional phenomenon- starting from: food availability at aggregate level; control of food prices; access to adequate quantity and quality of food; food entitlement through legal means; purchasing power to access to food; assurance of nutrient food; creating livelihood opportunities; and to right to food; food sovereignty/ food democracy (right to have own food) etc. It is also linked to other notions of security i.e. economic security, socio-political security and environmental security. It is equated with that of supply enough food and energy to live healthy, active and productive life at all the times. The public policies aimed at ensuring food security to the people and thereby elimination of hunger and poverty need to focus on the above factors. The Government of India and State Governments, during the post-independent period, repeatedly, paid attention to the problems of hunger/ food insecurity, poverty and launched several poverty alleviation policies such as asset-based programmes, wage-oriented programmes, social security programmes and food-grain distribution programmes to address the above concerns. However, the experience reveals that these programmes, including food security programmes, have not enabled many of the households to have adequate access to food and thus, are food insecure.

The intensity of the problem (food insecure) is highlighted by several studies. Decline in the direct food grains consumption per head; forced to manage to survive for long periods without sufficient food; decline of purchasing power and real consumption of majority; wide spread poverty; alarming food security status (67th rank of the 81 counties); population (more than one-third) consuming less than minimum human energy requirements; undernourished children (47 per cent) under the age of five; price hike of the most essential commodities; low body index; adding up number of hungry people to the existing population year-to-year; serious health risks and lack of initiative and drive due to the low calorie intake; etc, indicating the intensity of the problem of food security and the need for launching of food security policies in the country.

An examination of the reasons for the food insecure reveals that food inflation; reduction in public expenditure on agriculture sector; withdrawal/reduction in food subsidies due to the norms/conditions imposed by the World Bank; shortage of foodgrain availability for distribution due to the low production and procurement of grains; exporting large scale quantity of foodgrains in spite of shortage of its availability; lack of storage and distribution facilities resulting in wastage of grains; rise in the price of oil; use of cultivable land for bio-fuels; lifting the ban on the forwarding trading; market liberalisation; entry of multinational corporations in agribusiness; traders' taking protection under law; poor monsoon and uncertainty in harvests; reduction in cultivable land due to conversion of land for non-agricultural purposes and also erratic and scanty rain fall; commercialisation of agriculture; hoarding and hiking the prices of foodgrain commodities on the pretext of government announcement that reduction in sowing area in the coming days, etc, are collectively or individually contributing for food insecurity in the country. Further the analysis reveals that food insecurity is partly due to the launching of policies based on incremental approach- partly to tide over the unrest among the poor and get support in the election and partly to expand the market of Multinational Corporations and least is the fulfilling of constitutional goals.

The above concerns and others are incorporated in the FS policies, especially in the NFSA, 2013. Though the intentions of the government are good and rational in defining the core components of FS and norms for executing the scheme/s, they are not materialised at the field level. There is a wide gap between promise and performance of the FS schemes. In spite of specifying the norms for implementation, instances are not lacking where the state governments violate them or not adhere to the norms due to political compulsions or other reasons. The studies point out that the schemes were not access to all the people because of socio-economic, cultural and political compulsions and insufficient attention to the details of delivery mechanism (Khera (2010, IIPA, 2010-11). This is partly due to the acceptance of policies/ norms/ methods/practices, without taking account the socio-economic, cultural, political and administrative context of the country/state/ district. The field studies further confirms this fact.

Methodology of the Study

Despite above factors, the incremental policies are to be succeeded the role of governance of food security policies is all the more important. The governance, if properly designed and enforced, can address the issues related to food insecurity, poverty and inequalities in the society. Regardless of its importance, the studies on food security policies and programmes, in India, have neglected governance dimensions. The studies have mainly examined the quantity of foodgrain distribution and its effect on prices and impact on the living conditions of people. A few studies have examined the political dimension of the policies. The governance structures of food security policies and their dealings with actors have not been analysed with the same depth and rigor as the other dimensions of food security. It is pertinent to note that there is any study/ies, which examined the governance of food security policies, during the post-economic reforms where the State is withdrawing its socio-economic responsibilities and depending on the public-private partnership (PPP) for delivery of services. In this context, the present study on "Governance of Food

Security Policies in India: a Study in the Andhra Pradesh"[3], assumes considerable importance. The limitation of the study is that though the concept of food security encompasses several aspects of human beings, it mostly focused on agricultural production, procurement and distribution of foodgrains to the people of Andhra Pradesh (AP). In this study, AP means undivided State of Andhra Pradesh. Which was ppiturcated in to two states i.e. Telangana and residury Andhra Pradesh from 2nd June 2014.

Objectives of the Study

The study seeks to:

(i) To analyse the concept of food security and issues related to food insecurity;

(ii) To study the food security policies and programmes launched in India and Andhra Pradesh;

(iii) To study the organisational structures, process, methods and mode of operation of the different schemes in the State and identify strengths and weakness of governance;

(iv) To analyse the status of agricultural production, procurement and distribution foodgrains in the state; and

(v) To examine the perception of respondents on the governance of PDS in the state.

Hypothesis

1. The State's concerns, for formulating poverty alleviation/ food security policies ought to be: one, to undertake policies to increase the production/services and distribution of foodgrains or increase livelihood opportunities and reduce the poverty and misery of the people, as immediate concern; and two, enabling the policies to alter the existing unequal socio-economic system and emancipate the people from their hunger, poverty and wretchedness, as the long-term concern;
2. Food security policies are incremental or ad-hoc in nature and aimed at to benefit the ruling class in getting support of the poor in the elections. They do not have the capacity to intervene and also transform the existing conditions in which the poor people have been trapped for centuries;

3. The incremental policies like food security policies are to be succeed, they need to be formulated based on the local conditions and creation of institutions without being influenced by IGOs/ donor agencies;
4. Ensuring people's participation in food security policy/ies formulation, implementation, evaluation and sharing of benefits with equity and justice would address the issues related to governance dimensions.

Methods of Data Collection and Plan of the Study

The study has employed both the secondary and primary sources. For the purpose of study, one of the districts of Telangana i.e. Nalgonda district is selected. The detailed study is undertaken in five villages, selecting one village from each revenue division of the district. The villages have some common features and are diversified in certain characteristics such as size, location, irrigation facilities, type of soil, infrastructural facilities, number of BPL households (HH), number of ration cards, etc. It is hoped that these factors facilitate us to understand the governance of the food security policies in cross-cultural context. The field survey covers 100 respondents (20 respondents from each village). The data is collected through informal discussions with the Fair Price Shop (FPS) dealers, elite of the village and higher-level officials concerned.

Notes

1. The FAO through projects in over 100 countries worldwide, the programme promotes effective, tangible solutions to the elimination of hunger, undernourishment and poverty. Currently 102 countries are engaged in the programme and of these approximately 30 have begun shifting from pilot to national programmes. To maximise the impact of its work, FAO strongly promotes national ownership and local empowerment in the countries in which it operates.
2. John Williamson's list of 10 reforms of the Washington Consensus (1989) include: Fiscal discipline; Redirect spending priorities from things like indiscriminate subsidies to basic health and education; Lower marginal tax rates and broaden the tax base; Interest rate liberalisation; A competitive exchange rate; Trade liberalisation; Liberalisation of FDI inflows; Privatisation; Deregulation, in the sense of abolishing barriers to entry and exit; Secure property rights.

3. As per AP Reorganisation Bill, 2014 Andhra Pradesh State is bifurcated in to two States i.e. Telangana State and residuary Andhra Pradesh State from June 2nd, 2014.

References

Abeam Barman, (2010): *Economic Times*, 23 November.

Anupam Hazar, (2012): 'Food Security in Rural India; Poverty in the Land of Plenty', *Kurukshetra*, Vol. 60, No.5 pp. 7-10.

Aseem Shrivastava and Ashish Kothari, (2012): 'Churning the Earth- the Making of Global India', *Penguin-Viking group*, New Delhi.

Bala Ramulu, Ch, (2000): 'Technology and Rural Development', *Rawath publishers*, New Delhi.

———— *(2004)*: *'Development Policy and Governance in India from 1947 to 2003'*, Indian Journal of Public Administration, New Delhi, Vol. L, January-March, No.1.

Bryce, (2005): 'Human Rights and Global Health: a Research Programme', *Metphilosophy* Volume 36, Issue 1-2, pp. 182–209, January.

Erika Kinetz, (2010): 'What rots India as World prices at two-year High' CNBC, 6th August, http://www.msnbc.msn.com/id /38591224/ns/world news-south_and_central_asia.

Editorial note (2015), 'Volte-face on Food Security' *Economic and Political Weekly*, January 31, Vol. 5.

FAO, 'Indian Experience on Household Food and Nutrition Security', Corporate Document Repository, Regional Office for Asia and Pacific.

Gunnar Myrdal, (1970): 'The Challenge of World Poverty, A World anti- poverty Programme' pp. xvii + 518 pp.

Gupta et.al (2014): 'Manipulation by Association Is the Private Sector Undermining Nutrition'? *Economic and Political Weekly*, July 26, 2014 Vol. xl IX no 30.

Harisha Mander, (2011): 'Identification of poor: Errors of Exclusion and Inclusion', *Economic and Political Weekly*, February 26 Vol. XL No. 9.

Lester Brown, (2007): 'Bio fuels blunder: Massive Diversion of U.S. Grain to Fuel cars is Rising World Food Prices, Risking political Instability' testimony before the US Senate Committee in *Environment and Public Works, Earth Policy Institute*, 13 June, http://www.earth-policy.org/index.php?/ press-room/C68?Senatet EPW07.

Madhura Sawminadhan and Neeta Mishra, (2001): 'Errors of Targeting: Public Distribution of Food in a Maharashtra Village 1995-2000', *Economic and Political Weekly*, 30th June.

Mintz Sidney (1985): '*Sweetness and power: the place of sugar in modern history*' Harmondsworth: Penguin.

Misra, Ashok (2005): 'Food Assistance Programs and Food Security'.... Louisiana State University, the Effect of Food Stamps on Food Security: A Panel Data Approach.

Moreno-Black, G, (2003): 'Thailand In: The Encyclopaedia of Food' 3: 314 - 318, *Charles Scribes Sons Reference Books*: New York.

Rajamani, R.C (2012): 'The Imponderable Food Security Bill, 2011', Kurukshetra, Vol. 60, No. 5 pp. 3-6.

Rajesh Shukla, (2010): 'How India Earns, Spends and Saves', Sage, New Delhi, *Economic Survey*, 2010-11, see http://indiabudget.nic.in/.

Ravinder Bawa (2009): 'Pawar's rice shortage warning may lead to Hoarding', *India Today*. 24th September, http://indiatoday.intoday.in .

Reserve Bank of India, (2008-09): 'Annual Report (inflation rate data) 2008-09', Table 2.33, http://rbidocs.rbi.org.in.

Retika Khera, (2009) 'Right to Food' Act: Beyond Cheap Promises', *Economic and Economic Weekly*, Vol. 44, No. 29, Jul. 18 - 24 Page 40 of 40-44.

Saulo Araujo, (2012): 'Policies and Investments for Poverty Reduction and Food Security' September 27.

Sarris, AH Taylor, L; (1976): 'Buffer Stock Analysis for Agricultural Products: Theoretical Murk or Empirical Resolution'. FG Adams, S. Klein (Eds.), Stabilizing World Commodity Markets, Heat Lexington, Lexington (1978), pp. 149–160.

Sen, Amartya (1981): 'Poverty and Famines, an essay on Entitlement and Deprivation', Clarendon Press, Oxford.

Shankar Acharya, (2007): 'Intervention in a seminar on *India's Growth: Past and Future*, Beijing, 14-16 January.

Times of India, (July 2010): 'A Nation forced to go on Distress Diet'htpp://www.timesofindia.inindiatimes.com/India.

Upadhyay, V, and Shakti Kak, (2005): 'Prices, Food Security and PDS, in AES India 2004-05' New Delhi: *Daanish Books.*

Usta Patnaik, (2010): 'Changes in Urban Poverty under Economic Reforms', *Economic & Political Weekly*, 23-29 January.

Usta Patnaik, (2010): 'A Critical Look at Some Propositions on Consumption and Poverty'. *Economic & Political Weekly,* 6-12 February.

U Patnaik (2010): 'On Some Fatal Fallacies', *Economic and Political Weekly*, November 20, 2010, Vol. xlv No. 47.

Chapter–II

Food Security Policies and Programmes in India

Public policies for the socio-economic development of the people, especially weaker sections have come to assume vital importance in post-Independent India. The State, through a number of policies and programmes seeks to intervene in the development process in all the five-year plans. The policies are broadly of two types; one, policies which can alter the structure; and two, policies which are of incremental nature. The policies like land reforms, if enforced effectively, can touch the ownership of means of production and can lead to certain structural changes. The policies like educational loans/ scholarships; food security-public distribution system (PDS); subsidy-based poverty alleviation programmes- self-employment; wage employment; social security-lead to incrementalism and provide some relief to the deprived sections without affecting the basic socio-economic structure of the society. However, the State is giving more priority to the 'direct incremental policies than the structural change oriented policies'. The International Governmental Organisations (IGOs-WB, DFID, FAO), and others are promoting the incremental policies and assisting/ directing the Indian State to embark on them to eliminate the poverty and inequalities. The foremost concern of the Indian State ought to be that it has to operate in conformity with the Constitutional mandate-socio-economic justice and sustainable development, inclusive growth - and in the broader societal context and not to succumb to the pressure of ruling class/ industrial class or conditions/directions of

IGOs. Further, the policies are expected to combine resource management with production, creation of sufficient jobs, food security, fair access to products and opportunity, and equal distribution of resources to all the social groups. Development is about people and not about objects (Dwivedi, OP and Henderson, KM, 1996).

However, in practice, several factors collectively and severally have been affecting policy formulation, implementation and governance, during the post-independence period. The public policies are formulated and implemented mostly to: tide over the unrest among the poor; get the support of the poor in the elections in favour of the ruling party; take on of technological innovations; expand the market of MNCs; oblige the Judiciary directions; guard the ruling class power structure from the threat of the unrest masses; etc, (Bala Ramulu, Ch, 2004).

Today, the public policies and its concepts, norms and institutions, technology, capital, resources, of late, are globalised. The Indian state has little freedom to modify the norms of the policies/projects as most of them are financially and technically supported by the IGOs. In a way, it amounts to 'globalisation of democratic power' (formulation of policies) which ought to rest with the people and their representatives. Globalisation has changed the context, focus and the very notion of the constitutional mandate, nation state and the public policies and institutions. This model set two ways; one it heightened inequalities and two, it reduced access to services to the common people as the State gradually withdrawn from the activities/services, particularly subsidy, based policies, food security, health and education. As role of the State has been transformed to market forces, the Indian State either forcefully or voluntarily has been retreating from its role as 'nation state', 'development state', 'welfare state' and increasingly called upon to 'deregulate its role'. If this trend continues the role of the State would be instead of protecting the local capital, resources from the external capital, it is increasingly assuming the role of facilitating movement of the global capital and maintaining the order through law or even unlawful acts. Deregulated globalisation has taken away from nation states their power to enact and enforce policies that could- at least in principle- internalise external costs (Haragopal, G, 2012). The present National Democratic Alliance (NDA) government has brought several ordinances in six months, such as — the Textile Undertakings (Nationalisation) Laws (Amendment and Validation) Ordinance; the Coal Mines (Special Provisions) Ordinance; Andhra Pradesh Reorganisation (Amendment); Ordinance, 2014, and the Telecom Regulatory Authority of India (Amendment) Ordinance, 2014; Ordinance to hike the foreign direct investment (FDI) limit in the insurance sector to 49 per cent from 26 per cent; Land Acquisition, Rehabilitation and Resettlement Act, 2013, etc. the civil society bodies, opposition political parties condemned the actions of the government. In taking the ordinance route, the NDA government seems no different from the earlier UPA regime. However, its stance seems to have changed when facing the other side of the table. A day after the winter session of Parliament ended, 2014, the government decided to move ahead with reforms on further opening up the insurance sector and auctioning of coalmines, as "the country can no longer wait." Sitaram Yechury CPI(M) leader in Rajya Sabah, said: "To appease the domestic corporate sector and international finance capital, the NDA government is seeking to implement further neo-liberal financial and economic reforms to permit them to maximise their profit generation by further exploiting the Indian people and resources. This, the Modi government is doing by bypassing parliamentary procedures....The same BJP shouted from the rooftops against 'ordinance raj' during the last 10 years of the UPA governments. This is a shameless volte face."

The experience with the globalisation process world over reveals that there is widespread increase in hunger following the world food crises of 2007-08 (Sundaram, JK, 2010). It is evident from the people's movement to occupy the Wal-Mart in several countries in 2011-12 and latter. Further, the process of globalisation brought in new institutions and nomenclature with which the bureaucracy and social groups have to cope with. The terminology includes; structural adjustment, special economic zones, good governance, public-private partnership, outsourcing, consultants, decentralisation, empowerment, self-help groups, stake holders, users association, micro-finance, Millennium Development Goals 2000-15 and 2015-30, 20-20 vision. The essence of all these concepts is in the direction of what World Bank document 'State in the Changing World Order' stresses on minimalist state (Haragopal, G, 2012).

The institutions of governance have failed to meet the challenges of the societal development. On the other hand, the policies widened the gap between the better-endowed areas and backward areas and among the social groups. This retarded development in the society is mostly due to the ineffectiveness of the policies and institutions to alter the prevailing unequal socio-economic structure of the society. The Public policies are, more often than not, launched to meet the both internal demands (arrest the unrest among the poor and get the support of the poor in the elections and coming into power) and external demands (to expand the market of Multinational Corporations and capitalism); and the least is the fulfilling of constitutional goals (Balaramulu, Ch, 2004).

However, the effectiveness of any policy including incremental policies/ programmes meant for the welfare of OBCs depends on the State's autonomy to formulate policies, governance systems and levels of peoples' participation. The effectiveness of policies is also closely linked to the people living in the territory have a sovereign power to control the natural resources, cultural life styles and freedom to develop their own policies and institutions of governance to shape their own destiny in line with the needs and demands of people. Against this backdrop, an attempt is made to examine the Food Security policies/ programmes in India.

Food and Nutrition-based Policies of the Indian State

Pre-Independence Era

Historically, the objectives of the Food Security programmes in any society, including India, have been: (i) maintaining price stability; (ii) increasing the welfare facilities for the poor (by providing access to basic foods at reasonable prices to the vulnerable population); (iii) rationing during situations of scarcity, and (iv) keeping a check on private trade and domestic prices. Now they are also meant for ensuring right to food to the people. The origin of the food security in India dates back to the Second World War period. Before 1939, there was no experience of government food rationing, or of other forms of food control. Since the adoption of a laissez-faire policy in 1861, the then government refrained from interference with trade and prices of production (Bhatia, 1991). At the start of the Second World War in

1939 shortage of various essential commodities were anticipated. During the forty years of preceding the war, annual per capita food production had steadily declined from 254 kg (annual average in the decade from 1906-07 to 1915-16) to 181 kg ((annual average in the decade in 1936-37 to 1945-46) (Bhatia, 1991). The average level of consumption was very low. Imports especially rice imports from Barma made up for the difference between domestic production and effective demand.

The Indian State had an obligation to maintain supply lines to the armed forces for the conduct of the war, while, at the same time, supplying essentials to the citizens also. The government for the first time imposed controls on distribution of certain essential commodities under the Defence of India Rules, 1939 and ordered for the setting up of FPSs in the country. During this period India was a net importer of foodgrains, though the imports were small in size, they served to maintain public confidence during a critical period. The price of major foodgrains namely, rice and wheat sharply increased by 2.5 times during the war period. The government made efforts to control the prices of wheat in 1941. However, there was no control either on supply or on movement of wheat, which resulted in the failure of the wheat price control.

The 1940 to 1943 is the crucial period in the emergence of public distribution system. During 1942, there was a serious shortage of foodgrains and large sections of people were deprived of foodgrains. In order to address this issue the Government of India promulgated Rule 81-D under the Defence of India Rules empowering the Provincial Governments to regulate the shops dealing in food grains and even take over their business, if necessary. In the same year, the Government of India set up the Food Department, which was entrusted with the responsibility of regulating prices, procurement, movement and distribution of foodgrains on a centralised basis. A plan for the food economy of India called "The Basic Plan" was drawn up and put into operation from April 1943. The basic plan included issues such as procurement, contracts for purchasing agents, distribution of supplies received under the scheme, inspection, storage, finance and district administration (Chopra, 1988), all meant to keep down prices.

Price stabilisation was the principal objective of food the emerging food distribution policy.

Based on the anticipated harvest of the two major seasons (Kharif and Rabi) the Government of India ordered procurement from surplus States and allocation of food grains to the deficit States. The first Foodgrains Policy Committee was set up in 1943 to recommend a 'sound and effective food policy for the country, The Committee stressed the need for continuing the rationing in the urban centres and inclusion of certain rural areas under the scheme. Food rationing, which was introduced to cover 13 cities, in 1943 was extended to 103 cities and towns in 1944 and extended to 771 towns and rural pockets in 1946. The procurement in surplus States did not work out satisfactorily and the main source of supply of foodgrains during the period 1943-1947 was imports (Swaminadhan, AM, 2009).

The food situation in 1943 was critical and the Government of India modified the basic plan in such a way as to license dealers that are more private to encourage them to bring out the hidden stocks. The eastern region was first in the country implementation of this. However, the traders of Bengal captured most of the supplies intended for Bihar, Orissa and Assam resulting in further hoarding and rise in prices. The great famine of Bengal occurred during this period where the food entitlement failures caused a famine killing between 1.5 and 3 million people (Sen, 1981). Thus, the basic plan and its revised version ultimately failed. During the war period, three different types of rationing were in operation:

1. *Statutory or formal rationing*: Under this system, every cardholder was entitled to receive specified quantities of rationed articles from the ration shop at fixed prices. This was in operation in big cities of India.
2. *Non-statutory or informal rationing*: This was prevalent in the semi-urban areas and in some rural pockets. The system was flexible in such a way that the district authorities depending upon the availability of the stocks could alter the quantum of the rations.
3. *Sectional rationing*: In certain areas, sectional rationing was implemented to meet the foodgrain needs of certain specified

sections of the population like tea estate workers, members of essential services and non-producers of food grains in a region from which the entire marketable surplus was requisitioned.

Though the above three systems were found to render some service to the people, there were a large number of complaints about the foodgrain supply delivery systems and they were totally inadequate. The entire population was not covered and the persons left out had justifiable grievances. The entitlements also varied from State to State and within the State from region/area to region/area, giving rise to serious resentment. The prices also varied and there was not conscious attempt to subsidise the same. Further, there were complaints about the bad quality of the grains supplied by the government. Therefore, in certain areas where the quality was bad and prices were considered high, stocks accumulated due to poor off-take at the same time certain other areas that were ready to buy were waiting for the stocks. Lastly, the grain dealers indulged in various malpractices and the Provincial Governments were either unwilling or unable to take serious action against them, probably because they were also in-charge of the open market operations (Swaminadhan, AM, 2009).

For managing the above systems of rationing, local procurement of foodgrains was to be accomplished by the government apart from arranging for imports. The mode of procurement varied from Province to Province. The First Foodgrains Policy Committee recommended general expansion of statutory price control, extension of rationing the improvement of the procurement machinery. It suggested the creation of a single agency in each province for procurement of the surplus food grains both for civilian and military consumption. Each Province adopted its own machinery for procurement. The following three types of procurement were in vogue during the War period:

1. *Compulsory requisitioning*: The government requisitioned the entire marketable surplus after making provision for family consumption, wages in kind and seed purposes. However, there was much resentment against this and the administrative machinery found it difficult to carry out the operations.

2. *Partial requisitioning:* Here only a part of the marketable surplus was requisitioned. Though the resentment was much lower in this case, the cost of administration compared to the quantity requisitioned was found to be very high.
3. *Occasional requisitioning:* Occasional requisitioning was resorted to in certain cases depending on local conditions. This was tried only for a short while in Bombay and given up in view of stiff opposition.

As part of Grow More Food Campaign, the Government of India, during1946-1948, initiated measures to increase the foodgrain production. Among the other things, these measures involved minor irrigation works, distribution of fertilisers and seeds and land reclamation. After the end of war, the food situation was still seen as precarious by the government: production was insufficient, Grow More Food efforts were not successful and food security was far from imaginary. Overall, results of this campaign lagged behind the expectations. The situation became more difficult after Independence and partition. Independent got 82 per cent of total population of the subcontinent, 75 per cent of the central production and 69 per cent of the irrigated area (Chopra, 1988).

Thus, the food security programmes, during the pre-Independence period, especially during World War periods, were confined to meet the demands of armed forces and urban people of certain cities. In order to overcome the serious shortage of foodgrains, the then government initiated measures regulating prices, procurement and distribution of foodgrains on a centralised basis. It also initiated statutory or formal rationing, non-statutory or informal rationing and sectional rationing measures for supply of foodgrains to the people. However, there were a large number of complaints about foodgrain delivery system. They include: low coverage of households (HHs) and exclusion of large number of HHs, inadequate supply of ration items, variation in the entitlements from state to state and area to area, and variation in the price of the ration items, poor off-take ration by the HHs due to poor quality of foodgrains.

The colonial government failed to take necessary action in rural areas i.e. organising rural works programmes, particularly drought-prone areas. The British raj was obviously much more concerned with the military, civil defence works and strategic industries located in Calcutta and elsewhere in the country than with agricultural labourers, fishermen, transport workers and others who were among the most affected groups (Mooij, Jos, 1999). However, the then government also initiated measures like establishment of FPS, opening food zones, local procurement of foodgrains through compulsory requisition, partial requisition and occasional requisition, importing foodgrains, creation of single agency for procurement of foodgrains in each province, etc.

The Post-Independence Period

Food security has been a major goal of development policy since the beginning of planning. The State has been adopting different methods to achieve it. The government, time and again, initiating measures to promote growth of production, through producer-friendly food price policy, technological inputs, subsidies to farmers, etc.; organised interventions in the food system: procurement, maintaining of a buffer stock and distribution of subsidised food, and; introducing regulation and control of private trade practices through regulated markets and additional legal measures such as Essential Commodities Act, 1955. The Second Foodgrains Policy Committee (1947) favoured foodgrains decontrol and recommended to reduce the area of State intervention in the food market. This recommendation was to scrap the rationing system, to reduce the import of foodgrains and liberalise internal trade of foodgrains. The government initiated measures to implement the recommendations in November 1947. However, liberalisation of internal trade in a shortage situation resulted in sharp increase in foodgrain prices and very soon in September 1948, the government reverted to the price control mechanism.

The Third Foodgrains Policy Committee (1950) pointed out "a few serious contradictions in the policy like the existence of control over foodgrain prices vis-à-vis no control over other agricultural commodities and their influences on production." It further stated that the government is declared policy of feeding the vulnerable sections with an effort to reduce imports simultaneously was contradictory. Financial constraints rather than need, and the government is determined the reductions in imports; "trying to stabilise prices allowing at the same time the open market prices to find their own level" was not consistent. Therefore, the committee wanted the government to follow a consistent policy over a period. It recommended strict control by the government on the procurement and distribution of foodgrains including measures such as levy on producers statutory rationing in urban areas, fixation of open market prices etc.

The Five-Year Plans

During the plan periods, the Government of India and State Governments have undertaken several food and nutritional-based interventions with the technical and financial support or under the directions of the IGOs for ensuring of food security to the people. The rationale behind the food and nutrition-based intervention ought to be to provide a continued assistance throughout all stages of life- beginning even before the birth of an individual. Some of the important food security programmes (see the box-2.1) launched in different plan periods are discussed below, in brief, which would give us insights on the approach of the governments to address the problems food insecurity.

Box-2.1. Food and nutrition-based interventions of the Government: The important Food and nutrition-based interventions during post-Independence period and are in operation:

- Integrated Child Development Services (ICDS), 1975;
- Rajiv Gandhi Drinking Water Mission, 1991;
- Mid-day Meals Programmes, 1995;
- National Old- Age Pension Scheme, 1995;
- Village Grain banks Scheme for Chronically food scarce areas, 1996;
- Targeted Public Distribution System, 1997;
- Antyodaya Anna Yojana, 2000;
- Annapurna, 2000;
- Kishori Shakti Yojana, a nutrition programme for adolescent girls, 2000-01;
- Mahatma Gandhi National Rural Employment Guarantee Programme, 2005;
- National Rural Health Mission, 2005;
- Total Rural Sanitation Campaign, 2007;
- National Food Security Mission, 2009;
- National Rural Livelihood Mission, 2011;
- Rajiv Gandhi Scheme for Empowerment of Adolescent Girls, 2011;
- The National Food Security Act, 2013, (NFSA, 2013).

The First Five Year Plan (1951-1956) emphasis was to maintain the foodgrains distribution system related to the needs of urban and other highly deficit areas. For this purpose, certain cities and towns (selected according to varying criteria in each state) were chosen to be brought under statutory rationing: certain highly deficit areas were also given priority for distribution under non-statutory rationing. In 1952, the Foodgrains (Licensing and Procurement) Order was passed and FPSs were opened to prevent undue rise in prices consequent on the relaxation of controls. In 1953-54, the food zones, which were introduced during the war period to restrict the movement of foodgrains, were abolished. However, the zonal system was re-introduced in 1957 for wheat and rice distribution. By the end of 1954, rationing was very much reduced. This was a period of optimism for agricultural growth. Agricultural production was high in this year. Imports of foodgrains fell from 4.7 million tonnes in 1951 to 0.8 million tonnes in 1954. It was thought that India was nearing self-sufficiency and that government intervention and control could slowly be broken down (Chopra, 1988). However, the increase in agricultural production was confined to certain areas and category farmers, especially large farmers. The backward areas and marginal and small farmers faced the problem of food insecurity. Again, in 1955 food insecurity problems arose again in the country. The weather conditions were unfavourable and the low production prices have had an adverse effect on production. The year 1955 was an important one since it was during this year that the Essential Commodities Act was enacted. This Act, which is in force even today, has the objective of holding control over the production, supply and distribution of and trade and commerce in certain essential commodities. Subsequently, a number of Control Orders have been promulgated under this Act to cover various essential commodities.

The Second Five Year Plan (1956-1961) stressed the need to maintain adequate foodgrains reserve at all times, to be able to meet an adverse situation effectively and promptly. It felt that such a reserve is a necessary to safeguard against the inflationary pressures implicit in a big developmental programme. Actually, it went as far as to suggest that certain important raw materials and a few consumer goods also are to be included in such a measure. In fact, 1957 to 1965 is also the crucial period for emergence of public distribution system in India.

The demand for foodgrains was outstripping supply. The distortions of free market became increasingly evident. The Government of India again reversed food policy and reintroduced controls, in 1957 (Chopra, 1988). Based on the Report of the Foodgrains Enquiry Committee further strengthened the State intervention mechanism though controls over trade and its progressive socialisation. During this period, the State control was exercised though: foodgrains movement restrictions; price control; procurement, licensing and distribution control, and stock holding limits. The Committee stated that complete free trade was undesirable since it intended to increase the price fluctuations. Similarly, full control, in the sense of complete rationing and procurement, seemed undesirable as the government responsibility would become too large to carry (Ashok Mehata Committee Report, 1957), Accordingly, the committee argued in favour of controls of a flexible indirect nature, although in the long run, socialisation of wholesale trade was recommended.

In 1959, "Nationalisation of Wholesale Trade in Foodgrains" was attempted by fixing maximum selling prices at the wholesale and retail levels for rice and wheat. Due to large variations between the open market prices and the maximum prices fixed by the government, the market arrivals dropped. The important objective of food policy became distribution to the 'poorer sections' of the population. While sales from FPS should normally be made on a 'no profit no loss' basis, an exception was made for people in distress for whom even the normal fair price would be too high. The second objective of PDS- that is to help the weaker sections of the society. During the years 1956-1965 wheat and rice imported from the USA under Public Law 480 (PL 480) was pumped into the PDS at prices, which were lower than the domestic ones.

The Third Five Year Plan (1961-1966) formulated as its policy goals inter alia, price stabilisation and correction of seasonal and regional variations. Towards this end, it recommended strengthening the cooperative network for procurement and distribution, giving government agencies a more active role by extension of state trading regulation of private trade by licensing etc. The expansion of PDS in the period 1957-1965 both in terms of foodgrain distributed and number of shops, were greatly facilitated by large-scale imports under PL 480 conditions and pumped into the PDS at prices, which were lower than the domestic ones. The stated purpose was to protect the vulnerable sections of the population against the rising prices. India imported cheap wheat from USA, partly as gift and partly to be paid for in local currency. These rupees were put into a fund that could be utilised for development purposes. For the USA, PL 480 was a way to dispose of its wheat surplus and to support US domestic farm prices. At the same time, PL 480 was important in US foreign policy providing a powerful means to impose the US will on India. The USA extracted an economic and political price by suddenly withholding supplies and imposing conditions on the Government of India to modify its policies on currency valuation, fertilizer prices, foreign trade regulations etc (Mooij, J, 1999; Friedman, 1982), Byres and Crow mention that:

> ...Among other things, India agreed to the following: that for seven years the government should no longer have control over the pricing and distribution of fertilizers by private fertilizer firms; that the Indian government should its demand for fifty one per cent ownership of joint ventures in the fertilizer field; that greater latitude be allowed to American private firms operating in India; that India should stop trading with North Vietnam. Apart from this, India's devaluation of the rupee by 36.5 per cent on June 1966 was strongly influenced by American pressure (1983).

In the period 1958-66, India imported nearly 50 million tonnes of foodgrains, most of it under PL 480 conditions. In the peak year 1966, India imported more than 10 million tonnes, which was about 14 per cent of the total amount of foodgrains available in the country. It is doubtful that India needed this large amount of foreign cereals, and it may even be argued that these massive imports were counterproductive. The crises in domestic production that became clear in 1964-66 may well have been partly induced by the glut of cheap foodgrains in the Indian market (Bhatia, 1991). Due to these imports, foodgrains were relatively cheap in this period. According to Mundle (1981), there was specific price regime during these years in which the equilibrium price itself was reduced to a lower level due to extra, imported supplies. The result of this policy was that 'the government successfully blocked a potential shift of the terms of trade in favour of agriculture during this period' (Mundle, 1991).

That the Indian government was eager to keep prices down and to favour industry over agriculture is not surprising. It is in keeping with the general development strategy of that period. The Second and Third Plans (1955-65) specially emphasised the building of modern industrial sector. In these plans, food policy was predominantly regarded as a means to contain price rises and inflation. The Second Plan for instance, argues for imports and market control, as 'high or rising prices of primary necessities are apt to create serious difficulties…'[that could disturb the entire plan]' (GoI, 1956). In this period, the PDS supported the industrial labour class, the industrial capitalist class, and the urban-based politically important middle classes. With the help of cheap food and the expansion of a distribution system the government of India succeeded in maintaining a low rate of price increase (around 2.5 per cent per annum), which helped to maintain a sort of social equilibrium in the urban areas (Chakravarthy, 1987).

The establishment of Food Corporation of India (FCI) in 1965 with the objective of building up buffer stocks of foodgrains to achieve food security to the people was a major landmark of the Indian Food Policy. From 1965 onwards, the PDS became an important element in the planning process. The old FPSs scheme was re-designated as PDS shops. This has enabled the government to undertake trading operations through which it can influence the market prices and to achieve the third objective of food security i.e. to guarantee reasonable prices to the farmers and thereby act as an incentive to increase production. The Foodgrains committee welcomed the constitution of an agricultural price policy and price structure in the context of the need to raise agricultural production. In Mundle's terms, a new price regime emerged, in which the equilibrium prices were considered too low by the government. The objective of food policy now became to raise the level of the equilibrium price itself, while the earlier the thrust of policy was towards preventing agricultural prices from rising, [now] the emphasise was on establishing price levels which would act as an incentive to domestic production. PDS supplies changed from imported to domestic foodgrains, while procurement prices were fixed at an attractive level (Mundle, 1981; Bharadwaj, 1994).

The shift in foodgrain price policy had a lot to do with the desire to become self-sufficient in foodgrains. In view of the political conditions that accompanied US wheat under - PL 480, the then government has decided to scale up domestic production and protect its national sovereignty. The then Prime Minister's statement makes the stand of the government clear:

> *As early in 1951, Nehru argued in a broadcast: 'we have sought help from abroad...and we shall continue to do so under of necessity, but the conviction is growing upon me more forcefully than ever how dangerous it is for us to depend for this primary necessity of life on the foreign countries. We can never function, with the freedom we desire, if we are always dependent in this matter on others. It is only when we obtain self-sufficiency in food that we can progress and develop ourselves. Otherwise there is continuous pressure of circumstances, there is trouble and misery, and there is some times shame and humiliation' (Quoted in Bhatia, 1991).*

However, this stand was lasted for no longer period. The foreign experts especially advisors of the Ford Foundation, USA were very critical of India's food and agricultural policy. They insisted the Indian Government to adopt the Green Revolution (GR) strategy –application of modern technology- and large investments in modern inputs and price incentives to farmers to increase the production and overcome the issue of food insecurity. The IGOs- World Bank also supported this strategy. Though this strategy has enabled us to increase the production, it has contributed for expansion of the market of MNCs in the field of fertilizer and pesticides. The farmers, medium and large farmers in the better-endowed areas, used the modern seeds and applied the fertilizers and pesticides and benefited more. This has resulted in greater economic, regional and cultural disparities, across the castes and classes leading to rural unrest. This strategy destroyed not only the local technology, which was eco-friendly, but also foodgrain production suitable to our traditional/cultural food habits. This in a way has violated the food sovereignty right of the people.

The GR policy not only benefited better-endowed areas and groups, but also helped the Indian Monopoly houses, particularly those collaborating with the MNCs, in diverting its activities to agro-chemical and agro-machinery industries. The Industrial Big Houses (IBH) and other pressure groups Federation of Indian Chamber of Commerce and Industry (FICCI) have influenced the government to create new institutions like Fertilizers Corporation of India and Agro-Industries Corporation for expansion of agro-business of the private industries-chemical and agro-machinery (Ganguly, AS, 1983).

The IBHs have shown keen interest in the modernisation of agricultural production by providing financial assistance to the agricultural sector. The RBI reported that traders, especially dealers in fertilizers and agricultural goods, were giving short time loans to farmers accompanied by advice on improved methods of cultivation. The volume of such credit was considerable. Another factor that emerged simultaneously as noted by the RBI was that commercial banks were proposing to route credit to the cultivators through joint-stock sugar factories (RBI, 1969). At the same time political power of farmers, especially large farmers themselves had also gained considerable momentum. By the 1960s, agricultural lobbies had started to influence politics in several states. The introduction of a much more conscious producer price policy was a move to accommodate this increasingly powerful class of wealthy agriculturists (cf. Mitra, 1977; Varshney, 1993). Thus, there was close relation between Indian Capitalist classes and the State. The Industrial sector tried to enter the rural area and captures its markets and shift the development approach, especially food security policy, not directly but through the technique of diversification into agro-business and to allow its agro-based industries. The big farmers also influenced the agricultural policy in their favour.

The Fourth Five Year Plan (1969-1974): Until the end of Fourth Plan, India's main emphasis was on the aggregate growth of the economy and reliance was placed on the percolation effects of growth. This has resulted in mass movements; growing restlessness of the masses, which was reflected in Naxalbari uprising, tribal movement in Srikakulam of Andhra Pradesh and Separate Telengana State demand and other mass movements sent danger signals to the ruling classes and their power structures. These movements brought several questions on development and Governance in India (Hara Gopal, G, foreword, 1991). "In the face of continuing poverty and malnutrition, an alternative strategy of development comprising a frontal attack on hunger, poverty, unemployment and malnutrition became a national priority from the beginning of the Plan. This shift in strategy has given rise to a number of interventions to increase the purchasing power of the poor; to improve the provision of basic service to the poor and to devise a security system through which the most vulnerable sections of the poor, viz. women and children, can be protected."

The then government gave different approach to the development model i.e. **'Growth with Social Justice'** and announced several policy decisions and establishment of institutions in favour of the poor. It also tried to bring reforms to reduce inequalities among various regions and increase the efficiency of the administrative structure. The most important of them are Administrative Reforms Commission (1966-1969); Nationalisation of Banks (1969); Marginal Farmers Development Agency (1969); Small Farmers Development Agency (1969); Central Land Reforms Committee (1969-70); six-point formula for the development of the Telangana region. The plan recommended that the PDS be established on a regular basis and broadened to cover the rural areas also. It contemplated gradual replacement of the FPS System by Co-operative Consumer Stores or Multi-purpose Cooperative Societies. To make this viable, the Plan recommended that they should sell other articles of mass consumption also. This was expected to exert a downward pressure on open market prices. All these measures were undertaken to restrain the popular unrest and enhance the incremental capacity of the governance for better performance (Hara Gopal, G, 2003). In fact, if these programmes were implemented seriously the major problems of our country, especially food insecurity would have been solved largely. However, the policy-makers in this country are enthusiastic in announcing the programmes and do not take same interest in implementing them (Bala Ramulu, Ch, 2004).

The Fifth Five Year Plan (1974-1979) period is most important in the socio-economic and political history the country. The then government imposed National Emergency in 1975 to control the nationwide agitation by the opposition political parties. It also launched several anti-poverty programmes and established institutions to gain the support of the poor. Most important of them are: 20- point Economic Programme; Regional Rural Banks; Integrated Tribal Development Agency; Commissions for Scheduled Castes, Scheduled Tribes, Other Backward Classes and Women and Children; Integrated Child Development Services and Integrated Rural Development Programme in 1978. All these programmes were meant for providing employment and income for the poor and enabling them to have access to foodgrains.

Integrated Child Development Services

In addition to the supply of foodgrains under PDS, the Government of India also launched Integrated Childhood Development Services (ICDS) - the world's largest child development programme- in 1975, as Centrally Sponsored Scheme (CSS) to combat the problem of malnutrition in the country. One of its core aims is to improve the nutritional and health status of the children below the age of six years and pregnant and lactating mothers. The main purpose of the ICDS scheme is the distribution of supplementary nutritious food to children, adolescent girls and women and pregnant and lactating women in all rural habitations and urban slums. The programme is divided into three branches: the Supplementary Nutrition Programme (SNP), which addresses children and pregnant/lactating women: the Kishori Shakti Yojana (KSY) and the Nutrition Programme for Adolescent Girls (NPAG), which is aimed at girls in the age group 11-18 (19 in NPAG). The KSY is universally applied, while NPAG is conceived for underweight adolescents.

The plan, however, played down the welfare aspect of the PDS. Its emphasis was on productivity increases and increases in wages. It contemplated two main perspectives. (i) The PDS must avoid sizeable subsidy on the public exchequer, and (ii) the distribution basket should be reasonably small and the PDS commodities should be reasonably homogeneous in character. The rationale of a PDS according to this Plan must derive from the need to discourage speculation activities in trading on the one hand and the need to ensure steady growth of production on the other. The total amount of foodgrain handled by the FCI increased from 10 million tonnes per annum in 1965 to more than 18 million tonnes at the end of the 1980s. In the same period, the number of ration shops tripled. However, the end of the 1980s, there were more than three, 50,000 ration outlets. The system also became more and more costly. In 1965, there was hardly any subsidy involved, while twenty-five years later the subsidy given by the Central Government fluctuated around 25000-28000 million rupees. Apart from the quantitative enlargement, the system ruralised the PDS.

At the end of 1980s, approximately 75 per cent of the ration shops were located in rural areas (NSS, 42 round 1986-67).

The Sixth Five Year Plan (1980-1985) has reverted the food security policy to the old welfare approach. It wanted the PDS to be developed as a stable and permanent feature of the policies to control prices, to reduce fluctuations in supply, and to achieve an equitable distribution of essential consumer goods to the people. The Plan identified a list of essential commodities (i.e. apart from foodgrains) and recommended that all of them may be supplied in all the regions of the country. It anticipated horizontal linkages of the PDS with other Plan programmes, e.g., Mobile Fair Price Shops in areas where rural development works were in progress.

In addition to the above, the government launched wage and food security oriented policies such as Food for Work Programme (1977); National Rural Employment Programme (1980); Rural Landless Employment Guarantee Programme (1983) through which the foodgrains are distributed. These schemes have introduced an element of targeting within public distribution policy. While the PDS is a universal programme, these special schemes aim to guarantee that part of the foodgrains reach the neediest people. However, the studies on the wage-oriented programmes indicate that the goal of providing productive employment and distribution of foodgrains to the needy people remained a distance dream in the country. The reasons are: lack of manpower planning, undertaking un-productive works, selection of schemes without proper examination, lack of supervision, erratic distribution of foodgrains, supply of poor quality of foodgrains, undertaking the works on political considerations and on ad-hoc basis, undertaking the schemes near the residency of the rich farmer, frequent changes in the guidelines, lack of provision for the maintenance of assets, delay in undertaking the schemes and consequent non-completion of works, payment of low wages to the beneficiaries, lack of administrative staff, interference of political parties, corruption etc, which collectively contributed for the ineffectiveness of the programme (Bala Ramulu, Ch, 1996). Ironically, the contractors, rich farmers and bureaucratic agencies (Bala Ramulu, Ch, 1997) corner the benefits of wage-oriented policies. All these are the issues of governance.

Another strategy launched during 1975 was White Revolution Technology for providing food supply- milk and egg, meat- the most nutritious food- to the poor. The government initiated this strategy with the financial and technical assistance of WFP. Under this, the programmes called Operation Flood-I (OF-I) in 1975, OF- II in 1979, OF-III in 1985 were launched with a view to modernising dairy industry and promoting the quality of life by generating additional employment and income for a very large number of agricultural labourers, marginal and small farmers, as well as by supplying nutritious food to the people in the rural and urban areas. To fulfil these objectives, the government established National Dairy Development Board, Indian Dairy Development Corporation, National Milk Grid at the national level and cooperatives in various States for integrated production, processing and marketing of milk and milk products. Apart from this, under Integrated Rural Development Programme (IRDP) several thousands of poor farmers and agricultural labourers are given Jercy cows, Murra buffaloes and sheep to improve the milk production and also poultry-meat and eggs production in the country. These initiatives have made a positive impact on the milk producers and households in getting employment and income. Today, India acquired self-sufficiency in milk and poultry sectors and is ranked as second or third largest producer in these sectors in the world.

The Government of India announced de-licensing of the dairy sector in 1992 and this has facilitated several IBHs and MNCs to enter into dairy market and profits. The contribution of the OF-I, II, and III is that several thousands of IBHs and MNC companies (most important are Glaxo, Nestle, Cadbury, Noble Soya, Walls Ice-cream, Kisan Foods, Horlicks, General Foods, Raymonds Woollen, Apple Industries, Adi Godrej, etc,) have entered into dairy sector and producing the products-milk powder, ghee, baby foods, skimmed milk, biscuts, chocolates, ice-creams, etc. All these products are costly and the poor people cannot afford to purchase them. The experts in this field point out that the natural fallout of this could be a flood of milk based products in the Indian markets on the one hand, but an acute shortage of liquid milk on the other (Arindam Mukarjee, 1992). In the case of poultry sector, though there is enormous increase in the production, the average consumption of the people is less than 35 eggs in a year (as per the norms each individual is required to consume one egg every day to maintain the balance of the calories of nutritious food) indicating the lack of purchasing power of the people.

The Seventh Five Year Plan (1985-1990) emphasised on the human resource development (New Education Policy,1986) and technology mission (1988) (priority to literacy for adults, oil seeds, immunisation, protected drinking water, and communication) and continuation of asset and wage oriented poverty alleviation programmes. Along with these, the policy-makers made a strong plea to make the PDS supplementary to the poverty alleviation programmes. It wanted the PDS to be extended to un-served areas especially the remote and inaccessible areas. Expansion of PDS was made as one of the important points of the Revised 20 Point Programme (1986) and Minimum Needs Programme and more budgetary support towards food subsidies was assured. Thus, a close link of the PDS with food security for the vulnerable sections of the population was attempted during the seventh plan.

However, the studies reveal that in spite of the droughts, physical and economic access to food has increased. On the other hand, the PDS has not eradicated persistent hunger and malnutrition. Furthermore, the system did not succeeded in assuring reasonable prices to coarse grain producers. The system has concentrated on the rice and wheat, and hence on the relatively well-off farmers. Thus, Tyagi (1990) concludes, 'the food policy has not succeeded in protecting the interests of the most vulnerable sections of the population whether amongst the consumers of amongst the producers'.

Washington Consensus and Decline in the Public Expenditure in Agriculture Sector

As part of the expansion of globalisation process the IGOs, The term Washington Consensus was coined in 1989 by the economist John Williamson to describe a set of ten relatively specific economic policy prescriptions that he considered constituted the "standard" reform package promoted for crises-wracked developing countries, especially for the recovery of countries in Latin America from the economic and financial crises of the 1980s, by Washington, D.C.-based institutions such as the International Monetary Fund (IMF), World Bank and the

US Treasury Department. The prescriptions encompassed policies in such areas as macro-economic stabilisation, economic opening with respect to both trade and investment, and the expansion of market forces within the domestic economy.

One of the concerns of the consensus is provision for the redirection of public spending from subsidies ("especially indiscriminate subsidies", especially subsidies to farmers for fertilizers and other modern farm inputs) toward broad-based provision of key pro-growth, pro-poor services like primary education, primary healthcare and infrastructure investment. For decades, the World Bank and donor nations pressed developing countries to cut back or eliminate government fertilizer subsidies to farmers. World Bank experts also urged the countries to have farmers shift to growing cash crops for export and to use foreign exchange earnings to import food. This has affected the foodgrain production and several million of people needed emergency food aid. To meet this demand the governments in the developing countries reversed policy and continued subsidies to the farmers.

India also followed the above concerns to improve the governance and economy. This has affected the agricultural sector, as there is decline in the public expenditure. A number of authors stressed that the *Washington* Consensus has not contributed to the improvement of living conditions of people, particularly poor in the developing countries. According to Joseph Stanislaw and Daniel Yergin authors of *The Commanding Heights* the policy prescriptions described in the Washington Consensus were "developed in Latin America, by Latin Americans, in response to what was happening both within and outside the region." In view of the implication conveyed by the term Washington Consensus that the policies were largely external in origin, Stanislaw and Yergin report that the term's creator, John Williamson, has "regretted the term ever since", stating "it is difficult to think of a less diplomatic label.

The Eighth Five Year Plan (1992-1997) focused on poverty related issues, especially the demand for food for all. The political activists, NGOs, the economists working in international organisations agitated on the demand of ensuring food for all, the food, nutrition, security, and their efforts have finally led to adoption of a **World Declaration and Plan of Action for Nutrition** at Rome in December 1992. The Structural Adjustment Programmes (SAP) undertaken in many countries have also forced policy-makers and intellectuals to consider the impact of these adjustments on the nutritional status of people (Alderman, 1992). In India both the internal (severe economic crises balance of payment crises and the demand for reservation to the OBC in the government) and the external factors (Gulf war and Collapse of Communism in USSR and East Europe, etc) compelled the Indian government to accept the IMF and World Bank directed SAP. It emphasised on the process of abolition of import control over all items, privatisation of public sector and adoption of a better market economy to determine the pattern of investment and output. Since the SAP, emphasis was on reduction in government expenditure from 1991 onwards and cutting down the subsidies on food was mooted during this phase of the PDS. Towards this end, it recommended targeting of PDS assured supplies of essential commodities at subsidised prices to the population residing in disadvantaged and backward areas of the country. In the mid-1990s, the PDS suffers from financial un-sustainability combined with decreasing interest on the part of consumers.

The effect of the new economic reforms on food distribution has been two-fold. On the one hand, there was a tendency to stress the need for reduction, or at least rationalisation of government expenditure (Bhagavati and Sreenivasan, 1993; Pursell and Gulati, 1993). In the mid 1990s, government subsidy was approximately Rs 50,000 million per year, and it was argued that this was very high. The rise of the subsidy bill in the 1990s was seen considerable, but that this was only so at current prices. At constant prices, or as percentage of GNP, the rise of the food subsidy is much less dramatic. Periods of a rising subsidy have alternated with periods of a reduction (Swaminadhan, 1996). Nevertheless, popular phrases in the 1990s were 'streamlining of PDS', 'pruning of PDS', 'revamping of the system', 'making the PDS viable' and 'subsidy burden'. They all stress the lack of financial means to sustain the system. Targeting was depicted as the solution, as it would combine the provisioning of food to the neediest people with a reduction of government expenditure (Mooji, J, 1999).

On the other hand, the safety net aspects of the PDS came again to the forefront. In the 1990s, the PDS was regarded as a crucial component of safety net, meant to alleviate problems of poverty, partially induced or aggravated by structural adjustment. However, in actual practices a number of different policy changes occurred. The new economic reforms have resulted in increases in PDS prices. Between 1991 and 1994, the issue prices of PDS foodgrains selling price of the FCI-have gone up by more than 40 per cent. The result was that the price difference between PDS food grains and open market food grains has become small. Consequently, the off-take of foodgrains has come down. During 1993, against an allocation of 90.53 lakh tonnes of wheat, the off take was only 47.39 lakh tonnes and against an allocation of 121 lakh tonnes of rice, the off take was a mere 80.46 lakh tones (Gargi Pasai, in Hindu, 6th Feb. 1994). This increase in issue of prices not resulted in a reduction of overall food subsidy. On the contrary, food subsidy has nearly doubled in 1991-94 period. This is due to the simultaneous increase in procurement prices. Between 1990-91 and 1994-95, procurement prices were increased by 60 per cent in the case of rice and 66 per cent in the case of wheat (EPW editorial, 10th June 1995). Thus, in effect, the subsidy became more a producers' subsidy than a consumer subsidy (Varshney, 1993).

A paradoxical situation has emerged in that both procurement and distribution prices equal open markets prices. PDs off-take has come down and procurement was very high. Consequently, the buffer stock has tripled in three years (more than 37 million tonnes in June 1995, as compared to 12.2 million tonnes in April 1992) (Hanumanth Rao and Nayyar, 1994, EPW, editorial, 16th March, 1996). The maintenance of this buffer stock added to the food subsidy bill. In January 1996, the stocks were reduced again to 25 million tonnes, but not because of increasing PDS off-take but because of open market sales and exports (EPW, editorial, 16th March, 1996).

In the second half of the decade, the need for special attention to poverty issues induced or overlooked by adjustment programmes was widely acknowledged in Bank (World) documents. One component of the approach to poverty with adjustment was an attention to investments in human capital in general and nutrition in particular. More concretely, future interventions might benefit from continued assessment of whether explicit nutrition programmes are more appropriate than broad policy considerations, whether targeted programmes are more effectively implemented than broad based measures in all environments and whether nutrition is best promoted by food policy and food oriented subsidies or by health and sanitation programmes.

Mid Day Meal Scheme

As a part of safety net measures, the Government of India initiated several programmes for the benefit of children, women, tribal and others. The most important of them is Mid Day Meal Scheme launched in August 1995. The aim of the Scheme is two-fold: first, to ensure the necessary nutrition to every child in the age 6-10, and second to give it primary school instruction. A special focus is placed on children living in drought-affected areas, guaranteeing them adequate support during the summer vacations. The MDM is not just a programme to enforce the right to food, but is also meant somehow to attract the children to come to school, creating the basis for their future livelihood. Every child in government and government-aided primary and upper school and all schools run by a State Government, UT Administration, or with government money by a Local Body or Non-Governmental Organisation, in every part of the country, shall receive a cooked food ration with a minimum content of 450 calories and 12 grams of protein containing the necessary micronutrients (like iron or folic acid). The scheme covers students of Class 1-4 and in drought affected areas, the MDM is to be distributed during the summer vacations also. At least once every six months, de-worming tablets are to be given to the students. The Central and State Governments finance the scheme. However, major part of the funding is from Central Government.

Village Grain Banks Scheme for Chronically Food Scarce Areas

The main objective of the Village Grain Bank Scheme (VGBS) is to provide safeguard against starvation during the period of natural calamity or during the lean season when the marginalised food insecure households do not have sufficient resources to purchase the rations. Such people in need of foodgrains will be able to borrow foodgrains from the Village Grain Banks set up within their villages. It is primarily based an approach contribution, mutual assistance at the local level. The scheme has two components, viz, food component and cash component. Under the food component, each grain bank will store one quintal of foodgrains (Rice, Wheat or coarse grain of local preference) per family for an average 40 Below Poverty Line/ Antyodaya Anna Yojana families, which will be released as one time grant by the Central Government. During 1996-97, VGBs were established in 11 States. In 2001, the Government of India expanded the then existing Grain Bank Scheme to all the endemic, drought and migration prone areas with concentration of tribal population and in other non-tribal areas. Village Panchayat/Gram Sabah, self-help groups or NGOs identified by State Government are eligible for running the grain banks. In November 2004, the scheme was transferred to Ministry of Consumer Affairs, Food and Public Distribution for revision and implementation, as nodal Ministry.

This scheme was revised in February 2006 and Central Government has issued sanction for the establishment of 3282-grain banks in seven states, namely Andhra Pradesh, Orissa, Madhya Pradesh, Chhattisgarh, Jharkhand, Tripura, Meghalaya and Uttar Pradesh. The revised scheme envisages coverage of 30 to 40 Below Poverty Line and Antyodaya Anna Yojana families identified by the State governments as chronically food deficit areas for setting up the grain banks. Government of India provides one quintal of foodgrains per family as one-time grant. This is likely to meet about three months' requirement of grains for an average family of five persons. The Executive Committee, consisting of three to five persons, is expected to ensure proper storage of foodgrains and effective participation and management. Involvement of at least one woman in the committee would be essential. The implementation of the Scheme is the joint responsibility of the Central and State Governments. Zilla Panchayat/Deputy Commissioner/ Collector will consolidate the proposals received from the organisations i.e. GP/SHGs/NGOs and inform the State government, which in turn will consolidate the proposal for the State and do the needful for establishing the grain banks in the target villages by allocating foodgrains and sanctioning financial component out of the foodgrains and financial allocations made by Department of Food and Public Distribution for the respective State/UT.

The Government of India, during the financial year, under Village Grain Bank Scheme sanctioned food and cash components for establishment of 268 Grain Banks in Andhra Pradesh. Unlike other States, the government assigned this responsibility to the SERP for executing the Scheme- identification of Village Grain Banks, training the members, storage of foodgrains and monitoring of the scheme. The SERP has identified five districts viz, Chittoor, YSR Kadapa, SPSR Nellore, Sreekakulam and Adilabad for implementation of the scheme, during the year 2011-12.

The Ninth Five Year Plan (1997-2002) emphasised on developing strategies integrating the food production and distribution systems with the employment and poverty alleviation programmes. The structure of incentives for the producers of food was reviewed. While incentive pricing continued to remain an important element of the policy for boosting agricultural production in general, and foodgrains production in particular, the government focused more on devising cost-saving and yield-raising technologies and on creating rural infrastructure. This required increased investments in research, extension and infrastructure, which resulted in reduction and diversion of resources away from subsidies.

The Plan dispensed with the area-based approach and suggested that the PDS to be operated for the benefit of the poorer sections of the society in all the areas, especially in the remote and backward areas. It recommended a dual pricing formula for the BPL and APL cardholders, the subsidy being much higher for the former group (in terms of both quantity and price). From a Universal Delivery System the goal was shifted towards a Targeted Public Distribution System, which came into operation on 1.6.1997.

Targeted Public Distribution System (TPDS, 1997)

Following the advice given in an influential World Bank document (World Bank, 1996) the Government of India introduced the Targeted Public Distribution System (TPDS) in 1997 to restrict the food subsidy (GOI, 1997). The policy initiated targeting of households based on an income criterion to demarcate 'poor' and 'non-poor' households. The Targeted PDS differs from earlier variants of the PDS in certain key respects. The most distinctive feature of the TPDS in relation to previous policy i.e. Universal Delivery System is the introduction of targeting, specifically, the division of the entire population into BPL and APL categories, based on the poverty line defined by the Planning Commission. The government introduced a differential pricing system: poor HHs gets PDS foodgrains at a lower price than the APL HHs. However, the experts on the subject point out that this type of targeting can never contribute to a reduction of the system. It only means the PDS expands and becomes more expensive (Mooij, J, 1999).

Good Governance and Poverty Alleviation

The IGOs, along with the SAP, focused on good governance and the poverty alleviation. The World Bank stressed on the Good Governance for sustainable development. The World Bank Report (1997) on a State in the changing world stated that development is not just about getting the right or appropriate-economic and technical inputs but also creation of effective institutional environment. Further institutions' ability to focus on core public activities; underpinning the market transactions and civil society; increasing citizen's voice and partnership in design, implementation and monitoring of public goods and services; policy to decentralisation and sectoral approach; incentives to the public officials to make them more flexible; ensuring accountability and competition in the provision of public goods and services; controlling corruption and corrupt behaviour etc, are most essential for sustainable development. Good economic policies (including promotion of macro-economic stability), well-developed human capital, and openness to the world economy are necessary for broad based sustainable growth and the reduction of poverty. The governments are also expected to respond to the rapid diffusion of technology, growing democratic pressures, increased environmental concerns, greater global integration of markets and a shift to more democratic form of government (World Bank, 1997).

However, the studies indicate that the concerns for social justice have come to be abandoned with the inauguration of economic reforms in India. This shift in the role of the State from the interventionist to the role of regulator, calls for deeper mediation. The ineffectiveness of the governance and incompetence of instrumentalities, particularly the so-called meritorious bureaucratic apparatus is to be traced to the absence or marginal involvement of people in the very process of development (Kuldeep Mathur, 1999). The economic reforms led to the closure of several public undertakings managed earlier by the State, retreated from the welfare domain, and abandonment of agrarian reforms and relaxation of laws meant for protecting the industrial labour. The whole emphasis on privatisation led to downsizing of bureaucracy, including governance towards a greater maintenance of order, either through a rule or even without law. These factors rise to the emergence of people's movements for improving the quality of governance and demand for upholding rights (Hara Gopal, G, 2003).

Rural Poverty Reduction Programmes (2000)

The UNO declared 1997 to 2007 as Anti-Poverty Decade and committed for elimination of hunger and poverty. The World Bank recognised that India is in the forefront of economic reforms and initiating poverty alleviation programmes to reduce the poverty through accelerated economic growth with equity. The Bank sponsored District Poverty Initiative Project (DPIP)/ Velugu Projects in different states, including Andhra Pradesh. Latter it is renamed as Rural Poverty Reduction Programmes (RPRP) in 2000. This strategy is based on the principles that self-managed grassroots institutions and community participation in development of projects would improve material conditions and autonomy of the poor. It also aims at convergence of anti-poverty programmes at the state, district, mandal/taluk and village levels. The grassroots level institutions-SHGs networks from state to village- are expected to enable the poor to involve themselves actively in the entire process of decision-making leadership. They are also expected to generate additional profitable employment and income to the poor and making them accessible to market spaces and their life more sustainable. These measures are expected to enable the poor to increase their livelihood opportunities, purchasing power and ensure food security.

Though the project emphasised on the grassroots level institutions for generating rural livelihood opportunities to the poor, it is placed outside the umbrella of the democratically elected institutions-PRIs. The creation of multiple organisations (PRIs and SHGs) for mobilisation of the people led to contradictions among the people's institutions and working at cross-purposes. Further, the studies indicate that the land-based schemes have enabled the poor to derive benefits, while the non-land based schemes have not enabled the poor to get benefits from the schemes. The lack of freedom in choosing the scheme, lack of forward and backward linkages, lukewarm attitude of authorities concerned, market imperfections, lack of remunerative prices for the products produced by the poor, etc, reduced the livelihood opportunities, purchasing power of poor and denying access to food and their rights. All these are the challenges of the governance in ensuring food to the poor.

Antyodaya Anna Yojana

Antyodaya Anna Yojana (AAY) is for the 'poorest of the poor', particularly destitute and disadvantaged households, in which foodgrain is distributed with an additional subsidy. In order to make TPDS more focused and targeted towards the poorest section of population, the AAY was launched in December 2000. The beneficiaries receive an Antyodaya card, which entitles them to 35 kg of highly subsidised grains at FPS shops. The discount is considerably higher compared to the subsidy received with simple TPDS cards, since the programme addresses the poorest of the poor. Initially, AAY contemplated identification of one core poorest of the poor families from amongst the BPL families covered under TPDS within the states and providing those foodgrains at a highly subsidised rate of Rs 2 per kg for wheat and Rs 3 per kg for rice. In Andhra Pradesh it is Re. one per kg of rice. The AAY scheme has been extended in subsequent years. An Antyodaya card is assigned to: aged, infirm, disabled, destitute men and women, pregnant and lactating women, widows and other single women with no regular support, old persons (aged 60 or above) with no regular support and no assured means of subsistence; households with a disabled adult and no assured means of subsistence; households where no adult member can work. The scheme is entirely funded by the Central Government.

Annapurna

The Annapurna scheme was designed to give food security to those old people who have the criteria for being eligible under NOAPS, but do not get the money from the scheme. Under the Annapurna, 10 kg of grains are transferred monthly to old destitute people who are eligible for NOAPS but do not get the pension. Since 2003, the scheme was completely transferred to State level. Under this scheme, the BPL households are eligible to get 35 kgs of food-grains per month from public distribution centres. The foodgrain is supplied on free of cost to the beneficiaries.

The Tenth Five Year Plan (2002-2007) categorically rejected the idea of Universal Public Distribution System. It wanted the TPDS scheme to be implemented effectively and felt that the food security should be restricted to the BPL population alone. It wanted the TPDS to consist of only rice and wheat and specifically mentioned that sugar should be kept out of the PDS. As regards kerosene, the Plan recommended reducing the subsidy and eliminating the State's sales tax, to encourage supply that is more private. It also recommended the scaling down of the buffer stock with the option to go for imports or exports as the situation warrants. Finally, it recommended reduction of the number of FPSs and opening up the public distribution supplies through private licensed shops by introducing a system of food stamps, food credit cards etc.

Mahatma Gandhi National Rural Employment Guarantee Programme, 2005

The central objective of the Policy Integration Department of ILO is to further greater policy coherence and the integration of social and economic policies at both the international and national level. To this end, it works closely with other multilateral agencies and national actors such as governments, trade unions, employers' federations, NGOs and universities. As a part of its strategy ILO supported for rural employment programmes, including the National Rural Employment Guarantee Programme/Act (NREGP/A) in India launched in 2005. The Act guarantees 100 days of work to rural households who undertake unskilled manual work, with 33 per cent of all workdays reserved for women workers. The objectives of the programme as stated in the guidelines are to enhance livelihood security while producing durable assets, empowering women, reducing distress migration and promoting social equity. In October 2009, the programme was renamed as Mahatma Gandhi National Rural Employment Guarantee Programme (MGNREGP). It is different from previous employment programmes to the extent that it is rights-based and demand-driven, and envisages local government and community participation in its implementation. The return to power of the Indian National Congress government in the 2009 elections has been attributed to the implementation of this programme by some activists and political analysts in India (Roy and Dey, 2009; Bidwai, 2009, Kumbhar, 2009; Harikrishnan, 2009).

Though MNREGA was designed to minimise the well known problems of leakages and targeting in past programmes, including an incentive structure for performance and disincentive for non-performance and accountability through periodic social audits for evaluation and improvement (Mehrotra, 2008), the studies on the subject indicate that the programme also encountered several problems in the implementation. They are: wages paid are lower than minimum wages; distressing delay in the payment of wages; demand for work is not properly captured; dated receipts for work applications are not properly given; the payment of unemployment allowance is a rarity; shortage of staff; irregular flow funds; leakages and corruption etc are the universal problems across all the States (Sameeksha, 2012). The studies unfolds that the average man days employment generated to the poor is less than 45 days in a year, indicating that the programme has not made positive significant impact on the living conditions of the poor, particularly access to food security in the country. Further studies also highlighted that the assets created under the programme are mostly ad-hoc in nature and unproductive. To transfer Rs 50 to the beneficiary for the work done under this programme, the government is incurring Rs 180. The net result is that to transfer Re. one the government is spending Rs 5. Due to these and other considerations (as this is the pet programme of UPA government), the NDA government is contemplating to reform the programme by confining it to the most backward districts (200 districts or 2500 blocks) and change in wage and material component from 60: 40 to 50: 50. This amount to reducing the wage component would affect the employment and income opportunities and thereby reducing the food availability of the poor (Reforming MGNREGP- Essential or Death knell, NDTV, 30-10-2014).

National Rural Health Mission (2005-12)

Recognising the importance of health in the process of economic and social development and improving the quality of life of our citizens, the Government of India has launched the National Rural Health Mission (2005-12) to carry out necessary architectural correction in the basic healthcare delivery system. The mission adopts a synergistic approach by relating health to determinants of good health viz. segments of nutrition, sanitation, hygiene and safe drinking water. It also aims at mainstreaming the Indian systems of medicine to facilitate health care. The Goals are:

- Reduction in Infant Mortality Rate (IMR) and Maternal Mortality Ratio (MMR).
- Universal access to public health services such as women's health, child health, water, sanitation and hygiene, immunisation and nutrition.
- Prevention and control of communicable and non-communicable diseases, including locally endemic diseases.
- Access to integrated comprehensive primary healthcare.
- Population stabilisation, gender and demographic balance.
- Revitalise local health traditions and mainstream AYUSH.
- Promotion of healthy life styles.

National Horticulture Mission (2005)

The National Horticulture Mission (NHM) is a centrally sponsored scheme launched in 2005 to enhance production of every horticultural product (fruits, vegetables, flowers, plantation crops, spices, medicinal aromatic plants). The NHM aims to provide holistic growth of the sector, spreading technology, providing assistance to the farmers through regionally-differentiated strategies and creating employment opportunities in the agricultural sector; the ultimate objective is further improve food security by assuring a sufficient variety of nutrient crops in each area. The scheme instead of focusing on the quantity of food produced, with the purpose of growing enough for everyone, the NHM specialises on the quality and variety of nutrition and on the preservation of local crops. Every plant, with the exception of coconut (falling under a separate policy), is covered under the scheme: the farmers are eligible to receive a variety of services for the improvement of their main cultivation.

The thrust of the **Eleventh Five Year Plan period (2007-12)** was on **Inclusive Growth** – In 2006- World Bank describes - Inclusive Growth - "as growth with emphasis not only on the distribution of economic gains but also on the security, vulnerability, empowerment and a sense of full participation in social life. "It is akin to the development strategies such as growth with social justice", growth with equity, pro-poor growth, etc. In order to achieve these objectives, the Government of India proposed linking production and distribution systems with employment and poverty alleviation programmes. It emphasised on increasing higher production of food and its dispersal through an efficient marketing infrastructure, including the Public Distribution System. The thrust of the plan is to ensure adequate entitlements to access food to the poor either from the market or through the PDS. Entitlements are to be created and preserved through employment programmes such as MGNREGP, or income generation schemes such as National Rural Livelihood Mission. These programmes can be increasingly linked to creation of rural assets such as, irrigation and drainage channels, wells and tanks, check dams and bunds, roads, etc. These measures were expected to strengthen the production base and enhance productivity of the agricultural sector.

National Food Security Mission (2007)

The National Food Security Mission is recognised that the current path of grains production was not fast enough to cover for the increase in the population, leading to shortage of food at aggregate level. The major objective of this scheme is to increase production and productivity of wheat, rice and pulses on a sustainable basis, so to preserve the food security of the country. It is accomplished mainly by diffusion of new technologies as well as modern farm managing practices. The NFSM is entirely funded by the Central Government, and is divided into three branches: Rice, Wheat, and Pulses, each one specialised in the type of crop after which it is named. The quantitative objective of the scheme is increasing the production of rice by ten million tonnes, wheat by eight million tonnes and pulses by two million tonnes by 2011-12. Another objective of the policy is to creation of more job opportunities for the rural households.

The 12th Five Year Plan's (2012-17) vision is to bring 'Faster, Sustainable, and More Inclusive Growth', leading to broad-based improvement in the economic and social conditions of our people and achieve inclusiveness by both delivering benefits directly to the poor and the excluded groups and increasing their ability to access employment and income opportunities and nutritional food in the country. It is recognised that four per cent of growth of the agriculture sector is imperative for not only ensuring food security of the nation but more importantly to achieve inclusive growth. The twin objectives of ensuring food security and improving the lot of our farmers can be achieved through higher investments in agriculture and allied sectors, including irrigation.

National Rural Livelihood Mission (2011)

As a part of the inclusive growth, the Government of India launched the National Rural Livelihood Mission (NRLM) in 2011, which is aimed at Poverty elimination through social mobilisation, institution building, financial inclusion and a portfolio of sustainable livelihoods. The main objectives of the Mission are to: adopt saturation approach – cover all families; organise SHG at least one member from each HH, preferably women; cover all villages in phased manner; special focus on States with large tribal population; cover seven crore rural poor HHs; provide credit and subsidy (nearly one lakh in five to six years); generate income at least Rs 50,000; promote of self-employment opportunities; promote skilled wage-employment opportunities; eliminate hunger, malnutrition and rural poverty; and reduce inequalities. For implementing this project, the Central Government has bargained with World Bank for getting One billion dollars as loan. The Mission is designed to facilitate shift of the States from the allocation, based strategy to a demand driven strategy, enabling the States in the process to formulate their own poverty reduction plans. These measures would enable the poor to improve their nutritional status. The earlier poverty alleviation programmes aimed at directly attacking hunger and poverty received less priority in this plan.

The National Food Security Act, 2013

The National Food Security Act **(NFSA, 2013)** is the important programme launched in the 12th Plan Period. According the Act, 2013, the Food Security Law means that it is "an Act to ensure food security to enable assured economic and social access to adequate food and life with dignity, all persons in the country, at all times, in pursuance of their fundamental right to live with dignity." As per the Act Right to access of food security mean: (i) Every person shall have the right of access to, at all times, either directly or by means of financial purchases, to quantitatively and qualitatively adequate, sufficient and safe food, corresponding to his or her cultural traditions and which ensures a physical and mental individual or collective fulfilling and dignified life free of fear of hunger or malnutrition; (ii) No person shall be discriminated against on the basis of caste, creed, colour, religion, race, gender, disease or disability on the matter of access to food and other entitlements under this Act. It also adopts the life cycle approach, which means food security shall be based on the delivery of services from pregnant women and children to senior citizens to ensure access to food in adequate and appropriate quantities calories and proteins and other nutrients for healthy body and mind. The other main objectives of food security Act are: (i) safe drinking water; (ii) effective public distribution system; (iii) proper sanitation; (iv) hygienic toilets; (v) primary healthcare; (vi) special schemes for those who are economically vulnerable or physically handicapped. *Jean Drèze summarised NFSB/ A, 2103,* as passed in the Lok Sabah on 26 August 2013).

The Act provides for coverage of upto 75 per cent of the rural population and upto 50 per cent of the urban population for receiving subsidised food-grains under Targeted Public Distribution System (TPDS), thus covering about two-thirds of the population. The eligible persons will be entitled to receive five Kgs of food-grains per person per month at subsidised prices of Rs 3/2/1 per Kg for rice/wheat/coarse grains. The existing Anthodya Anna Yojana (AAY) households, which constitute the poorest of the poor, will continue to receive 35 Kgs of food-grains per household per month" (Government of India, 17, September 2014).

The Act has a special focus on the nutritional support to women and children. Besides meal to pregnant women and lactating mothers during pregnancy and six months after the childbirth, such women will also be entitled to receive maternity benefit of not less than Rs 6,000. Children upto 14 years of age will be entitled to nutritious meals or take home rations as per the prescribed nutritional standards. In case of non-supply of entitled food-grains or meals, the beneficiaries will receive food security allowance. The Act also contains provisions for setting up of grievance redressal mechanism at the District and State levels. Separate provisions have also been made in the Act for ensuring transparency and accountability (Government of India, 17, September 2014). All these provisions would enable the people, especially the poor to have access and equity of adequate quantity and qualitative food-grains and thereby eliminate hunger, poverty and inequalities in the society. The main features, in a nutshell, are presented in box-2.2.

Box-2.2. The main Features of Food Security Act, 2013:

1. 75 per cent rural and 50 per cent of the urban population are entitled for three years from enactment to five kg foodgrains per month at ₹ 3 (4.9¢ US),₹ 2 (3.3¢ US),₹ 1 (1.6¢ US) per kg for rice, wheat and coarse grains (millet), respectively;
2. The states are responsible for determining eligibility;
3. Pregnant women and lactating mothers are entitled to a nutritious "take home ration" of 600 Calories and a maternity benefit of at least Rs 6,000 for six months;
4. Children 6 months to 14 years of age are to receive free hot meals or "take home rations";
5. The Central government will provide funds to states in case of short supplies of food grains;
6. The current food grain allocation of the states will be protected by the central government for at least six months;
7. The state government will provide a food security allowance to the beneficiaries in case of non-supply of food grains;
8. The Public Distribution System is to be reformed;
9. The eldest woman in the household, 18 years or above, is the head of the household for the issuance of the ration card;
10. Establishment of state- and district-level redress mechanisms; and
11. State Food Commissions will be formed for implementation and monitoring of the provisions of the Act.
12. The cost of the implementation is estimated to be $22 billion (1.25 lac crore), approximately 1.5 per cent of GDP.
13. The poorest that are covered under the Antodaya yojna will remain entitled to the 35 kg of grains allotted to them under the mentioned scheme.

1 Preliminaries

The Bill/Act extends to the whole of India and "shall be deemed to have come into force on the 5th day of July 2013." [NB: This is the date when the National Food Security Ordinance 2013 came into force.]

1. Entitlements

Priority households are entitled to five kgs of food grains per person per month, and Antyodaya households to 35 kgs per household per month. The combined coverage of Priority and Antyodaya households (called "eligible households") shall extend "up to 75 per cent of the rural population and up to 50 per cent of the urban population." The PDS issue prices are given in Schedule I: Rs 3/2/1 per kg for rice/wheat/millets. These may be revised after three years.

Other Provisions

- ***PDS Reforms :*** In Chapter V, the Bill/Act states that central and state governments "shall endeavour to progressively undertake" various PDS reforms, including: doorstep delivery of food-grains; end-to-end computerisation; leveraging "aadhaar" (UID) for unique identification of entitled beneficiaries; full transparency of records; preference to public institutions or bodies in licensing of fair price shops; management of fair price shops by women or their collectives; diversification of commodities distributed under the PDS; full transparency of records; and "introducing schemes such as cash transfer, food coupons or other schemes to the targeted beneficiaries in order to ensure their food-grain entitlements" as prescribed by the central government.
- ***Obligations of Government and Local Authorities:*** The main obligation of the Central Government is to provide food-grains (or, failing that, funds) to state governments, at prices specified in Schedule I, to implement the main entitlements. The Central Government has wide-ranging powers to make Rules "in consultation with the state government."
- The main obligation of State governments is to implement the relevant schemes, in accordance with the Central

Government guidelines. State governments also have wide-ranging powers to make Rules. They are free to extend benefits and entitlements beyond what is prescribed in the Bill/Act, from their own resources.

- Local Authorities and Panchayati Raj Institutions are responsible for proper implementation of the Bill/Act in their respective areas, and may be given additional responsibilities by notification.

Assessment of Food Security Policies

The studies on food security policies present mixed opinion. Contrary to the common belief in policy debates and academic circles that, the policies/programmes are dysfunctional schemes, a survey of the PDS in nine Indian states, conducted during May-June 2011 finds that many State governments have undertaken a series of measures that have made the PDS functional. By providing assured supply of foodgrains at nominal prices, the PDS has become an important source of food security for rural households, or more precisely for eligible rural households. With notable exception of Bihar, BPL households in the nine sample States reported receiving almost their full entitlement of grain (rice and wheat) on a regular basis. The study further point out that the PDS performs a very useful role in ensuring food security for the rural poor as it ensures a regular supply of foodgrains even in the remotest parts of the country. As things stand, rural markets are underdeveloped and private markets seem to fail at the last mile in many areas. It is not easy to predict what would happen in the event of a dismantling of the PDS. This stabilisation role of PDS is not adequately recognised by the scholars even to date (Reetika Khera, 2011).

The report/study on the implementation of PDS in Orissa State indicates that there has been vast improvement in operation of PDS; BPL households are receiving their entitlements; strong preference for distribution of grain over cash; etc. Further the report highlights that poor households wanted larger quantity of rice; inhabitants of villages which are far from the PDS outlet preferred PDS shop to be located in the village/hamlet itself; willing to purchase coarse grains such as bajra, jowar or makka, which are more nutritious than wheat or rice from PDS (Aggarwal, A, 2011) .

The studies also highlighted several issues that hampered the progress of food security programmes. Though the intentions of government, IGOs/NGOs/CBOs are good and rational in defining the core components of FS policies and norms for executing the scheme/s, they are not materialised at the field level. There is a wide gap between promise and performance of the FS schemes. This is partly due to the formulation of policies or norms sometimes stipulated by IGOs/NGOs/ Donor agencies, without taking account the socio-economic, cultural, political and administrative context of the country/state/ district. However, many columnists on the subject are of the opinion that the existing administrative arrangements are not conducive to deliver the services to desirability of the target groups.

The studies highlighted several issues. They are: violation or not adhering to the norms by the State governments due to political compulsions; inaccessibility of the schemes/food to all the people due to the socio-economic, cultural compulsions; (Khera, 2010; IIPA, 2010-11); lack of freedom to the beneficiary to choose the food items and inadequate attention to the cultural diversity and diversity in the food habits of people representing different areas/ states, while framing the FS policies; insufficient attention to the details of delivery mechanism; many families which had their names in the BPL HHs list did not have actually had a BPL or Antyodaya card; cardholders being forced to pay money to get their ration cards or get extra pages added to their ration cards; 'the transition from universal PDS to TPDS has neither benefited the poor, nor helped the government to its reduce budgetary food subsidies; targeting has affected the functioning and economic viability of the PDS network adversely and led to a collapse of the delivery system; large-scale leakages from the PDS, that is, grain being diverted and not reaching the final consumer (Planning Commission, Programme Evaluation Organisation, 2005); the relatively better-off or ineligible households obtained ration cards and availed benefits under PDS and sold rice in open market (Aggarwal, A, 2011); large proportion of agricultural labour and other households in the lowest expenditure classes are excluded from the PDS (The data from the NSS 61st round); 67 per cent of the wheat meant to reach the poor end up missing the target, being pilfered or sold on the open market en route; many a times the godowns authorities sending less grain to the ration shops than they are supposed to get, which forces PDS outlet managers, in turn, to distribute less grain to cardholders; etc, (Khera, 2010).

On the other hand the relatively better-off or ineligible households obtained ration cards and availed benefits under PDS and sold rice in open market ((Aggarwal, A, 2011); considerable leakage of wheat in rice eating states, ranging from one-third to 100 per cent and in contrast, the leakages for rice were lower; wide prevalence of diversion from one category of beneficiary to another, either due to wrong identification or misallocation; identification errors as well as the possession of multiple cards by a significant number of beneficiaries; the poor state of monitoring and grievance redress mechanisms; lack of procedural and institutional changes for proper implementation of programmes (IIPA, 2011). These factors mostly related to administrative dys-functionalities and contributed for ineffectiveness of FS policies.

Assessment of the National Food Security Act, 2013

Though the Act came into operation from 5th July, 2013, many State Governments and Union Territories have not yet adopted the Central Act (as per the norms State Governments have to adopt it within one year i.e. 4th July 2014). The Government of India extended the period up to March 2015 and directed the State governments to adhere to the instructions. The major reasons for non-compliance of the Central Governments directions mostly are: the UPA Government has enacted the Act at the end of the term of the Government/ Parliament; the opposition political parties both at the Central and State levels were indifferent as it is considered as a 'pet project' of Indian National Congress president Sonia Gandhi and 'vote security, for Congress and not the food security to the people; the need for huge budget allocation for implementation of the Act; the newly elected NDA Government is not serious about the implementation of the Act.

However, the initial response of on the Bill/ Act indicates weather it is possible for the government to ensure food security to the entire citizens and all the times? If it fails to do so, then this simply devaluates the meaning of a right and perpetrates the culture of having laws that are meant to be violated. Therefore, it is necessary to identify the problems that are likely crop up in the implementation of the NFSA. Here an attempt is made to analyse the opinion of the views of the Central and State Ministries, experts, other stakeholders are presented here under, and they are relevant even to date, which would provide insights on the phenomena. Indian National Congress President Sonia Gandhi remarked the passage bill would be a "chance to make history." Former Minister of Consumer Affairs, Food, and Public Distribution K.V. Thomas stated in an interview (2011):

> "This is no mean task, a task being accomplished in the second most populated country in the world. All the while, it has been a satisfying journey. The responsibility is not just of the Central Government but also equally of the States/ [Union Territories]. I am sure together we can fulfil this dream. The day is not far off, when India will be known the world over for this important step towards eradication of hunger, malnutrition and resultant poverty...By providing food security to 75 per cent of the rural and 50 per cent of the urban population with focus on nutritional needs of children, pregnant and lactating women, the National Food Security Bill/Act will revolutionise food distribution system."

Former National Advisory Council member and development economist Professor Jean Dreze, reputedly one of the architects of the original, 2011 version of the bill, wrote, "...the Bill is a form of investment in human capital. It will bring some security in people's lives and make it easier for them to meet their basic needs, protect their health, educate their children, and take risks." (NFSB, 2013)

The experts, political leaders, stakeholders have expressed doubts on the proper implementation of the bill. One senior opposition politician, Murali Manohar Joshi (2011) went so far as to describe the bill as a measure for "vote security" (for the ruling government coalition) rather than food security. Another political figure, Mulayam Singh Yadav (2011) declared, "It is clearly being brought for elections...Why didn't you bring this bill earlier when poor people were dying because of hunger?...Every election, you bring up a measure. There is nothing for the poor."

The report of the 33rd meeting of the Technical Advisory Committee on Monetary Policy stated, "...Food prices are still elevated and the food security bill will aggravate food price inflation as it will tilt supply towards cereals and away from other farm produce (proteins), which will raise food prices further...Members desired that the Reserve Bank impress on the government the need to address supply side constraints which are causing inflationary pressure, especially on the food front." Surjit S Bhalla warned, "The food security bill...if implemented honestly, will cost three per cent of the GDP in its very first year." The writer Vivek Kaul noted,

> "The government's estimated cost of food security comes at 11.10 per cent...of the total receipts. The Commission on Agricultural Costs and Prices (CACP) estimated cost of food security comes at 21.5 per cent...of the total receipts. Bhalla's cost of food security comes at around 28 per cent of the total receipts...Once we express the cost of food security as a per centage of the total estimated receipts of the government, during the current financial year; we see how huge the cost of food security really is."

The Indian Ministry of Agriculture's CACP warned that enactment of the Bill could be expected to "induce severe imbalance in the production of oilseeds and pulses," and "...will create demand pressures, which will inevitably spill over to market prices of foodgrains. Furthermore, the higher food subsidy burden on the budget will raise the fiscal deficit, exacerbating macro level inflationary pressures." The Commission argued further that the Bill would restrict private initiative in agriculture, reduce competition in the market place due to government domination of the grain market, shift money from investments in agriculture to subsidies, and continue focus on cereals production when shifts in consumer demand patterns indicate a need to focus more on protein, fruits and vegetables. This can devaluate the efficacy of all laws of the nation (Basu, 2010).

The Former Union Agriculture Minister Sri Sharad Pawar (2013) opined that it is difficult to implement the proposed Act under the present administrative system. He lamented that there are serious limitations on all fronts like financial position of the State agencies, manpower, quality inspection mechanism, storage and movement.

Even at the level of operation, the railways are finding it difficult to handle the movement. A massive programme to enhance foodgrains output would require huge investments in irrigation, power and fertilizers.

Ashok Gulati, Chairman of the CACP commented that, no promises on inclusiveness and long-term food security would be sustainable unless growth in agriculture is propelled to more than four per cent per annum. It is important to mention that agriculture growth, during the last three five year plans, is below the four per cent of the target. Gulati further lamented that fifteen years of continuous failure should be sufficient to teach any nation a lesson that business as usual will not deliver. But it seems we refuse to learn.

The Expert Committee on National Food Security Bill-2011 identified the following major operational issues, which need to be addressed to realise the goals of the proposed NFSA. They are:

- Given current trends of food-grain production and government procurement, and the likely improvements in these over time, will there be adequate availability of grain with the public authorities to implement the full entitlements for the priority and general category as proposed in the NFSA?
- What will be the impact of such large government foodgrain procurement on the open market prices? This is relevant since the both priority and general category will be purchasing a part of their consumption needs from the open market.
- What are the subsidy implications for the both phases and can these levels is sustained in the future?
- Arriving at a clear definition of priority and general households and the methodology of identification of these households is not an easy task.
- Given the inefficiencies and leakages in the current distribution system, identify the principal areas of reform of the PDS and the alternative mechanisms of reaching the foodgrain/subsidy to the entitled households is a major challenge of the governance.

The experts feel that the main problems rest on a complicated division of the population into three groups: priority, General and

Excluded households. Each group is to have different PDS entitlements: major benefits, token entitlements and nothing, respectively. There is no clarity, however, as to how these groups are to be identified. The National Advisory Council (NAC) was unable to resolve this problem. It merely recommended the coverage of priority groups should be no less than 46 per cent in rural areas and that of Excluded households no more than 10 per cent corresponding ratios in urban areas are 28 per cent and 50 per cent. Identification criteria –indeed the entire identification process- were left to the State government. The Rangarajan Committee, in its evaluation of the NAC proposal, took the view that the foodgrain requirements were too high. Therefore, the committee recommended legal entitlements for priority households only, and ad-hoc provisions for general households. It did not take issue with the proposed division of the population into three groups, or with proposed coverage of different groups (EPW December 24, 2011).

The identification of households, which are below poverty/hunger line has two important magnitudes: (i) in India, poverty estimation and identification is a highly contested domain with no agreement among experts as to how many people are poor (which vary between the range of 25 per cent to 77 per cent) and; (ii) the tying of PDS to poverty measurement makes BPL process open to the 'vagaries of politics of patronage' that plague the Indian democracy. The people who are close to the centres of localised power manage to get themselves counted as poor and avail of the various benefits that the state has to offer, mainly the PDS among others. The government/ economists, on the other hand, have the onerous task of finding suitable statistical methods to show lesser number of poor people and hence the success of inclusive growth policies (Banerjee, K, EPW, 2011).

Another problem NFSB/A is how to ensure a larger goal of nutritional security suitable to their cultural traditions rather than just food security? Presently, certain food-grains like rice, wheat and sugar are mostly supplied under PDS to the targeted groups in most states. The 'other crops' like millets, coarse cereals, pulses, oilseeds etc, which are part of the diet of people across the country are not available in the ration shops. It is pertinent to mention here that food-basket of people differ from place to place and among social groups. The agencies of the Central and State Governments are not focusing on the procurement of the other crops for the purpose of inclusion in PDS, as availability of these items on large quintiles is limited in the country. The 'other crops' are grown in rain fed conditions, which are scanty and erratic, and the output is also uncertain. The main reason for this can be attributed to flaw in the Green Revolution strategy of our country. The GR strategy mostly focused on the promotion of wheat and rice and neglect on other crops.

The government agencies – FCI- adopt the centralised mechanism akin to a monopolistic buyer to buy from the grower of rice, wheat and sugar at a fixed minimum support price (MSP) and the same facility is not extended to other crops. Even if MSP is extended these crops, it is low compared to rice and wheat. The MSP policy has resulted in the increase in the proportion of area under rice and wheat cultivation accompanied by a decline in the proportion of area under jowar, bajra and other coarse cereals (Banerjee, K, EPW, 2011).

Right to food, in theory and practice, seems to have a basic contradiction as far as modern democratic governments are concerned. Theoretically, the right to food is universal, i.e. every citizen has to be guaranteed a life free from hunger. In practice, authorities concerned plead helplessness to be able to honour such a guarantee. They cite supply of foodgrains and fiscal constraints as reasons for ensuring right to food to every household. The present centralised procurement of foodgrains is not enough to be able to provide 35 KGs of foodgrains to every household, who deserve help under NFSA, 2013. This situation also make implementing agencies to realise the objectives of NFSA difficult, as it adopts the life cycle approach, which means food security shall be based on the delivery of services from pregnant women and children to senior citizens so as to ensure access to food in adequate and appropriate quantities calories and proteins and other nutrients for healthy body and mind.

An analysis shows that despite the several provisions and safeguards, the story of the Act will not be much different to that of earlier food security policies. The major challenge to the Act lies in its governance, particularly at the field level. The centralised decision making (the central government has wide range of powers to frame the rules for implementation); inadequate electricity supply for end to end computerisation; linking Aadhar (UID) for identification of entitled beneficiaries; non-compliance of Central Government directions for implementation of Act by the State governments; change in the regime and its indifferent attitude to the Act (the Act was enacted by UPA government and the NDA government has to implement it); low agricultural growth; conversion of agricultural land to non-agricultural purposes; reduction in area under foodgrains; procurement of foodgrains in adequate quantity; impact of foodgrains procurement on the prices in the open market; commercialisation of agriculture has changed the production from foodgrains to non-foodgrains or consumption purpose to market purpose); determining the food basket items by the market; subsidy implications on procurement and distribution of foodgrains (11.10 per cent to 28 per cent) of the total receipts of the government.

Further, micro-level inflationary pressures; methodology for identification of 'priority, general and excluded HHs' (priority groups should be no less than 46 per cent in rural areas and excluded HHs no more than 10 per cent); identification of principal areas of PDS and devising alternative mechanism for implementation of the Act; ensuring nutritional security suitable to cultural/traditions of people /food sovereignty; lack of incentives to the farmers for producing the coarse cereals, millets, pulses (MSP is applicable to only certain crops); fiscal deficiency of the State governments; lack of manpower and quality inspection mechanism; physical infrastructure (storage, transportation); severe imbalance in the production of oil seeds and pulses; etc, are the formidable challenges of governance of food security policies/ Act in the country. Further, the NFSA, 2013 remains silent on the issues mentioned below. They are:

- Use of the productive natural resources-land, water- for real estate business, special economic zones, and other non-agricultural purposes, this reduces cultivable land and production. Further, the productive resources are under the control of the rich, Multinational Corporations, private agencies;
- Sluggish growth rate in the agriculture sector (less than four per cent) for the last one and half decades. There is no

additional infusion of resources in agriculture, irrigation, power, infrastructure, and technological and financial support to the farmers, especially to the small farmers to enhance agriculture production;

- Lack of freedom to the farmers in selecting the seeds, which are eco-friendly and cost-effective and are important from the point of nutrition and food sovereignty. In India, there were variety of seeds-2000, 1500 kinds of paddy and wheat, respectively. Today, the private companies, especially Multinational Corporations are controlling the seed production and distribution, which are not cost-effective and have no nourishment value;
- Adoption of centralised mechanism akin to a monopolistic buyer of the government agencies like Food Corporation of India to buy from the grower of rice, wheat and sugar at a fixed minimum support price (MSP) and not extending the same facility to other crops;
- Fixing uniform standards for covering the target group across the states/country and limiting subsidies to be provided by the central government. This would not only reduce the entitlements of the poor, but also impinge on federal spirit of the Constitution; There is no choice to the State governments in formulating the policy; There is additional burden on the state governments to implement the Act, as the subsidy for distribution is limited; Further there is inadequate budget allocation for the implementation of Act (Rs 79,800 crore in 2013), which is not even about two-thirds of what is actually needed;
- Merger of many ongoing programmes meant for women, children and the weaker sections in the Act;
- The non-supply /non-availability of safe food and nutritional security corresponding to his or her cultural traditions- millets, coarse cereals, pulses, milk, meat, fish etc, which are part of the diet people across the country- in the ration shops;
- Lack of emphasis on access to safe drinking water, sanitation, healthcare education, which are complimentary conditions for nutritional absorption;

- The variations in the existing government mechanism, financial position of the State agencies, manpower, inspection mechanism, storage and movement of food-grains across the states and their non-compatibility with the spirit of the Act;
- The concerns of political parties in taking forward the Central Government's neo-liberal agenda by incorporating a scheme for cash transfer (Chapter 13, Section 3(g), of the Act states: "Introducing scheme for cash transfer to the targeted beneficiaries in lieu of their foodgrain entitlements"). Bill/ Act is prepared/ enacted without making proper arrangements for foodgrains and budget allocation and it is election stunt of the government for political mileage.

Summing Up

Public policies to alleviate poverty, unemployment etc, have come to assume vital importance in post-Independent India. The Millennium Development Goals (MDG) 2000-15 and the proposed MDG 2015-30 also emphasise the elimination of hunger and poverty. The policies such as self-employment, wage employment, social security, and food security are aimed at direct attack on hunger, malnutrition and poverty and are considered the important programmes for providing employment, income and foodgrains to the poor. An examination of public policies reveals that the Indian State is giving priority to the incremental policies neglecting structural change oriented policies. Further, the public policies are formulated and implemented mostly to tide over the unrest among the poor; get the support of the poor in the elections; take on technological innovations; expand the market of MNC; oblige the Judiciary directions; guard the ruling class power structure from the threat of the unrest of masses; etc. Today, the public policies and the related concepts, norms and institutions, technology, capital, resources are globalised. The Indian State has little freedom to modify the norms of the policies/projects as most of them are financially and technically supported by the IGOs. In a way, it amounts to 'globalisation of democratic power', which ought to rest with the people and their representatives. Globalisation has changed the context, focus and the very notion of the Constitutional mandate, nation state and the public policies and institutions. The analysis shows that the present globalised model is the new face of development, where the State either with private sector or with voluntary organisations / civil society organisation work in collaboration and cooperate with each other to further common goals of market – driven, growth oriented agenda. Given the unequal socio-economic structure of India, this approach to development further accentuates the inequalities and in access of poor to employment, income and foodgrains in the country.

An examination of food security programmes, during the **pre-Independence period**, especially during World War periods reveals that they were meant to cater to the needs of armed forces and urban people of certain cities. In order to overcome the serious shortage of foodgrains, the then governments initiated measures to regulate prices and procure and distribute foodgrains on a centralised basis. However, there were a large number of complaints about foodgrain delivery system. They include low coverage of households (HHs) and exclusion of large number of HHs, inadequate supply of ration items, variation in the entitlements from state to state and area to area, and also variation in the prices of the ration items and poor off-take of ration by the HHs due to poor quality of foodgrains.

An assessment of the food security policies, during the **post-Independence period**, shows that they have undergone changes plan after plan- from the provision for procurement and distribution of foodgrains to whole population to cover only BPL households. The major reasons for this are: change in the regimes; withdrawal of assistance/ support for foodgrain supply by USA under PL- 480; application of modern technology in agriculture and diversification of cropping pattern, particularly from food crops to non-food crops/ commercial crops; declining growth rate in agriculture sector; reduction in public investment in agriculture sector; IGOs-WB's directions to the government to supply foodgrain only to the BPL households; the election strategy of the political parties to get 'vote security' in the elections; formulation of price policy in favour of the powerful class of wealthy agriculturists; priority to white revolution and expansion of the market of MNCs; low priority to the coarse grain producers; focus more on the promotion of paddy /wheat and neglect of the traditional crops due to GR technology, etc. All these factors have affected the governance of food security policies. However, the food security policies have contributed to increase the purchasing power of the poor; meeting the basic needs of poor, especially children, women, and the elderly and extending the PDS to the entire country; raising the level of the equilibrium price itself; reducing the imported foodgrains and promoting domestic foodgrains by giving MSP.

The State intervention to ensure food security can be broadly categorised into five phases. The first phase from 1945 to 1960, the focus then was achieving self-sufficiency in agricultural production especially in foodgrain production and stabilising prices. PDS was expanded to selected cities and it was generally dependent on imports of foodgrains. The second phase, from 1960 to 1978, was one, which saw major organisational changes. Specifically, in response to the food crisis of the mid-1960s, the Government of India took a holistic approach to food security, and set up the Agricultural Prices Commission and the Food Corporation of India in order to strengthen domestic procurement, storage, and supply of foodgrains. The third phase, from 1978 to 1991, was marked by large-scale expansion of the PDS, supported by domestic procurement and stocks. The fourth phase, from 1991 to 2010, is one in which the policy of universal food security has been replaced by a targeted policy in line with the directions of World Bank and objectives of economic liberalisation. The fifth phase, from 2013 onwards, is making food security a fundamental right. It adopts life cycle approach and gives priority to the cash transfers replacing the distribution of foodgrains to the people. Thus, over the period, the food security grew from a rationing scheme in selected cities to a national programme of food distribution, to a policy targeted at the income transfers to the poor and now to fundamental rights of the people.

The NFSA, 2013 is hailed as an important step towards eradication of hunger, malnutrition and resultant poverty and towards ensuring right to food and fulfilment of basic needs such as protection of health, education and other risks of the people thereby investment in human capital. The main features of the Act are laudable, especially adoption of life cycle approach, provision of safe drinking water, proper sanitation and hygienic toilets, primary healthcare, special schemes for those who are economically vulnerable and the physically challenged and reforms in PDS and involvement of local governments in the implementation of the Act.

An analysis shows that despite the several provisions and safeguards, the story of the Act will not be much different to that of earlier food security policies. The major challenge to the Act lies in its governance, particularly at the field level. The centralised decision-making (the central government has wide range of powers to frame the rules for implementation); inadequate electricity supply for end to end computerisation; linking Aadhar (UID) for identification of entitled beneficiaries; non-compliance of Central Government directions for implementation of Act by the State governments or amending the State food security policies in accordance with the Act; change in the regime and its indifferent attitude to the Act; low agricultural growth and enhancement of agricultural production and procurement foodgrains in adequate quantity; impact of foodgrain procurement on the prices in the open market; subsidy implications on procurement and distribution of foodgrains (ranging 11.10 per cent to 28 per cent) of the total receipts of the government; micro-level inflationary pressures; methodology for identification of 'priority, general and excluded HHs' (priority groups should be no less than 46 per cent in rural areas and excluded HHs no more than 10 per cent); identification of principal areas of PDS and devising alternative mechanism for implementation of the Act; ensuring nutritional security suitable to cultural/traditions of people / food sovereignty (the GR strategy and commercialisation of agriculture has changed the production from foodgrains to non-foodgrains or consumption purpose to market purpose); determining the food basket items by the market (change in the food basket of people from place to place and among the social groups; lack of incentives (MSP) to the farmers for producing the coarse cereals, millets, pulses (MSP is applicable to only certain crops); fiscal deficiency or poor financial position of the State governments; lack of manpower and quality inspection mechanism; physical infrastructure (storage, transportation); severe imbalance in the production of oil seeds and pulses; restricting private initiative in agriculture due to government control on foodgrain market; etc; are the formidable challenges of governance of food security policies/ Act in the country.

A close examination of government policies, particularly in the economic reforms period reveals that the government focused on four important aspects i.e. decontrol of foodgrain production and distribution; regulation of foodgrain production and distribution; special provisions for the benefit of marginalised sections; and organisational reforms. One, the decontrol of foodgrain production and distribution includes: promoting growth of production; limiting State intervention in the food market; elimination of state's sales tax benefiting the traders, scaling down the buffer stock and encouraging more exports/ imports; liberalising internal trade of foodgrains; stabilising the prices of the commodities by releasing more foodgrains to open market; reduction in distribution of basket items and confining to homogeneous goods; cutting down the subsidies on food items and targeted PDS and dropping the sizeable subsidy on the public exchequer; dual price policy for the BPL and APL card holders; reduction in number of FPSs and encourage private limited shops for distribution by introducing a system of food stamps, food credit cards, etc.

Two, the measures to regulate foodgrain production and distribution include: maintaining adequate foodgrains reserve at all times; opening of FPSs and supply of foodgrains; issuing foodgrains licensing and procurement order 1952; enacting Essential Commodities Act, 1955 to have control over the production, supply and distribution and trade and commerce in certain essential commodities and directing the State governments to adhere to the Act; State government restrictions on foodgrains movements; price control and stock holding limits of foodgrains; nationalisation of wholesale trade in foodgrains and fixing maximum selling price for rice and wheat; correction of seasonal and regional variations; strengthening of cooperative network for procurement and distribution of foodgrains.

The Central Government, recently, has communicated its decision to procure only 25 per cent of the requirement of the foodgrains for distribution to the target groups and institutions and the remaining 75 per cent has to be procured by the respective State governments. This amounts to shifting its financial burden to the State governments, which would cost heavily to the State exchequer. Though the State government has the autonomy to undertake food security policies or modify the norms, they do not have the adequate infrastructure- such as market yards, storage facilities, transportation facilities, power to maintain cold storages- and adequate number of skilled personnel to cope with the procurement and distribution of foodgrains. Added to these, the deficit budget of State government makes it to depend on the Central Government and adhere to its norms set for implementation of food security programmes. Nevertheless, the State governments are bringing pressure on the Central Government to procure 75 per cent of the requirement.

Three, the Central and State governments have initiated special programmes to improve the nutritional and health status of the children and women and developing human capital; increase in the budget allocation for food subsidies; strategies for integrating the food security with other PAPs; organising Village Grain Banks for the benefit of the poor; food and cash component supply to the poor; priority to the poorest of the poor in the distribution of foodgrains; encourage the farmers to raise the horticultural crops for assuring variety of nutrient foods; etc.

Four, the government measures for organisational reforms include establishment of FCI and separate government Agencies/ Corporations and involving Multipurpose Cooperative Societies; the NGOs, SHGs, PACs, AMCs, SERP and PRIs Societies, promoting PPP in procurement and its storage, transportation and distribution to targeted group and social welfare institutions and application of e-governance for implementation of the food security policies in the State.

Despite government's initiatives for ensuring food security to the people, reports of hunger and malnutrition have been pouring in from different parts of the country. An assessment of the governance of food security policies reveals that there is a wide gap between promise and performance, mostly due to the failure of governance of food security programmes. Firstly, there is no democratic governance. The real beneficiaries are not involved in core components of democratic governance- the formulation, implementation, monitoring and supervision and evaluation of policies. These are prerequisites for effective governance of any policy, including FS policy. Secondly, most of the provisions of the FS projects / policies are supported/directed by the donor agencies or IGOs, as the latter extend financial and technical support for the projects. With the result the policies have not taken into account the cultural habits or food habits/practices, food sovereignty, regional and seasonal variations, family size, age group, gender, and adequate quantity and quality of foodgrains. Thirdly, at the State and below levels, the decision-making on the issues like, procurement and distribution of foodgrains, minimum support price is mostly influenced by multiple actors like agricultural commission agents, rice millers, fair-price shop dealers, transport agents for their benefits, which affect the proper implementation of programmes. In fact, they determine 'what a Food Security policy should accomplish'. Fourthly, the lack of integrated administrative structure is causing for ineffectiveness of the policies. Multiple Ministries/Departments such as Agriculture; Food and Consumer; Rural Development; Revenue; Civil Supply; Marketing; Food Corporation of India; Railway; Social Justice and Empowerment; Women and Child Welfare; are associated with the decision making on the issues related to the FS policies. Ensuring coordination among these Ministries/departments is a formidable task to the authorities concerned at all levels of government. Fifthly, ensuring availability, accessibility of nutritious food in adequate quantity and food sovereignty to all the people and on a consistent basis are the formidable challenges of the governance, especially at the grass-root level. Sixthly, the foodgrain items like red-gram dal, Palm oil (edible oil) etc, distributed under PDS are imported from other countries, which are not tasty or normal/ habitual food of local people. Lastly, privatisation of agriculture sector, and priority to commercial crops, allowing Foreign Direct Investment (FDI) in food and agriculture related segments would not only undermine India's sovereignty, but also make the country to depend on the food crops industry, located within or outside the country. The genetically engineered crops are major invaders on the food crop area. For instance, 30 per cent of food production area had been occupied by BT cotton in the past decade and this situation is threatening the food security and food sovereignty of communities in several States.

All the above factors collectively and individually are weakening the development policies and its governance. Even the 'so called NPM model'–efficiency, effectiveness, economy, transparent, responsive and accountability have not succeeded in managing the Food Security policies in India. Therefore, the potential of these policies, largely depend, on the community participation in evolving the policies based on the ground realities; ensuring food sovereignty to the beneficiaries; regulating the private traders in procurement, storage and distribution of foodgrains; allocation of more budgets to agriculture and taking necessary measures to increase the production. These factors in fact, would ensure democratic governance of FS policies - legitimacy; accountability; competency; participatory; consensus; equitable and inclusive; respect for law and protection of human rights, etc. Democratic governance is recognised as one of the important strategies of FS policies to identify the eligible target groups; make the target group/s access to adequate quantity and quality of food; ensure food sovereignty of the people; etc., rather than mere receivers of foodgrains supplied by government agencies. Thus, people-centred governance in the design, implementation, monitoring and evaluation are prerequisites for the success of the programme. The policy-makers may consider the above factors in implementing the NFSA.

In this context, the democratic governance, with emphasis on involvement of community (all the social groups) in the management of FS policies, appears to be better model, compared to State-centred model (bureaucratic) and NPM model (more incentives to the individual or private agencies) to overcome the obstacles of FS policies. The Deccan Development Society (DDS) an NGO based in Medak District of Andhra Pradesh has developed an alternative strategy for PDS on the lines of democratic governance. It is an innovative programme. It has evolved local solutions for local problems, where foodgrain production, procurement, storage and distribution are done at community/village level and are entirely managed by the women sangham members. The programme integrates sustainable agricultural goals such as bio-diversity and soil fertility with community goals of rural livelihoods, food security and socio-economic empowerment of dalits and women based on plural values, local customs and practices and indigenous knowledge. The governance strategy of DDS is based on the principles: evolving strategy/ planning with community participation; taking decisions based on the ideas that originate in the village; local community and their traditional knowledge, community spirit are the main resources; flexibility in framing the rules suitable to the local conditions; mutual learning and sharing experience; continuous monitoring of the programme by the community; and, the main goal is to think systemic, holistic that integrates bio-diversity, natural resource management with rural livelihoods and empowerment of community (DDS, 2004).

Notes

1. The Essential Commodities, Act, 1955 (No. 10 of 1955) (1st April 1955), an Act to provide, in the interest of the general public, for the control of the production, supply and distribution of, and trade and commerce, in certain commodities.
2. The Concurrent- evaluation studies of Indian Institute of Public Administration, New Delhi, in 14 states (Orissa, West Bengal, Tripura, Nagaland, Arunachal Pradesh, Manipur, Haryana, Chandigarh, Punjab, and Tamil Nadu. Jammu & Kashmir, Himachal Pradesh, Andhra Pradesh, and Karnataka) noted several administrative dysfunctionalities.
3. The experts, political leaders, stakeholders have expressed doubts on the implementation of the bill. Ashok Gulati, Chairman of the Commission for Agricultural Costs and Prices, cited by Rajamani, RC, 2012; Chief Minister Bihar 19th December 2011, PTI; Chief Minister of Tamil Nadu, 22nd December, 2011, Economic Times Bureau; Chief Minister of Uttar Pradesh, 22nd December, 2011, PTI; Sharad Pawar, the Union Agriculture Minister, 2011, PTI; Thomas, KV, 22nd December 2011, PTI; Subodh Varma, 12th March, 2012, PTI; Brinda Karat (2011) Food Security Bill needs amendments, The *Hindu,* July 22, Editorial, The problem of Ending Hunger, Seminar, 634, June 2012, pp. 12-13.

References

Agarwal, A (2011): 'The PDS in Rural Orissa: Against Grain'? *Economic & Political Weekly,* September, 3, Vol. XLVI, No, 36, pp. 21-24.

Agarwal, A and Narain, S (1997): 'Dying Wisdom: Rise, fall and Potential of India's Traditional Water Harvesting Systems, 4th State of India's Environment Report, *Centre for Science and Environment,* New Delhi.

Anupam Hazar, (2012): 'Food Security in Rural India; Poverty in the Land of Plenty', *Kurukshetra,* Vol. 60, No.5, pp. 7-10.

Ashok Mehata Committee, Report, (1957).

Bala Ramulu, Ch, (1996): *'Human Resource Development and Liberalisation Policy: A Study of Rural Employment Programmes in India', Special Number on Liberalisation Policy and Social Concerns,* Indian Journal of Public Administration, New Delhi, Vol. KLII, No.3, July – September.

——— *(1997): 'Poverty Alleviation programmes and Right to Work to Rural Poor', Special Number of Fifty Years of Indian Administration – Retrospect and Prospects*, Indian Journal of Public Administration, New Delhi, Vol. XLIII, No.3, July – September.

——— *(2004): 'Development Policy and Governance in India from 1947 to 2003'*, Indian Journal of Public Administration, New Delhi, Vol. L, January-March, No.1.

————,(2014): 'Governance of Poverty Alleviation Policies in India: a Study of Food Security Policies to Rural Poor', *Journal of Land and Rural Studies,* Volume 2, Issue 2, July, Sage publication, New Delhi.

Bala Ramulu, Ch, and AVN Reddy, (2014): 'State, NGO and Development Experiences in India- Need for Stronger Relationship', *Indian Journal of Public Administration,* April-June, Vol. LX, no. 2.

Banerjee, K (2011): 'Decentralised Procurement and Universalised PDS', *Economic & Political Weekly,* December 24, Vol. XLVI, No. 52, pp. 19-26.

Basu, K (2010): 'Beyond the Invisible Hand; Ground work for a new Economics', Princeton University Press.

Basu, K (2011): 'India's Food-grain policy: An Economic Theory Perceptive', *Economic & Political Weekly*, January 29, Vol. XLVI, No, 5, pp. 37- 43.

Bhatia, BM (1991): 'Famines in India', *Konark Publishers*, New Delhi.

Bhagavati, J and Sreenivasan, TN (1993): 'India's Economic Reforms, *Ministry of Finance, Government of India,* New Delhi.

Bharadwaj, Krishna (1994): 'Agricultural Price Policy for Growth: the Emerging Contradictions' in TJ Byres (ed) *The State and Development planning in India,* Oxford University Press, Delhi.

Chakrabarthy, Bidyut and Bhattacharya, Mohit (2008): (Ed) 'The Governance discourse- A Reader' Oxford University Press, pp. 15-18.

Chakravarthi, Sukhamoy (1987): 'Development Planning: the Indian Experience', Oxford University Press, Delhi.

Chopra, RN (1988): 'Food Policy in India, A survey', Intellectual Publishing House, New Delhi.

Dreze, Jean and Amartya Sen (1989): 'Hunger and public Action, Clarendon Press, Oxford.

Editorial Note (1995): *Economic & Political Weekly.*

Editorial Note (1996): *Economic & Political Weekly.*

Editorial Note (2011): 'Food Security Bill: Simpler the Better', *Economic & Political Weekly*, December 24, Vol. XLVI. No. 52, p. 7.

Deccan Development Society (2004): 'A Study on Alternative Public Distribution System', *Bookline,* Hyderabad, pp. 21-25.

Dwivedi, OP and Henderson, Km, (1996): The Politics of the Administrative Process, 2nd edn....

Gargi Pasi, (1994): The Hindu, New Delhi, edition.

Government of India, (2002): 'Towards Sustainability; from the Past, Innovating for the Future: Stories from India', Centre for Environment Education and Ministry of Environment and Forests Ahmedabad.

Government of India (2005): 'Food Security in India', Planning Commission, *Programme Evaluation Organisation,* New Delhi.

Government of India, 'Economic Survey', 1991-92.

Government of India, (2012): 'Sameeksha, Compilation on MGNREGA' (Ed) Mahir Shah, Member of *Planning Commission,* New Delhi.

Government of India, (2013): 'Expert Committee on Leveraging Panchayats for Efficient Delivery of Public Goods and Services'.

Hanumantha Rao, Ch, and Roshini Nayyar, (1984): 'New initiatives for Rural Poverty Alleviation, paper presented at IDPAD seminar *'Structural Adjustment and Poverty in India: policy and Research Issues,* 29-30 November, 1994, *The Hague.*

Haragopal, G, (1991): *Foreword to a book Bala Ramulu, Ch. 'Public Policies: An Evaluation of Integrated Rural Development Programme',* Ajantha Publications, New Delhi.

Haragopal, G, (2003): *'The Failure of Organisational Reforms: a Tragic Story of Indian Adminstration'.*

Hara Gopal,G, 2012: 'An Elementary Note on Status of the Discipline of Public Administration in a Globalising World', paper presented at *International Conference on Public Administration, organised by Osmania University, Hyderabad,* AP. India, during 25-27 October, 2012.

Jean Drèze (2013): Prepared Summary of 'National Food Security Bill 2013' on behalf of TEHELKA.

Khera, (2010): *'BPL Census and Possible Alternative', Economic and Political Weekly,* February 27, Vol. xlv. No. 9.

Mahendra Dev, S Sharma, AN, (2010): 'Food Security in India: Performance, Challenges and policies', Oxfam India, Working papers Series, OIWPS-VII, p.1.

Mitra, Ashok, (1977): 'Terms of trade and class relations' Frank Cass, London.

Mooij Jos, (1999): 'Food Policy and the Indian State- The Public Distribution System in South India', Oxford University Press, Delhi, pp. 36-40.

Mundle, Sudipto, (1981): 'Surplus Flows and Growth imbalances- The Intersectoral Flow of Real Resources in India, 1951-71, Allied Publishers, Bombay.

Mundle, Sudipto and Govindarao, M (1991): 'Volume and Composition of Government Subsidies in India, 1987-88, *Economic and Political Weekly,* 26, no.18.

Pursell, G and Ashok Gulati, (1993): 'Liberating Indian Agriculture: An Agenda for Reform', Policy Research Working papers, September, World Bank, Washington.

Rajamani, R.C (2012): 'The Imponderable Food Security Bill, 2011', *Kurukshetra,* Vol. 60, No. 5 pp. 3-6.

Reetika Khera (2011): 'India's Public Distribution System: Utilisation and Impact', *The Journal of Development Studies,* Vol. 47 issue 7.

Sathesh, PV (2002): Crops of Truth: 'Farmers' Perception of the Agro-biodiversity in the Deccan Region of South India', *Deccan Development Society,* Hyderabad; for several dozen case studies see the Planning Commission Reports, http//planningcommission.nic.in.

Sen, Amartya (1981): 'Poverty and Famines, an essay on Entitlement and Deprivation', Clarendon Press, Oxford.

Tyagi, DS, (1990): 'Managing India's Food Economy: Problems and Alternatives', Sage Publishers, New Delhi.

Varshney Ashutosh, (1993): 'Self-Limited Empowerment: Democracy and Economic Developmentand Rural India, *Journal of Development Studies,* 29, no. 4.

Vyas, VS, 2000: 'Ensuring Food Security- The State, Market and Civil Society', *Economic and Political Weekly,* December 9, pp.

Chapter III

Organisational Structures and Operational Process of Food Security Programmes: Issues and Challenges

Proper organisational structure is pivotal to every administrative action, for no administrative action can be implemented without the organisation. In any organisation, the governance engrosses administrative actions to transform the four systematic processes viz, inputs, transformation, outputs and feedback relating to achievement of its goals. Further it involves cooperative effort by a number of institutions/units and people to achieve certain objectives. It is obvious that the number of units/people must be organised and given adequate powers, budget, and provide forward and backward linkages to realise the desired end. They should work in cooperation with each other and all their cooperative energy should be directed towards the same end. A reasonable or rational purpose of governance might aim to assure that an organisation produces worthwhile pattern of good results for the whole society, particularly the marginalised sections, while avoiding an undesirable pattern or bad circumstances. As mentioned earlier, during the end of the twentieth century or early twenty first century, in India, the concept of governance has undergone change, especially in the government sector, and adopting the New Public Management approach- emphasising on the outright privatisation of activities/ services, competence, accountability, voice and partnership/ networking with market and civil society bodies, etc, - for achieving the set goals. In an unequal socio-economic system, the organisational structures and the governance mostly serve the interest of the relatively better-off sections rather than the poor. The supporters of the ruling class- political parties, top bureaucracy, contractors, intermediaries, etc, benefit from the execution of any policy, including the food security policies. Against this background, in this chapter an attempt is made to analyse the organisational structures devised for realisation of the goals of food security policies.

Section-I

Organisational Pattern at the Central Level

The Indian food security system is operated under the joint responsibility of the Central and the State governments. At the Central level the Ministry of Consumers Affairs, Food and Public Distribution, headed by a Cabinet Minister in charge, is responsible for public distribution in the country. The Ministry has two departments viz., the Department of Consumer Affairs and Department of Food and Public Distribution. The main concern of the Ministry is on incentivising farmers through fair value of their produce by way of minimum support price mechanism and distribution of foodgrains to BPL families. While evolving the policy and programmes the Ministry has to seek the cooperation of several Central Government Ministries such as Agriculture; Women and Child Development; Rural Development; Health and Family Welfare; Social Justice and Empowerment; Human Resource Development. The Planning Commission, Government of India, will assist the Ministry in monitoring and evaluation of the FS policies. The Government of India through FCI allots rice, wheat and levy sugar to the state governments. The Director of Food and Civil Supplies of the respective state in turn sub-allocate the said commodities to the districts. The allocation foodgrains to districts is mainly based on the population, number of ration cards and quantity of allocation received by the respective State government from Government of India. The Department of Consumer Affairs is responsible for administering policies relating to consumer cooperatives, monitoring prices, availability of essential commodities, consumer movement and controlling bodies like Bureau of Indian Standards and Weight and Measures etc. The main functions Department of Food and Public Distribution are:

- Formulation of national policies relating to export and import, buffer stocking, quality control and specifications of foodgrains;

- Procurement of foodgrains for the central pool and is done by the FCI complemented by the State Civil Supplies Corporation under a de-centralised procurement system;
- Allocate foodgrains to States and provide for its transportation to depots in each state;
- Fixes uniform Central issue prices for issue of foodgrains under the PDS;
- Provision of storage facilities for the maintenance of central reserves of foodgrains and promotion of scientific storage;
- Administration of food subsidies relating to rice, wheat and coarse grains;
- Control over price and inter-state trade and commerce supply and distribution of sugar, vanaspati, oil seeds, vegetable oils, cakes and fats;
- Implementation of the PDS with special focus on the poor; and,
- In case of short of foodgrains, the Central government shall provide funds to State governments to the extent of such short supply.

The Department of Food and Public Distribution issue circulars, notifications, orders from time to time, to regulate the PDS in the country. The PDS is governed and regulated under Essential Commodities Act 1955. In the interest of public, Section-3 of the Act confers powers on the Central Government to control production, supply and distribution of essential commodities. Prevention of Black Marketing and maintenance of supplies of Essential Commodities Act is enacted in 1980 to prevent unethical trade practices like hoarding and black marketing and to detain persons whose activities are found to be prejudicial to the maintenance of supplies of commodities essential to the community. The Government of India has issued order called the Public Distribution System (Control) Order 2001, which is also amended subsequently in 2008. For all practical purposes, the Ministry of Consumers Affairs, Food and Public Distribution role is confined to policy formulation and ensuring coordination from the Central Ministry's/Departments and between the Centre and State governments in the implementation of food security programmes.

For discharging its various functions the Ministry/Department has under its administrative control three public sector undertakings, viz., Food Corporation of India, Central Warehousing Corporation and Hindustan Vegetable Oils Corporation: two attached offices, viz., Directorate of Sugar and Directorate of Vanaspati. Except for supply of oils and vanaspati, all the other responsibilities are discharged through the respective State governments and the Central Government role is confined to policy formulation and co-ordination. The PDS operates through a national network of about five lakh retail outlets (owned by Civil Supplies Corporation, cooperative, voluntary organisations and private agencies) controlled by the respective State governments. The Central government and every State government shall constitute a National and State Food Commission, respectively, for monitoring and reviewing implementation of the food security policies/ Act.

Organisational setup at State Level in Andhra Pradesh

In Andhra Pradesh, the Civil Supplies Department was originally functioning as part of the Board of Revenue. One of the members of the Board was the Commissioner of Civil Supplies. The Department was called Board of Revenue (Civil Supplies). The designation of the Commissioner of Civil Supplies was Commissioner of Civil Supplies and Excise or Commissioner of Civil Supplies and Relief. In addition to Civil Supplies, the Commissioner of Civil Supplies was entrusted with the Departments pertaining to Excise, Relief etc. The Member was assigned the status of Ex-Officio Secretary in Food and Agriculture Department at Secretariat level. In 1977, the Board of Revenue was abolished and Commissioners were appointed exclusively to head the Departments. Since then the Commissioner of Civil Supplies has been functioning as an independent head of the Department and Ex-Officio Secretary to Government.

A Cabinet Minister is in-charge of Portfolios of Food, Cooperation and Consumer Protection is responsible for public distribution – procurement, transport, storage, distribution of foodgrains in the State. The Secretary to Government in-charge of department coordinates the activities of Civil Supplies Department and the Civil Supplies Corporation. The important functionaries of the department are Commissioner of Civil Supplies, Chairman, Civil Supplies Corporation,

Registrar Cooperative Societies, and Additional Director General of Police. The Commissioner of Civil Supplies, is responsible for: (i) procurement of food-grains; (ii) distribution of essential commodities under PDS; (iii) enforcement of various control orders issued under the Essential Commodities Act, 1955; (iv) create awareness among public on consumer rights and responsibilities; (v) implementation of Consumer Protection Act, 1986; vi) price Monitoring and Control. These activities are enforced through its administrative units and agencies. The department also relies on the other institutions such as FCI, Legal Metrology, GCC, ITDA, PRIs.

The Commissioner of Civil Supplies is assisted by the Director of Civil Supplies, three Joint Directors, two Deputy Directors, one Assistant Directors, one Accounts Officer and one Assistant Accounts Officer with support staff at State level. In each district, except in Visakhapatnam, there is one district supply officer to look after the Civil Supplies matters. In Visakhapatnam District, two District Supply Officers are functioning. These District Supply Officers with the support staff will be functioning under the control of the District Collector. The Legal Metrology Department, which was under the control of the Industries, recently, is transferred to Food and Civil Supplies Department.

The Government of Andhra Pradesh in pursuance of PDS (Control) Order 2001 has issued Public Distribution System (Control) order, 2008, for the purpose of maintaining supplies and securing equitable distribution of essential commodities in the state. The major concerns of the governance of food security policies are ensuring coordination various departments/wings and monitoring of programmes for achieving the common goal- food security to people. The operational responsibilities of the State governments include: allocation of foodgrain within the State, identification of families below and above the poverty line, issue of family cards and supervision and monitoring of the functioning of the PDS. The State government is responsible to: (a) create and maintain scientific storage sites; (b) suitably strengthen capacities of their Food and Civil Supplies Corporations; and (c) establish institutionalised licensing for FPS; (d) directing the field agencies to display the list of identified priority and general households prominently in the public domain; (e) ensure the delivery of foodgrains to the target group as per their entitlements, etc.

Andhra Pradesh State Civil Supplies Corporation Limited

The Government of Andhra Pradesh, with a view to procure, storage, transportation and distribution of essential commodities, established the Andhra Pradesh State Civil Supplies Corporation Limited (APSCSCL) in the year 1974 as a Public Limited Company under the Companies Act, 1956. As per the memorandum and articles of association, the main objective of the Corporation is as follows:

> "To engage in, promote, improve, develop, counsel and finance, production, purchase, storage, processing, movement, transport, distribution and sale of food-grains, food stuff and any other essential commodities and to establish laboratories for the purchase of ensuring quality control, to train personnel in the techniques of quality control, and to provide service and assistance of all kinds of them said purchases including capital credit, means resources, technical and managerial services, advice and assistance."

Activities of APSCSCL

The Corporation discharges its duties as per the directions of the State government. The Corporation, during last four decades, is undertaking various activities. They include: Procurement of rice from millers and procurement of paddy from farmers, (1975-76); opening of paddy purchase centres for purchasing damaged paddy (1978-79); distribution of imported RBD (refined, bleached and de-odourised) palmolien oil (1979), Levy Sugar distribution (1980); Cement Distribution (1981); LPG centres and retail counters (1981); implementation of Rice Subsides Scheme (1983); Manabiyyam – Manakosam, which means 'Our Rice for Our Purpose' (2012-13); Amma Hastam (2012-13) – distribution of nine items at subsidised price. Some of the activities such as cement distribution are undertaken on ad-hoc basis as when the State government direct them to do so. The major activities are procurement of paddy and rice and distribute the rice to the target group at subsidised rate.

Organisation of APSCSCL

The "APSCSCL" is responsible to curb and prevent shortages, misappropriation and diversion of stocks. It exercise internal controls, improving the procedures, installation of computers, electronic weighing scales and training of the staff to ensure clean Public Distribution System without any scope for loss of the Government (GO No. 83, 2006). It is the responsibility of the Corporation to undertake transportation, storage and delivery of the stocks under PDS at the doorstep of the FPS Dealers.

The Board of Directors consisting of not less than two and not exceeding eight members at any time is managing the Corporation. The Chairman is appointed by the government and in the absence of such an appointment; the Commissioner of Civil Supplies is the Chairman of the Corporation. Normally the Board consists of Officials and Non-officials as appointed by the government. The Vice Chairman and Managing Director is the Chief Executive of the Corporation. At the corporate office, four Functional Managers, an Executive Engineer and eight Managers assist him / her. The District Managers of the Corporation maintain a close liaison with the District Administration with regard to distribution of Essential Commodities to the target group in the district. The Managers are under the administrative control of the Joint Collector of the respective district, who is also Ex-Officio Executive Director of the Corporation.

The FCI, APCSCL, Legal Metrology Department, Revenue officials are responsible for making stock physical verification and maintenance during transportation to MLS points and to take suitable measures for ensuring fair distribution of foodgrains (GO No. 83 dated 21.12.2006). Most important functionary, in this regard, is District Manager, APSCSCL. He/ she is responsible to: depute one representative (in-charges at MLS points) at each loading point of FCI; ensure that the representatives furnish particulars of movement to MLS points daily; reconcile movement particulars with reference to the stocks received at MLS points; ensure that necessary entries are made in the goods received register, stock register and issue register at MLS point; ensure receipt of stock report from MLS point every month and sending a consolidated report for the entire district to the VC and MD of APSCSCL; ensure proper securitisation of the bills of the transporters with reference to the registers at the MLS points.

The Girijan Co-operative Corporation Limited (GCC), a public sector undertaking of the Government of Andhra Pradesh established in 1956, is responsible for ensuring the availability of

Essential Commodities in the interior agency areas through a network of Daily Requirement Depots (DR Depots). These Depots sell essential commodities as well as commodities of day-to-day needs of the tribal like soap, detergent, etc. The affairs of the Corporation are administered by the Vice-Chairman and Managing Director. The Project Officers of the Integrated Tribal Development Agencies (ITDAs) act as Executive Directors of GCC in the area of their operation. The GCC has 10 Divisional Offices, 43 Girijan Primary Cooperative Marketing Societies, and 839 DR Depots in tribal areas to cater to the needs of the tribals by supplying essential commodities under the PDS and other daily-required commodities.

The Organisational setup at the District Level

The district government/agencies and below are responsible for distribution of foodgrains to the target groups. At the district level, the Joint Collector and Chief Rationing Officer (in Hyderabad and Vishkapattanam) are responsible for implementation of food security programmes in the rural and urban areas, respectively. They are assisted by the officials of both Civil Supplies Department and Civil Supplies Corporation such as District Supply Officer, Tahasildar and Dy Tahasildhar, Revenue Officer, and District Manager, Assistant District Manager and other officials of the Corporation in the implementation of food security programmes. Every local authority, as authorised by the State government, shall conduct or cause periodic social audits on the functioning of TPDS, and other welfare schemes, and take necessary action. In addition, every State government shall set up Vigilance Committees at the state, district, block, and FPS levels. As per NFSA, 2013, State governments shall appoint District Grievance Redressal Officers.

Mandal Level Stock Points Management

The APSCSC has 439 Mandal Level Stock (MLS) Points @ one per three Mandals and supplying approximately 3.6 Lakh Metric Tonnes (LMT) of raw rice (the quantity of supply varies from month to month) to cardholders, social welfare hostels and mid-day meals programme. Out of the 439 MLS points, 28 MLS points are being handled by GCC and the Civil Supplies Corporation manages the remaining 411 MLS points. The present capacity of these MLS points is 3.2 LMT with a capacity of storing one-month stock. Anticipating in the increase in the procurement of rice due to Decentralised Procurement (DCP), the Corporation has increased the capacity of godown space by hiring the space from the Department of Marketing and AP State Warehousing Corporation.

The Joint Collector (twice in a month), District Supply Officer (four times in a month), Revenue Divisional Officer (four times in month) are expected to visit MLS points in their respective jurisdiction and make physical verification of the stocks. The Corporation is contemplating to adopt Public-Private Partnership (PPP) by appointing an agency as third party for inspection and physical verification of stocks at all MLS points in the State.

At the level of MLS points the functionary of APSCSCL / GCC is expected to look after the Stocks to be received at MLS points by 100 per cent weighment; Entries of all transaction to be made in all the registers – Truck Chits and release orders to be maintained date-wise; Delivery stocks to FPS under various schemes by 100 per cent weighment; prepare the claims of Hamali (loaders) and transporters. However, in many places, only manual weighing scales of 0.3 Metric tonnes (Mts) capacity are installed and it is becoming very difficult to weigh the PDS grains at MLS points. As per the GO No. 83, dated 21.12.2006 the FCI shall ensure that Electronic Weigh Bridges are installed at all loading points by replacing the Mechanical Weigh Bridges within a period of six months. However, GO is not being implemented properly in the State. Wherever they are being installed, the power cut in the State is major constraint for its operation. As a result there is no way of ensuring that they received the full quantity of rice and other commodities from Stage I transport contractor. The MLS points also do not receive any samples from FCI along with the stock and hence no verification of proper quality can be made. The Truck chits and the Weight Check Memo is received at MLS points are handwritten and not electronically printed Thus, there are possibilities of diversion of foodgrains (Justice Wadhwa Committee, 2009).

Responsibilities of Route Officer

Route Officer, the rank of Junior Assistant, is responsible for delivering stock at FPS and to ensure that there is no diversion en-route and full quantity is delivered at FPS. He/ She obtain acknowledgement from the FPS dealer after delivering the foodgrains at FPS under the witness of the Sarpanch or ward Member or the Panchayat Secretary of Gram Panchayat and acknowledgement from two other persons Vigilance (Food Advisory) Committee members or elders of that area in token of receipt of the stocks. The Route Officer is expected to immediately enter the details of the stocks delivered in the stock register of the FPS dealer and attest the entry.

As per standard sampling procedure, two samples are to be taken out by the authorities of MLS point at the time of delivery of stock to the FPS. Each sample has to be marked showing the particulars of the MLS point, the FPS, the month for which the commodity has been issued, the date on which the sample is drawn and the signature of the in-charge of MLS point. The samples have to be sealed with the seal of MLS point. The Route Officer is required to ensure that one sealed sample given by the MLS point in-charge prepared in duplicate containing the signature of MLS point-in-charge and Route Officer at the time of the weighment is delivered along with the stocks.

The Governance at the Grassroots Level: The Role of Panchayat Raj Institutions

Under the existing instructions issued to States/UTs from time to time by the Ministry including the Public Distribution System (Control) Order, 2001 notified on 31.8.2001, various roles/responsibilities have been assigned for the Panchayat Raj Institutions (PRIs) in implementation of TPDS in States/UTs. In view of the large number of complaints about diversion of essential commodities, the government emphasised on the role of PRIs to monitor the functioning of PDS at the grassroot level (G.O. vide G.O. Ms. No. 7 dated 01.02.2006).

However, the Expert Committee of Government of India on Leveraging Panchayats for Efficient Delivery of Public Goods and Services (2013) is of the view that the State Governments, including Government of Andhra Pradesh, are not giving due weightage to the PRIs as instructed in Public Distribution System (Control) Order, 2001. The guidelines must make this role mandatory to follow the aim of the 73rd Constitutional Amendment Act, 1992 and to ensure that the intended beneficiaries can have effective access to the TPDS commodities in terms of timeliness, quantities and quality. This issue has acquired urgency with the National Food Security Act, 2013 to provide food security to the targeted population.

The Act provides for the local authorities, which includes Panchayat to be responsible for the proper implementation of the Act in their respective areas. Section 33(2) further provides that State governments may assign additional responsibilities for implementation of TPDS to local authorities. Under Section 37 (1) of NPSA, Vigilance Committees are to be constituted by State government at State, district, block/ mandal, FPS levels. It also provides for due representation to local authorities in Vigilance Committee. The Act provides for preference to public institutions or public bodies such as Panchayats, self-help groups, cooperatives in licensing of FPSs and its management by women collectives. The Expert Committee (2013) deliberated on this critical issue and considers that the PRI representatives are not only to be involved in the implementation of the new law, but these institutions will have to play the principal role for realising the goal of "advancing food and nutritional security" and this has to be clearly stated in the Act itself. The elected panchayats have important role for the last mile delivery of foodgrains and other essential commodities. This can be ensured if the Food Security Act is made consistent with the provisions of Part IX and IXA of the Constitution as well as Panchayat Extension in Scheduled Areas (PESA).

The PRIs, responsibility and powers will be particularly significant in the PESA areas where the vulnerabilities are high and the delivery of crucial public goods and services face weak infrastructure and leakages. The PRIs as the local elected bodies and embedded in the local context will be in the best position to set things right and to respond to the local needs, problems and grievances. The Committee therefore, recommends that the panchayats at the district, intermediate and village levels should be given the total responsibility for implementation of the food security for the last mile delivery at the district, sub-district and village level after the commodities are arranged and made available by government agencies concerned. They may be kept informed about the arrangements planned and finalised. The agencies working for food security at district and sub-district levels must be brought under the disciplinary and regulatory authority of the appropriate tier of panchayat system.

Further, the Committee is of the view that the PRIs should be the licensing authority for FPSs in the rural areas and not be mentioned only as receiving preference as is often seen recently. The Grievance Redressal Mechanisms must involve the elected women and men of the panchayats. This mechanism should be under the district panchayat at the district level with the concerned bureaucracy serving under this body. At higher levels, adequate representation of DPC (District Planning Committees) established under Article 243ZD, the panchayats, especially district panchayats would be crucial to ensure a people-run, and people oriented Grievance Redressal Mechanism. The PRI committee overseeing the food security system needs to be headed by seniormost women PRI representative. Finally, in the Transparency and Accountability mechanisms, these local self-governing institutions and especially the Gram Sabha should be made the pivot of transparency and accountability

Fair Price Shops

The Fair Price Shops are the final link in the chain of distribution of foodgrains to the consumers. As per the GO Ms. No. 35 dated 17.9.2007 the district administration is authorised to grant new FPS or bifurcates the existing FPS based on convenience of the cardholders and economic viability of managing the FPS and intimate the same to the government within 45 days of opening of FPS. The norms to be followed in the rationalisation of the FPSs are: (a) Rural areas: The number of Iris-based ration cards to be attached to each FPSs is 400 to 450 BPL and 50 pink cards; (b) Urban areas: The number of Iris-based ration cards to be attached to each FPSs is 500 to 550 BPL and 250 pink cards in Municipalities and erstwhile Taluk Headquarters; and (c) Corporations: The number of Iris-based ration cards to be attached to each FPS is 600 to 650 BPL Cards and 400 pink cards. In practice there are variations in number of Cards attached with a shop ranging from 400 to 800 cards out of which 80 were of AAY category and 720 of BPL category. In some cases the number is 2,558 ration cards (2406 White cards, 147 AAY cards, 5 Annapurna cards (Justice Wadwa Committee, 2009).

Appointment of FPS Dealers

As per the APSPDS (Control) Order, 2008, the FPS dealers posts are reserved for Scheduled Castes (15 per cent); Scheduled Tribes (six per cent); Physically Handicapped (three per cent); Backward Classes (25 per cent); Women (30 per cent). The Revenue Divisional Officer (RDO) or the Sub-Collector in respect of rural areas and District Supply Officer in respect of Hyderabad and Visakhapatnam are competent authority for appointment of dealer. The Dealer is only a licensee for a fixed period. As per the norms, the validity of license is for two years and the same needs to be renewed for every two years. The license should run the FPS personally and no agent or *benami* is permitted to run the FPS on behalf of the licensee. However, in the case of woman dealer, this rule is relaxed.

Though the dealer is to be appointed based on merit by following reservation rule of the State government, the authorities concerned are granting license either on the recommendations of politicians, MLA or taking bribe. In addition to this, dealer has to pay bribe every month (depending upon the number of ration cards) to the higher-level authorities and local area inspector for renewal of license. In turn, the officials help dealer to make bogus ration cards normally made for five years. FPS dealers make use of these cards and sell commodities in the open market at the higher/market rates. The guidelines such as acquiring SSC or X class qualification, submission of solvency certificate and Affidavit, depositing the amount in the bank, etc are the major drawbacks for the weaker sections for obtaining the license. All these factors are helping the relatively better off, who can manage/ fulfil all the above, in getting the license to manage FPS. In fact, there are several instances where the influential persons are obtaining the license in the name of their family members or persons who are loyal to them and managing the FPS. This has enabled them to enter into local and state politics and occupy the political executive positions in rural and urban local bodies and State government (field notes).

Duties and Obligations of a Fair Price Shop Licensee

The PDS Order, 2001, under Clause 7 and GO Memo no. 3396 dt 20-10-2003 specifies the duties and responsibilities of the FPSs owners. They are: selling essential commodities as per the entitlement of ration card holders and at the retail issue prices fixed by the concerned State Government; display the information such as List of BPL and Antyodaya beneficiaries, entitlement of essential commodities, retail issue prices, timings of opening and closing of the FPS, stock of essential commodities received during the month, opening and closing stock of essential commodities; and the authority for redressal of grievances/lodging complaints with respect to quality and quantity of essential commodities on a notice board on a daily basis. Further, FPS owner is also responsible for furnish copies of specified documents such as the ration card register, stock register, sale register to the office of the Gram Panchayat or Nagar Palika or Vigilance Committee or any other body authorised by State Government for the purpose of verification.

Viability of the FPS

The major concern of the FPS Dealer is to meet expenditure in managing it as per the guidelines of the government. The government pays the commission to the Dealer for distribution of ration items to the cardholders and to meet the expenditure on the items such as rent for the shop, electricity charges, salary to the assistant, charges to the hamalies, stationery, etc. The Dealers allegation is that the commission paid by the government to them is inadequate to operate the FPS. On an average each dealer, who is supplying the ration items to 400-450 cardholders, would get about Rs 4000 as commission from the government. However, the expenditure on the above-mentioned items would be more than what they get from the government. In addition to this, they are expected to invest more than Rs 50,000 per month for lifting the ration items. The Justice Wadhwa Committee has observed that there are other factors affecting the viability of a FPS. Some of these are: delay in supply of foodgrains; losses suffered by FPS dealers due to blockage of working capital invested for the stock and transport, for long periods; losses suffered on account of short supply of goods; unequal distribution of ration cards; high transportation costs; Commission for organising FPS being too low to generate moderate income.

Despite dealers repeated requests the government is not revising the commission rate keeping in view the rising cost in operating the FPS. The general understanding of the officials and public is that the dealers acquire bogus cards, claim the ration from the government, and sell it in the open market for higher price and gaining profits out of managing the FPS. On this assumption, the government is not revising the commission rate based on the actual income and expenditure in managing the FPS. Nevertheless, this in a way is encouraging the dealer to resort to malpractices. This is the biggest challenge of governance of food security policies, which is continued right from the implementation of TPDS i.e. 1997 onwards. No government is willing to address this issue for the past two decades or even more.

Food Advisory Committees

The State Government appoints the members of Food Advisory Committees (FAC), which are also known as the Vigilance Committees, at all levels of administrative units (G.O. Ms. No. 470 dated 10th November 1995 and GO No. 93 dated 13-7-2005). The Committees are to be constituted at District, Mandal and Village level in the rural areas and Municipal Corporation Circle, Division, Municipality, Ward, and FPS level in urban areas. District level and Mandal level committees are required to meet bi-monthly and all other level to meet monthly and discuss the issues related to PDS. The District Joint Collectors / Chief Rationing Officer are responsible for the conducting committee meetings. The FAC/ Gram Panchyat is authorised to certify the proper utilisation/ distribution of foodgrains and the same has to be communicated to higher level bodies for taking further action and release of foodgrains to the dealer for distribution to the card holders. Nevertheless, in practice, the State government is on paper and the higher-level officials are not serious about its implementation.

Food Advisory Committees at the Village Level

As per the GO. Ms. No. 495 dated 16th December 1995, the FAC were to be constituted at all levels starting from state to village levels. Based on the experience the government revised the guidelines in 2005 (GO. Order Nos. 4/6699/04 dated 16.5.2005 and GO. MS. No.93, dated 13-7-2005). The government has issued amendment to the then existing GO by issuing GO. Ms. No. 7 dated 01-02-2006 for reconstituting the FACs duly involving the representatives of PRIs, as they play a vital role in strengthening the PDS at the grassroots level. The GO. No. 53

dated 07-11-2007 and GO no. 58 dated 24-11-2007 provide provision for the inclusion of Member of the Legislative Council and District Managers of APCSC as members of the FAC at the District level.

As per the GOs the village level the FAC is headed by the Sarpanch and it is expected to meet every month, preferably 1st Monday of the month. The Tahasildhar of the concerned mandal is responsible for conducting FAC meetings. The role of FAC at the village is to: review the allotment of essential commodities made to the FPS; review the closing balance of the essential commodities of previous month with the FPS; conduct enquiry by the team of not less than a minimum of three members of the committee at the Gram Panchayat Level and placing the matter before the Gram Sabha for public hearing; passing a resolution on the action to be taken and forwarding the same to the Licensing authority under copy to the Mandal Revenue Officer (MRO) concerned for taking action. During the field survey it is observed that no such committees are in operation. The authorities concerned are not taking initiatives to form and activate the FACs at the grass-roots level. Unless this is done no amount of, monitoring or any modern methods would arrest the leakages in PDS at the grass-roots levels.

Allocation and Release of Foodgrains

The Commissioner of Civil Supplies (CCS) issues a notification of monthly district-wise allocation of foodgrain for each food security scheme. The District Collector/ Joint Collector in turn make FPS-wise allocation in the district. On receipt of this order, the District Manager of APSCSC deposits a demand draft against the value of foodgrain to be lifted for public distribution with concerned Area Manager of FCI. The FCI issues the Release Order after obtaining the stocks from FCI. The District Manager positions the stock at various MLS points. The stocks are transported from the FCI godown to the MLS points through transporters appointed on contract by APSCSC known as Stage I transporters. No officer of the department accompanies/ escorts the truck while transportation of foodgrain from FCI to MLS and Stage-I Transport Contractor is responsible for any short delivery of foodgrains. The District Supply Officer thereafter makes allocation for each FPS. The District Manager APSCSC issues release order for each FPS in terms of the allocation. The FPS owner deposits the money to get the foodgrain through a Demand Draft with the District Manager APSCSC.

On receipt of the Demand Draft from FPS owner, the release Order is required to be issued by the Mandal Revenue Officer on the same day. MRO is required to issue Release Order/ allotment orders FPS wise with reference to the net requirement based on the gross allotment of FPS and the closing balance available with the dealer on the last day of the month. MRO /ASO has to report the allotment, lifting and distribution for each FPS commodity-wise duly totalling for the Mandal for the particular month by third of the next month to the Collector / CRO, Hyderabad to consolidate and report the district-wise position to the commissioner of civil supplies by fifth of every month. In accordance with the release order, the foodgrain is transported by Stage -II transport contractors to the FPS. At the time of transportation of foodgrains to the FPS, the Route Officer is expected to accompany the truck.

Transportation of Foodgrains

The APSCSC Ltd. appoints Transport Contractors under Stage I for transportation of foodgrain from FCI godowns to MLS points by floating tenders every year. Along with the Tender, the transporter has to furnish earnest money of Rs 6 lakhs. The main criterion prescribed for transporters is that he/she must have minimum five trucks of his own and five hired trucks. He/she has to furnish a security deposit of Rs 15 lakhs and a Bank guarantee of Rs 20 lakhs, which vary from time to time. Tender process involves calling of technical and financial bids.

The government monitors the movement of vehicles through SMS messages from the officials at FCI godown to the District Manager's Office. Once the vehicle is received, it is informed by the official at the MLS point to the District office about the receipt. The stocks received are weighed at the MLS point and if there is any variation in stock, double the value of the stock at actual cost is collected for that shortage from the contractor. However, Justice Wadhwa Committee, during its visit to the field units, observed that the said SMS system actually does not exist in practice. The Committee found that MLS point in-charge and other officials do not use SMS system as they found it very cumbersome to type SMS. Similarly, the weighment at MLS point while receiving stock from FCI is not done in practice as they do not have weighing machines to weigh such huge quantity of foodgrains and hence weighment is not practically possible by using small weighing machines.

The District Manager of APSCSC is responsible for entering into contract with Transporters under Stage II. The Transport contractor is responsible for transporting essential commodities from MLS Points to FPSs within the Mandals attached to MLS points. Separate agreements are done for each MLS point. Distribution and transportation of foodgrain to the retail units from MLS points is done as per norms of Stage II transportation. Except for the cities of Hyderabad, APSCSC Ltd does Secundrabad and Vishakhapatnam the transportation of PDS foodgrain from the MLS point to the FPS through Stage II transport contractors. The appointment of Stage II transport contractors is done MLS point-wise/Mandal-wise by District administration by floating tenders. The period of contract is two years (Circular No. PDS 2/Govt/F.G.5 (9)/599/2005-06 dated 20-05-2005). The criteria are that the transporter must have at least two Vehicles for transportation from MLS points to FPSs. The tender has to be accompanied by earnest money. The rates of earnest money, security deposit and Bank guarantee vary based on the allotment of essential commodities allotted to the contractors.

The individuals / firms, who are blacklisted by APSCSC Ltd, at any time, are prohibited from participating in the tenders. The Rice Millers Association / Rice Millers Lorry Owners Associations or their Associates are also prohibited from participating in tenders. The contractors are prohibited from engaging the Trucks of the Stage I contractors existing in the districts or the Rice Millers or their Associations or persons involved in diversion of stocks or with criminal record or issues involved in 6-A case under EC Act for the purpose of transportation of foodgrains under PDS and they should not have any tie-up arrangements with the above said person. In practice, the family members of traders/millers and lorry owners associations are taking the contracts and transporting the foodgrains to the MLS points and FPSs in the State.

Norms Regarding Stage II Transportation

As per norms Stocks should be transported under stage II transportation from MLS point to door step of the FPS as per the route plan evolved under escort of a government official to ensure proper delivery without diversion or leakage en-route. The validity period allowed by the GOI for lifting of stock allotted to State is 50 days i.e. from 1st day of the preceding month to 20th of the month for which the allocation pertains. To ensure that allocated food grain is delivered to FPS within the first week of the month for which allocation is made the FPS dealers are instructed by the State Government to file their Demand Drafts on 18th of preceding month. The release orders are sent to the MLS points on the same day to commence transportation from MLS point to FPS.

Section-II

Governance Issues and Challenges

The food security programmes, like any anti-poverty programmes, encountered with several problems, which are hampering the progress of the programmes. The Independent Evaluation Committee appointed, recently, by the Planning Commission reported that in certain places, the foodgrains to be distributed under PDS are not reaching to the real beneficiaries. More than half of the targeted group, especially in Delhi, is not getting the ration items. Further, the Committee observed that the government is incurring about Rs 3.65 to transport the foodgrains worth of Re 1. The inability of the organisations to deliver the services to the targeted groups is the serious issue. The following are the governance issues and challenges of the food security programmes, which need to be addressed by the government.

Official Procedures

The major concerns of the Civil Supplies Department/Corporation are: competition from the private traders in procurement of foodgrains; negotiation with producers, cooperative societies, market federation and other government departments; adhering to the officially prescribed procedures- tenders in purchasing/ storing/transporting the foodgrains; etc. The department/corporation discharges most of its activities through the private firms (traders, millers, commission agents, and transport agents, warehousing corporations/owners, recruiting the lower level workers/hamalies, FPS dealers, sub-contractors or other intermediaries). Therefore, it has to follow officially prescribed procedures in dealing with the private traders and ensure fair transactions. This sometimes would be counterproductive. For instance, tenders involve high transaction cost; there is a bureaucratic hassle and they often take more time; or collude with large trading companies or big traders; or the traders form the ring and monopoly the trade. Furthermore, tender purchase does not easily combine with the flexible market intervention. Many levels of hierarchy and lack of autonomy to the field staff; bureaucratic culture; fear of allegations for overlooking the procedures or allegations for showing favouring suppliers; illegitimate interference of politicians in administrative matters in the corporation/department, etc, does not provide right environment for an entrepreneurial spirit. Thus, multiplicity of objectives; the lack of operational autonomy; constraining purchase procedures; unreasonable and shortsighted demands and political interference, etc, are affecting the functioning of the department/corporation in the state.

Enforcement of Essential Commodities Act, 1955

The purpose of EC Act, 1955 is to provide for control of production, distribution and trade in certain essential commodities in the interest of public. The Government of AP in pursuance of PDS (control) Order, 2008, for the purpose of maintains supplies and securing equitable distribution of essential commodities in the State. These measures would enable the authorities to prosecute any agency- private trades, rice mill owners, transporters of essential commodities, cooperative marketing societies, and ration shop dealers- if they contravene the provisions of the Act. In spite of these procedures, the traders are indulging in malpractices. In certain cases, the Vigilance and Enforcement authorities are booking the cases but the traders, with their economic and political power are in a position to bring pressure on the administration to fizzle out cases; and sometimes get relief from the court taking the advantage of loopholes in the Act. The officials and politicians extract money from the culprits and help them to come out of the case.

Identification of the target group/beneficiary

Under the subsidised foodgrain scheme, it has become necessary for the governments to identify the target group households using verifiable economic criterion that could be uniformly applied all over the State. For the purpose of distribution of foodgrains, the Central Government has formulated guidelines for issuing ration cards to the different categories of target group i.e Above Poverty Line (APL), Below Poverty Line (BPL), Antyodhya Anna Yojana (AAY), Annapurna (AP). The Clause 3 and clause 4 of the Public Distribution Order, 2001 State governments shall identify the families and issue distinctive ration cards to different categories of HHs mentioned above. These clauses further mandate the State government to make periodical review of the ration cards and eliminate the bogus ration cards.

However, the State government has freedom to formulate guidelines for the purpose of identification of BPL/AAY/AP within the framework given by Central government. The government has issued GOs (57 dated 13-05-2005; 27 dated 23-07-08) time to time keeping in view the changing pattern of income and economy of the people. The income criterion is enhanced from Rs 20,000 and Rs 24,000 in 2005 to Rs 65,000 and Rs 75,000 in 2008 in rural and urban areas, respectively, for identification of BPL HHS in the state. In 2009, the then government has enhanced it up to below Rs one lakh. The Telangana State government enhanced identification criterion for granting Aahara Badaratha Card (Food Security Card) up to Rs One lakh and fifty thousand per HH or seven acres of dry land or three and a half acres wet land in rural areas and Two lakhs per HH urban areas (November, 2014).

The Government of Andhra Pradesh prescribed norms for exclusion of certain groups. They are: (a) Cultivators possessing the land more than the above ceiling; (b) Persons owning two wheelers, three wheelers, four wheelers (other than provided under govt. schemes); (c) Persons whose electricity consumption is more than Rs 6,000 per annum; (d) A *pucca* building having plinth area of 500 sq.ft. alternatively, more either owned or rented out; (c) Permanent employment in government/ organised sector like companies, industries and firms.

The main criteria adopted for the purpose of identification of target group in the State are: (i) households annual income or (ii) land holdings (less than five acres). The annual income criteria was/is considered in the urban areas, while in the rural areas it is landholdings in granting the cards. The designated authority (MRO) is authorised to issue the ration card/s to the above poverty line (pink card), below poverty line, Antyodaya and Anna Yojana families (BPL/ White cards) within one month of the date of receipt of the application. The clause 11 (2) of PDS order 2001 provides that any person aggrieved by an order of the designated authority denying the issue or renewal of a ration card or cancellation of the ration card may appeal to the appellate authority within the thirty days of the date of receipt of the order. In practice due to the cumbersome rules and procedures it is herculean task for the poor man to submit the application and securing the card. Along with the application, the applicant has to enclose the residential certificate endorsed/authenticated by Sarpanch and Village Revenue Officer (VRO). These functionaries, most of the times, do not stay/reside in their respective villages and pay visit to the village/s as and when they have official or personal work. The poor, who are otherwise busy in search of livelihood, are unable to meet the functionaries and get their signatures endorsement. Sometimes they are taking time on the pretext that they have no time to verify the records, especially his/her parents' ration cards and number of members included in the card, whether her/his name/family members name/s figure in or verify it from the dealer of the ration shop, whether he/she has already availed card or not, etc. If the applicant belongs to the opposition political party or not voted in favour of the Sarpanch in the panchayat elections, he/she has to undergo these difficulties. Many a times the applicants are not approaching the higher authorities for justice, partly they are not aware of the provision mentioned in the clause 11 (2) of the PDS order 2001 or partly they do not have faith in the higher authorities.

In many cases, the assessment is done without any scientific method and it is manipulated and relatively better off households in the rural areas obtained the income certificate below the stipulated income and secured the BPL ration card/s. The landowners submitting wrong information/hiding the information on the ownership of the land of the household also misuse even the land criterion. The officials also do not take into account the land value and there are huge variations within and between the villages, which are proximity to the urban areas and connected to transport and to that of the villages located in the backward and rural areas. The one acre of land value in the semi-urban areas / mandal headquarter is equivalent to five to 10 acres of land in the rural areas. These variations are not taken into consideration in granting the ration cards.

The conversion of wetland into dry land and vice-versa is a major problem to arrive at correct decision to determine the eligibility criteria for issuing ration cards. The existing criteria of issuing white card to households having less than two acres of wet land or less than five acres of dry land which is causing for imbalance in the issuing of cards in the villages. The households with one-acre of wet land are much better off than households with more than five acres of dry land. Therefore, in the irrigated areas almost all the HHs, who possess 2.5 acres of wet land are likely to be covered while in dry areas many poor HHs, who possess more than five acres, are likely to be excluded from the scheme within the same village. Some HHs will have fertile land with adequate water and others do not possess such resources. The HHs who have better endowed resources and the HHs, who have poor endowed resources, are equated on equal footing while issuing the ration cards. This is causing for wrong identification of HHs. While fixing the ceiling on land for the distribution of white cards in the State, the variation in land productivity across the districts and regions, villages must be given due importance (Indrakanth, S and S. Harikishan (The Telangana).

There are also instances where some of the household members working in the private sector earning up to Rs 10,000 per month are obtaining BPL ration cards by claiming that they are unemployed or income is less than that of the government criteria. The households, who are migrated to the urban or other areas in search of livelihood for more than five years, are taking the BPL cards or detaining cards already taken. The reasons for this are: (i) the government/private agencies are considering/insisting the ration cards as one of the documents for identification proof for issuing of driving license, passport, railway tickets, (ii) claiming for housing, medical and educational benefits from the government schemes, (iii) opening bank account and securing personal loans, (iv) taking mobile connections, etc. The most important of all these, is the launching of 'Arogya Sri Programme' where in the BPL/white card holders get the medical relief up to Rs one lakh for chronic diseases. The relatively better- off or large farmers/employees earning more than Rs 10,000 per month are manipulating the information or bribing the officials in getting White cards. All these factors are resulting in issuing bogus ration cards and sometimes more than households in a village issue.

Issue of Bar Coded Biometric Ration Cards

The government is issuing bar coded Iris Technology based biometric ration cards to the eligible candidates since 2005 in the State. However, the guidelines and the procedure adopted for issuing cards is not based on any scientific manner. As per the guidelines, any person who desires to obtain ration card has to submit the fill the declaration form cum household information sheet to concerned Mandal Office. No additional document or affidavit with regard to age, identity proof, annual income, etc, except a Xerox copy of the residential address, is required to be submitted by the applicant. The designated inquiry officer has to make an enquiry and verify the information furnished by the applicant through 'circumstantial evidence'. Thereafter Iris image of both the left and right eyes retina and photographs of all the family members will be captured. Finally, the ration card duly signed by the Tahasildar will be issued to the cardholder. However, in practice there is no proper verification of the information submitted by the applicant due to political intervention. The Wadhwa Committee (2009) recorded the officials' version that 'there were unwritten instructions to issue ration cards to all the applicants without verification. This has caused for issue of bogus ration cards and it reached to the extent of 50 lakh in 2008. The lack of availability of instrument or technology at FPS to read the Irish-based ration card to determine the genuine cardholder or not, is letting the bogus ration cardholders to avail the benefits from TPDS. The Committee reiterated that end to end computerisation of PDS is the only answer to arrest the problems in the system, including the weeding out the bogus cards in the State. But the 'end to end computerisation' at the grass-roots level is not implemented due to the lack of required infrastructure and personnel- computer/ laptop, power/ power backup- and also lack of skilled employees to do the task of computerisation of the programme.

Computerisation of PDS

It is believed that computerisation of PDS is necessary for strengthening and revamping the system and for addressing the challenges faced by PDS i.e. inclusion/exclusion errors, leakages/ diversion of foodgrains, lack of transparency, weak grievance redressal and social audit mechanism. Based on the recommendations of the High Power Committee constituted under the Chairmanship of Justice DP Wadawah, Honble Supreme Court in its order dated 14.09.2011 directed the Central government to computerize the PDS. Accordingly, the Department of Food and Public Distribution, GOI has issued guidelines to all States/ UTs for Computerisation of TPDS, which need to be implemented in a time-bound manner as stipulated by the Court. End to end computerisation of PDS in States/UTs has to be implemented in two parts as follows:

Component I: Supply-Chain Computerisation of the entire TPDS operations should cover monitoring of foodgrains allocation, storage and movements starting from the base depots of FCI till the FPS. The information related to the supply-chain should be made available in public domain through the Transparency Portal. The portal will have different dashboards catering to the varying information needs of various stakeholders involved in TPDS operations. States/UTs are to implement this within a period of three months. The Chhattisgarh State model of Computerisation of TPDS may be adopted for the purpose.

Component II: This component relates to the computerisation of operations at the FPS. The issuing Smart Cards/Food coupons, etc. require reengineering and replacement with online Aadhaar authentication at the time of foodgrains delivery. In Gujarat, new Bar Coded Ration Cards were issued to all existing cardholders as well as for fresh Ration Cards also. The new Ration Card System captured the biometric information of at least one adult member depicted in the Ration Card. Along with Bar Coded Ration Cards, Bar Coded Food Coupons are issued to the beneficiaries.

The Department of Food and Public Distribution, Government of India has identified four key components for computerisation of PDS in all the States/UTs as below:

- Creation and Management of digitised Beneficiary Database;

- Supply-Chain Management of TPDS commodities from FCI till FPSs;
- Sale of TPDS commodities at FPS including identification and authentication of beneficiaries and recording of transactions; and
- Transparency and Grievance Redressal Mechanism.

Though the Andhra Pradesh is one of the leading States in the country in the advancement of in the Information sector and its application in different departments, many of the activities are not implemented properly. This indicates the failure of the institutions of governance meant for the implementation of food security programmes.

Government Reluctance to Transfer or Grant New Ration Cards to the APL HHs Migrated to the Urban Areas

Prior 1997, the pink cardholders used to purchase sugar and rice from FPS. After launching of TPDS, the government reduced the allocation of budget to supply the ration items to the pink cardholders with a view to reduce its burden on subsidy. Further, the APL families who are separated from the joint family or migrated to the urban areas in search of livelihood opportunities are demanding for transfer of the cards or granting new cards. The government is/was reluctant to do so. Due to this many APL households produced false evidence income certificates/manipulated the records and obtained white cards. They used this white card for mostly availing the medical benefits under Arogyasree Programme. Nevertheless, this has given scope for the FPS dealers to claim ration of these cardholders from the Corporation and resorting black marketing the ration for higher price (Eenadu, 8th December 2013). The officials' indecisiveness to act on the demands of the applicants has not only denied the rights of the genuine families but also gave scope for the dealers to resort to the malpractices and earning easy money.

Food Coupons System

In order to arrest the malpractices (false entries in ration books by the FPS dealer) and keep track of the allocation and distribution of grains, the government has introduced the system of food coupon system in 1999 and issued bar coded coupons to the cardholders for distribution of rice and kerosene oil in 2006. The cardholder is expected to submit the coupons to dealer of FPS for claiming the ration items/ entitlements. As per the norms, the FPS Dealer has to submit his/her collected coupons to the higher officials every month for lifting the monthly quota for next month.

The major problem in this system is that the authorities have distributed the coupons to the cardholders more than the actual requirement ration cards in the State. The extra coupons, along with the bogus cards, leave a lot of scope for diversion of PDS commodities. The food coupons being distributed are said to be bar coded, it is of no use as there is no bar code reader either at MLS points or FPS in the entire state. Another problem is the authenticity of the coupons supplied by the higher officials to the cardholders and the coupons submitted by the cardholder, especially in view of the fact that several bogus cards are in circulation in the State. In the absence of bar code reader instrument at FPS there is no way to ensure the authenticity of the coupons and defeat the basic purpose of introduction of this system. Presently this system is not in operation in the State.

Corruption Rendering PDS Ineffective

The Centre for Media Studies and Transparency International, Delhi-based research firm conducted a study on 'Corruption in India's Public Distribution System' (covering 4,405 respondents over 20 states, in 2007) conclude that PDS needs a total overhaul to get rid of its dubious distinction of being one of the most corrupt sectors in the country. The study point out that what is ailing India's Public Distribution System (PDS). "Corruption" is the one and only answer to that question. Even the Central government's TPDS is in no way helping to weed out graft in the entire sector. FPSs have been the breeding ground for corruption right from its inception. The main reason for short supply of ration is diversion of grains to open market. Registering complaints against the shop owner is a complicated task. Again, consumer is unaware that he/she is being overcharged. About 60 per cent of the respondents to the survey felt that corruption increased in 2006 in high poverty states and people paid Rs 50-500 as bribe to get new ration cards. The survey has found out that 60 per cent households using PDS are not getting ration supplies. The survey further said in high-poverty states, 'out-of-stock' scenarios were as high as 80 per cent. In addition, 34 per cent of those visiting PDS offices had to make four or more visits before their voice could be heard and suitable action was taken. Moreover, nearly 50 per cent of them paid bribe for obtaining a new and legitimate ration card. Andhra Pradesh Government is no exception to these issues.

Monitoring of the Food Security Policies

As mentioned earlier, the Civil Supplies Department and Corporation are responsible to monitor the programmes, especially in procurement, transport, storage and distribution of foodgrains. The civil supplies department, as mentioned earlier is expected to: rationing of essential commodities in scarcity conditions – procurement of specified commodities through levy or through direct or indirect procurement, seizures, imports, etc.; fixation of entitlements; ensure the availability of food-grains (both produced by the farmers and imports and open market) in the state throughout the year and in all the districts; make the people to have access to foodgrains; control the price hike of the foodgrains; control terms of trade between the rice millers and the farmers and corporation; provide forward and backward linkages – construction or hiring of godowns for storage of foodgrains arranging vehicles for transportation of foodgrains, identifying the place/building for establishing FPS, appointment of dealer, on-line transactions etc.; organisation of transport and storage network to move and store the commodities; organisation retail outlets to distribute the commodities; coordinate with the other functionaries involved in food security programmes such as MGNREGP; release food subsidies, maintain the foodgrain stocks for future needs, etc; ensuring utilisation of foodgrains, supplying suitable food grains to the target-group members; ensuring sanitation and safe water for drinking water to the target group; addressing the issues involved in the transportation of the foodgrains; organisation of vigilance set up to supervise the distribution of foodgrains and punish the offenders; banning of private trade in the commodity which is rationed; undertaking operations to unearth holders' stock, etc.

All these activities require close monitoring of civil supplies department /corporation. However, the higher-level officials are mostly confined to office work, conducting official meetings and reviewing the progress of the PDS and many a times they are confined to compilation of data/ figures. Sometimes the figures reported to the higher-level officials and the figures available with district and below level are not tallying. Nevertheless, the validation of figures /reports with the ground reality is lacking. The variation is mostly due to the lack of monitoring by the higher-level officials over the district and field level functionaries. It is also due to the frequent transfers of the higher-level officials, lack of adequate staff to supervise the regional and district level officers. The officials knew about prevailing of malpractices in granting tenders to purchase procurement of essential commodities such as sugar, palm oil, chilli powder, tamarind; granting permission to private vehicles to transport the foodgrains to the MLS point and FPS level; fixing the price of the commodity, quantity and quality of the foodgrains, etc. They are helpless due to the lack of adequate staff and others. The corrupt practices of traders, black-marketers, officials, are unchecked. In addition to these problems, there is a general feeling that the officials are not participating whole-heartedly in the work. It is complained that they lack commitment and sympathy for the poor. There are instances, where the officials commented that distribution of foodgrains at subsidised rate is not desirable as it makes the poor as 'parasites' on the society. Any programme, including PDS, designed to provide service on nominal price (Re one) or free of cost, every agency/stakeholder involved in its implementation would like to grab the opportunity and make use it for personal ends rather than for the intended purpose. This is the general psychology of the human beings in the class society.

The target group members or their associations or civil society organisations do not take much interest in watching the programme. Though the provisions of PDS provide the scope for constitution of food committee, social audit, public audit, in which the target group members/ representatives are the members and authorised to monitor the programme, they hardly take any interest to perform their role. Majority of the target group members and the field level officials are not aware of the constitution of such committees. Similar situation is prevailing all most in the entire state –the officials commented. Thus, there is a gap between the promise and performance of the programme (field notes).

The Coordination

The linkage and control are the essential integrating process between one part of the system and the other with the main purpose of enabling the machinery to function effectively and smoothly. If the links are not well tailored and connected, the system cannot function properly. Therefore, if the food security policies, especially PDS have to function well, it becomes essential to have connecting themselves with several departments/agencies. The government depends on the active involvement of FCI, Revenue, Weights and Measures and Financial Institutions, Warehousing Corporations, Railway department, Vigilance/Police department etc for the purpose. The cooperation and coordination between and among these agencies/departments is often lacking. This is causing for delay in procurement, transport, storage and distribution of foodgrains to the people. Further, there is shortage of functionaries in all the departments mentioned above and unable to cope with their regular work and establish rapport with the departments concerned. This situation is more at the district and below levels.

The Problem of Coordination at the District Level

The District Collector is the overall coordinator of all the programmes, including the food security programmes, and this office enjoys particular prestige, and is expected to ensure coordination, among various departments mentioned above for implementing PDS in the district. However, the District Collector is pre-occupied with so many other programmes that he/she hardly has time to look into the matters of the TPDS or civil supplies corporation. This is one office on which the demands are so heavy that the office hardly can do justice to the tasks assigned to him/her. Further, his/her capacity to coordinate the work is rendered ineffective, as he/she has no direct control over the FCI, warehousing corporations, financial institutions. The office of the District Collector in rural unified Andhra Pradesh is a best example to Riggsain observation that while there is increasing differentiation in the developmental tasks, the capacity for coordination is dwindling gradually.

The Joint Collector of the District is in-charge of implementation of the food security programmes in the district and exercise control on all the departments involved in the implementation of PDS at the district level. He/she has to ensure coordination from all the departments/ agencies/corporations involved in the implementation of all the activities of food security programmes – procurement, storage, transport and distribution of food-grains. He/she is expected to visit the mandal level stock points at least twice in a month and guide and monitor the functioning of the functionaries and inspect five FPSs in a month under the his/her jurisdiction. But in practice he/she is not able to do so for various reasons – such as frequent transfers, pre-occupation with other revenue and developmental works, organising meetings for ministers' visit, lack of interest to intervene in programme implementation as it is already dubbed as 'trouble task to reform', or due to political intervention and pressure from rice millers.

Problem of Coordination at the Field Level

Lack of coordination between the field functionaries of Civil Supplies department/ corporation and other governments such as revenue and panchayati raj, especially gram panchayat posed one of the major hurdles in the distribution of foodgrains to the ration cardholders. The revenue and gram panchayat functionaries do not cooperate with the civil supplies department/ corporation functionaries in providing necessary information i.e. income and land and nativity particulars of the prospective target group for identification and issuing of ration cards to the real target group households. In certain cases, the revenue and gram panchayat functionaries manipulated the records to the advantage of big farmers. The big farmers manage the revenue and gram panchayat functionaries in getting necessary certificates within the permissible limits to get the White cards. It is evident from the fact that more than 100 per cent of HHs in 2001 and 98 per cent HHs in 2011 have obtained ration cards in the State. This indicates that majority of the non-poor HHs acquired the White cards in the State (the details of the distribution of cards are presented in the subsequent pages). It is also true in all other anti-poverty programmes where the non-poor availed the programmes by registering themselves as poor (Bala Ramulu, Ch, 1981 and 1991). In the absence of proper response from the field functionaries of revenue and gram panchayat, benefits tend to go most undeserving HHs. The civil supplies department / corporation officials knew that in majority of the cases the relatively better-off enjoining the benefits intended for poorer sections because of such manipulations. The officials pleaded their helplessness, as they have no control over the field functionaries of the revenue and Gram Panchayat.

Middleman/ Intermediary

Another major constraint of the Civil Supplies Department/ Corporation is the emergence of intermediary (middlemen) who mediates between the bureaucracy and the target-group. The institution of middleman is an outcome of cumber some rules, lack of proper response from the officials to the stakeholders – traders, FPS dealer, SHGs, target group, etc. The middle class members and political leaders have entered into these new roles to make easy money. The bureaucracy is also pleased to deal with intermediary, who gives them money, parties and other facilities. Parallel to the bureaucracy, there are private agents/ intermediaries who collect money from the traders, transport vehicle owners, dealers illegally and distribute it to the officials every month. Though there is a transfer to the officials, there is no transfer to the private agents and the latter establish rapport with the officials, who comes on transfer, and the same process continue.

The intermediary also plays an important role in granting FPS and dealership at the field level. Though, there are prescribed norms for granting them, in practice they are materialised based in the political considerations and payment of bribe to the higher-level authorities. Latter this practice is giving scope for the dealers to procure bogus cards and diversion of ration items to the private traders and earning easy money. It is known fact that the relatively better-off farmers, who are availing the ration items, are selling them in the open market or private agents or FPS dealers at higher price.

Recycling of Ration Rice

The APL HHs or non-poor, who secured White ration cards purchase the rice at Re one per kg. not for the purpose of their consumption but they do this for selling to the petty merchant at the rate of Rs 12-15 per kg. The un-official sources indicate that about 20-30 per cent of ration cards do ineligible persons under PDS i.e., secure bogus cards. These families do not consume the rice supplied by the Corporation, as its quality is very low and sometimes contain insects. Their assumption is that they would become ill health, or face the problem of indigestion, if they eat the rice supplied by the Corporation.

In certain cases, the FPS dealers promote this process. They collect the BPL cards from the APL householders or those, who do not collect the allotted quota for various reasons in a particular month/s, claim the rice allotted to them by paying Rs 7-10 per kg. Some of the FPS dealer or moneylenders advance the amount as loan to the poor by mortgaging their White ration cards. The borrower/ poor households have to pay the monthly interest and collect the ration card from the FPS dealer/moneylender and claim the rice from the FPS, failing which the latter claims the rice on behalf of the poor households and sell it in the open market for higher price.

The general practice both in the rural and urban areas is that the petty merchants/or the persons interested in the recycling of rice collect the information either from the dealers or informers about the date/s of distribution of rice in the village/ward and visit the village on the next day or two-three days later and contact the APL HHs or HHs willing to sell the rice claimed under PDS and purchase the rice at Rs 12-15 per kg. They in turn sell it to the rice millers or poultry farms. The rice millers re-polish the rice and sell it in the open market or to hotel at higher price ranging between Rs 18-20 per kg. alternatively, supply it to the Corporation under levy system. The poultry firm owners mix the rice in the preparation of feed and fodder of the birds.

Cardholders' Reluctance to Purchase Ration Items

Although the red gram dal, chilli, haldi/tarmaric powder and tamarind are included in PDS charts, the cardholders are reluctant to purchase them from FPS owing to its poor quality. According to the reports, quite a few beneficiaries of the PDS, who purchased the above items from FPSs as part of their monthly ration, found its quality is extremely low. They have reportedly stopped purchasing commodities from the next month onwards, leaving the dealers in a fix. Subsequent months, the dealers too have stopped lifting commodities, despite force by officials. This is also partly due to import of the commodities from other States/Countries and partly beneficiaries are interested in local variety or produced in their village. Unlike the rice, quantity of consumption of these items by the beneficiaries is very less and, therefore, they prefer to purchase them from the local variety. FPS dealers are not lifting the stock from the Civil Supplies Corporation, as much of the stock in gowdown is not in a position for human consumption and officials are unable to understand how to get rid of existing stock in godowns.

According to the Civil Supplies officials of Ranga Reddy district, the red gram dal is imported from Malaysia and sometimes it is stored in godowns for more than two years as there is no demand for it from the takers. It is evident from the response of the cardholders "we have not been taking red gram dal from ration shop for the last four months, before that for two months, the quality of 'dal' was not good. It would take five whistles in the pressure cooker even before the outer crust of the dal was cooked." The cardholders are now purchasing it in the open market at Rs 70 per kg. However, the officials' version is that: "Other varieties of cheaper pulses are available in the market and people are choosing them over the Malaysian red gram dal. We have written to the Head office seeking permission to sell off the stock in auction", the District Manager Civil Supplies Corporation informed. It is pertinent to mention that instead of taking remedial measures by replacing the commodity with that of higher quality, all that the officials have done is just turn a blind eye to the issue (Swathi, V, Hindu, and 23-10-2012).

Universal Public Distribution to Arrest Malpractices in Public Distribution System

In the context of enacting of NFS A, 2013, many scholars, political parties, members of National Advisory Committee on Food Security Act and others argued that Universal Public Distribution System (UPDS) would not only ensure Food Security to all the individuals, but also arrest the problems such as bogus ration cards, cornering of ration benefits by the relatively better-off sections, diversion of ration items to the black market, control food price inflation, etc. Further, they also maintained this would also reduce the burden of storage of foodgrains and maintenance of godowns, as the production is in surplus and lying in the godowns. Their main argument is that the governance at the grass-roots level is very weak i.e., skelton staff, biased and corrupt officials and lack of coordination among the functionaries, subjected to political pressures – and incompetent to handle the issues involved in the implementation of the Act or PDS. Further, they cited the examples of the states, especially Tamil Nadu where the UPDS is in operation without any flaws in the implementation of food security programmes.

The supporters of TPDS argue that it is not UPDS vs. TPDS, what is important is the good governance, committed officials for the implementation of the Act/PDS. Even under UPDS, the issues in procurement, transport, storage and distribution of foodgrains are inevitable. On the other hand, the real beneficiaries will be neglected in getting the required commodities, especially when there is shortage in the availability of foodgrains in the country. The real issue is not UPDS/TPDS, but availability of adequate quantity of foodgrains. There are several instances where there is a shortage of foodgrains partly due to the failure of monsoon and low production and partly due to the hoading of foodgrains. In this situation it is very difficult to implement the UPDS, thus implementation of the TPDS is an alternative to protect the rights of the poor in the country (Venugopal, K.R., 2013).

Section-III

Innovative Practices

The National Food Security Act, 2013, states that the Central and State governments shall undertake reforms of the TPDS, including: (a) doorstep delivery of foodgrains; (b) application of information technology and computerisation; (c) leveraging Aadhar for unique identification; (d) full transparency of records; (e) preference to public bodies in licensing of FPSs and management of such shops by women or their collectives; (f) diversification of commodities offered by TPDS; (g) support to local public distribution models and grain banks; and (h) schemes such as cash transfer and food coupons in lieu of foodgrains. All these measures are the challenges to the authorities concerned of FS policies at the grass-roots level. These concerns demand for modernise the procedures and structures to cope with the ever changing issues The Government, in the recent past, has initiated measures to improve the organisational capacities to improve the delivery of services to the target group. Some of them are discussed below.

Weeding out Bogus Ration Cards and Issue New Cards through Mee-Seva Centres

In order to weed out bogus ration cards and reduce the subsidy burden the government is contemplating to issue new ration cards to the real target group/poor families through the Mee Seva Centres. The present government view is that the earlier governments have issued ration cards to the families indiscriminately without seriously examining the eligibility criteria and as a result, today the cards are more than the households in the State are. Of the total cards (263.18 lakhs) in the State, 30 lakhs ration cards are bogus cards (20 lakhs in Andhra Pradesh and 10 lakhs in newly formed Telangana State. (Eenadu dated 28-8-2014 and 03-9-2014). However, the official sources reveal that, out of the total cards, more than half of them are bogus cards and need to be weed out them. As a part of this the government announced that bogus card holders or dealers who possess bogus ration cards should voluntary surrender their cards to the authorities concerned, failing which action would to be taken against the guilty. In order to arrest these loopholes in granting of ration cards the government is contemplating that to make a door-to-door survey in rural and urban areas, collect the information, and issue a new ration card, preferably in the name of women. For this purpose, the government makes use of modern machine to take fingerprints of the members, as it is/was done while issuing Aadhar Card. This work has to be processed through Mee-Seva centre (Eenadu, July 12th, 2014).

The Samagra Kutumba Survey - 2014 in Telangana State

The Government of Telangana State has conducted the Samagra Kutumba Survey (Integrated Household Survey-IHS) on 19th August 2014 closing all the public and private institutions, shops and even public transport services. The IHS was carried out to identify the bogus beneficiaries' cards of welfare schemes since the government estimates are that while there are 84 lakh HHs in Telangana State, as many 91 lakh White ration cards have been issued. The success of the survey, according the Chief Minister of the State, is an ominous signal to State agencies elsewhere in the country who wish to identify particular groups. These agencies now know what needs to be done to force universal participation in surveys that may be designed to identify unwanted others (EPW Editorial, 30th August 2014).

However, the intension of the government policy is good, it is very difficult to implement, if not impossible task. This method is also not a foolproof method as the persons/officials, who are assigned the responsibility of collecting the household information, is subjected to pulls and pressures based on political party, caste, religion, region, bribe, etc., and manipulate the records. This is evident from the experience not only in food security policies but also in other anti-poverty programmes, where huge numbers of ineligible persons are/were identified as target group members and availing/availed the programmes intended for poor. As mentioned earlier, verification of land holding and income of the family is very complicated process as it depends on various factors such as conversion of land (wet to dry) ; value of land and income generation from it; division of land among the family members without proper recording; separation of households (though all the family members stay in the same under one roof with common cooking but furnish the information as separate families); not furnishing the secondary source of income of the family members, etc. In this context, what is important is the sincerity of the cardholders in furnishing factual information and commitment of the officials and other stakeholders to implement the PDS more effectively. The field reports indicate that IHS has further complicated issue as it reported more number of HHs than the existing HHs. In fact, all the opposition political parties questioned the reliability and legality of the survey and blamed the government for wasting of public money and resources.

Application of Global Positioning System (GPS)

The Civil Supplies Corporation, as mentioned earlier, procure the rice from the FCI and rice millers and transport it to the MLS point and from there to the FPSs for distribution to the targeted group. For this purpose, the government invites the tenders from the vehicle owners and allots the job to the bidders, who quoted lowest amount. At this stage, the vehicle owners form the 'syndicate' and influence the decision-making of the authorities concerned and enter into the contract with the corporation to transport the foodgrains. It is observed that during the process of transportation the transporters and dealers of FPS in collusion with the officials divert the vehicles along with the foodgrains to the traders/ rice mills or blackmarket and earn easy money. Further, the vehicle owners in collusion with the field functionaries make wrong entries in the concerned records by showing more number of trips for transportation of foodgrains from one place/ FPS to another place/point and claim more amount from the Civil Supplies Department/Corporation. Because of this, the government is incurring couple of cores. In fact, there are several instances, where higher-level officials/ vigilance authorities on the complaint from the public or their own investigated the matter and seized the vehicles/ mills/foodgrains. Nevertheless, the culprits come out of the problem with the help of political leaders or higher officials or making use the loopholes in the law in their favour.

In order to control the above problems the government is contemplating to introduce GPS and connect it to the main server, which would give information on the every movement of the vehicle, This would enable authorities to monitor the transporting of foodgrains in the State. Further, the Civil Supplies Department/Corporation is also contemplating to give a special colour to the transport vehicle and also rice gunny bag and FPS and printing the specific logo on these items. The department assigned the responsibility of stock verification to the third party i.e. the Tata Organisation/agency and it is expected to do this for every three months. During the informal discussion, the officials accepted that though the application of GPS is good to arrest the malpractices, in practice it is not being implemented as the vehicle owners are not showing interest to insert the machine related to the GPS into the vehicle. However, they also expressed doubt that the GPS would only enable the department to know about the movement of the vehicle, but not how much quantity is transported.

Ration Distribution by Acquiring Cardholders' Fingerprints

The civil supplies department/corporation with the technical support of the Centre for Good Governance, Hyderabad has evolved an e-PDS strategy i.e. acquiring cardholder's fingerprint before distribution of the ration items at the FPS. The government has made efforts to experiment this strategy in six districts viz., Chittur, Ananthapur, East Godavari, Hyderabad, Rangareddy and Karimnagar districts in August 2013. The fingerprints taken for issuing Aadhar cards are uploaded to the machine. The official's version is that the government has installed modern machine e-PDS in each FPS, which will record the details of the card holders i.e., finger prints, claiming of ration items, time, person, etc. While taking the ration items the card holders are expected to undergo finger print test and the machine would tally the prints and identify the guilty, if any. The estimated cost for each machine is Rs 40,000. As per the official's sources, in 20 FPSs of East Godavari district, where this method is experimented, 20 per cent of malpractices are arrested. Nevertheless, the progress of the method is standstill as the Supreme Court gave judgment that producing Aadhar card for claiming any benefit, from including ration items from the government is not a mandatory. Further, the reorganisation of AP, 2013 and change in the regime in two States also contributed for this state of affair.

Minimum Government and Maximum Governance Order of Merit Award

The Government of India is promoting the concept of Minimum Government and Maximum Governance in all the government activities. As a part of this, it has awarded the Order of Merit Certificate to the Civil Supplies Department, Government of Telengana state on 20th September, 2014 for application of e-PDS software to weed out the bogus ration cards in the state. The Civil Supplies Department seeded the Aadhar cards with e-PDS software, identified 10.13 lakh bogus cards within three months, and could save 16.54 Metric tonnes of rice (Eenadu, 21st September 2014).

Public Switched Telephone Network (PSTN)

The Civil Supplies Department has entered into an agreement with the BSNL for providing separate telephone line at the FPS and connects it to the modern machine called POS (Point of Service) and it is being implemented in 45 FPS in Hyderabad and East Godavari districts on pilot basis in 2013 to arrest in loopholes in the distribution of foodgrains. Through the mobile signals or network supplied by BSNL, the FPS dealer is expected to send SMS alert about the arrival of foodgrains to the ration cardholders. This service will be connected to the main server located at Hyderabad. Further, this machine would identify the persons or display the photo of the cardholders within a minute and help the FPS dealer whether the person is the real cardholder or not. The Civil Supplies department would pay Rs 350 per POS machine every month to the BSNL towards service charges. Though it is the first of its kind in the entire country, the machines are not working properly due to the frequent failure of BSNL network and power failure/ cut in the State. As a result, the authorities concerned are unable to send the SMS to the target group. This is also mainly due to optimum use of telephone network for other purposes and always one would get the automatic answer that network is busy or it is out of service. Sometimes each card holder has to wait about 10-20 minutes at the FPS for verification of their identity and to collect the ration items (Eenadu, December 19, 2012).

Foodgrains Supply in Pocket Bags to the Cardholders

The government is distributing about 3.50 lakh tonnes of rice every month to White cardholders—least 4 kgs. in addition, maximum 20 kgs to BPL card holders. The government at present is supplying foodgrains in gunny bags with a capacity of 50 kgs and dealer in turn distributes the foodgrain, particularly the rice to card holders as per their entitlements. According to the informal sources, this practice is more convenient for the dealer/transport agents to divert the foodgrains to the blackmarket and it is very difficult for the Vigilance and Enforcement Officials concerned to identify the stocks while transporting to the blackmarket or preserved in the godowns of rice traders or blackmarketeers as there is no difference between the packages of bags made by the Corporation and private traders. In order to arrest this problem the government, recently decided to supply the rice in small pockets – i.e., 4 kgs, 8 kgs, 12 kgs, 16 kgs, and 20 kgs to the cardholders as per their entitlements. Similarly, the other ration items – sugar, wheat/ wheat – aatta, dal, salt are also to be packed in small packets. All these items/packets are to be packed in a big woollen woven bag and supply it to the ration cardholders. This scheme is being implemented under 'Amma –Hastam Scheme' for couple of months in 2012 in the State and latter it is discontinued. This responsibility – packing the ration in small pockets and filling them in a bag – was assigned to the private contractors (Eenadu 18th November 2012). The government assumption was that the transporters or authorities incline to sell/divert the ration items packed in small pockets as they are easily identifiable in the blackmarket and subjected to punishment, if found guilty. Even the blackmarketers also do not show interest to purchase the ration items in small pockets. Though intention of the government is good, this system also gave scope for the contractors to indulge in malpractices, particularly packing less quantity of foodgrains in the pockets. These issues and other factors, particularly the weak governance in the State due to the agitation for separate State compelled the authorities to withdraw the Amma Hastam schemes and packing of foodgrains in the pockets.

Vigilance and Enforcement Department

The loopholes in the operation of PDS, largely, can be arrested if the Vigilance and Enforcement Department (VED) make regular monitoring over the activities of the functionaries. For instance, based on the complaints received from the public/civil society organisations, the VED has made surprise visits to the MLS points located in 20 districts of the State and verified with the stock availability and its records in 2012. As per the Director of VE department, in all Rs 145 crore worth of foodgrains are seized and booked 55 cases against 55 MLS/ration shop functionaries under Essential Commodities Act/ section for holding the foodgrains especially pulses illegally. In Kurnool district alone 1.78 lakh bags of pulses, which equals to Rs 50 crore as per the market value (Sakshi, 2013)? However, the basic problem with the Civil Supplies Department/ Corporation is lack of the adequate staff to monitor the programme. The Department/ Corporation is contemplating to recruit the officials for the purpose (Eenadu, December 10, 2012).

Summing up

The Central and State governments are responsible for implementation of food security policies in India. Nevertheless, the decision-making on the formulation and implementation of policies is centralised, as the Central government determines the extent of procurement and allocation of foodgrains and the norms for its distribution to different categories of target groups or social groups and institutions, including criterion for identification of target groups. The Central Government under Essential Commodities Act, 1955 and subsequent amendments, orders/circulars exercises control over production, supply and distribution, prices of the commodities and directs the State governments to adhere to the provisions of the Act. It also exercise control on inter-state trade and commerce, quality control and specifications of foodgrains, fixation of price of levy of sugar and other commodities, granting funds to the State governments for construction of godowns, etc.

The Central Government, recently, has communicated its decision to procure only 25 per cent of the requirement of the foodgrains for distribution to the target groups and institutions and the remaining 75 per cent has to be procured by the respective State governments. This amounts to shifting its financial burden to the State governments, which would cost heavily to the State exchequer. Though the State government has the autonomy to undertake food security policies or modify the norms, they do not have the adequate infrastructure- such as market yards, storage facilities, transportation facilities, power to maintain cold storages- and adequate number of skilled personnel to cope with the procurement and distribution of foodgrains. Added to these, the deficit budget of State government makes it to depend on the Central Government and adhere to its norms set for implementation of food security programmes. Nevertheless, the State governments are bringing pressure on the Central Government to procure 75 per cent of the requirement.

An examination of the organisational pattern for implementation of food security programmes shows that the Andhra Pradesh Government has a separate Ministry for Agriculture for production and Ministry for Consumer Affairs Food and Civil Supplies and autonomous Civil Supplies Corporation for procurement and distribution of essential commodities to the people. Though the Corporation has the autonomy in its day-to-day operations, for all practical purposes it is working as per the directions of the State government. The analysis reveals that, during the four decades of its existence, the Corporation has been undertaking several activities such as opening foodgrains purchasing centres; purchasing damaged paddy; opening retail counters; distribution of essential commodities such as rice, wheat, sugar, dal at subsidised rate/ free of cost, cement distribution (as and when the situation demand due to the shortage or hoarding by traders); opening LPG centres and retail countres, etc. It is also implementing the special schemes – Mana Biyyam- Manakosam and Amma Ahstam, as per the directions of the State government. Today, the Corporation is overburdened with multiple activities.

The effectiveness of the Civil Supplies Department/Corporation, to a large extent, depends on the cooperation of Central Government, State Warehousing Corporations, GCC, ITDA, district administration Units/wings – revenue, agriculture, AMCs, PRIs, SHGs, and the private agencies i.e, traders/ millers, transporters, NGOs, etc. An examination of functioning of the Civil Supplies Department/Corporation uncovers that it is encountering several problems in the implementation of food security policies. They are: illegitimate interference of politicians in the administrative matters; legal loopholes in the provisions of government orders/circulars; lack of coordination between government departments/agencies at all levels; cumbersome official procedures in procurement and distribution of foodgrains; lack of autonomy to the field functionaries; fear of allegation for overlooking the procedures in the interest of public; malpractices of traders/millers in levy of commodities; lack of clarity on the criterion of identification of target groups; lack of monitoring by the higher authorities on the implementation of activities at the grass-roots level; non-availability of instrument to read Irish-based ration cards at FPSs; lack of infrastructural facilities and skilled personnel for making end to end computerisation of the operational details of the programme; non-existence or non-functioning of food advisory committees; involvement of middleman in the implementation of activities; availing foodgrains by non-poor; circulation of bogus ration cards; recycling of ration rice/ wheat; diversion of foodgrains to the blackmarket; importing foodgrain-red gram dal from other States /countries; cardholders' reluctance to avail the ration items owing to its poor quality; dubious distinction being most corrupt sectors of State/ Country; etc; collectively affecting the functioning of the Civil Supplies department/ Corporation in the State.

The analysis also reveals that the State government has initiated several measures to arrest the malpractices in the implementation of the programmes. They include: application of global positioning system and monitoring the movement of foodgrains transportation vehicle; third party verification of quality of foodgrains; instalment of modern machine (point of Service), application of e-PDS and acquiring finger prints of the cardholder/person collecting the ration while distributing the foodgrains; linking the Aadhar card for identification of the beneficiary and distribution of foodgrains; weeding out bogus ration cards and issuing new cards through Mee-Seva centres; conducting Integrated kutumba survey for identification of the real beneficiaries; sending SMS to the cardholder about the arrival/availability of foodgrains at FPS; activating the vigilance and enforcement to file legal case against the culprits or hoarder or diversion of foodgrains to the blackmarket, etc. However, not all these initiatives could deter the illegal activities of traders/millers, corrupt bureaucrats, FPSs dealers and politicians. Above all, lack of political will to ensure food security to poor is the major concern of the governance. Every political party/ government viewed the PDS as an instrument to get 'vote security' system and remain in power.

References

Andhra Pradesh G.O. vide G.O. Ms. No. 7 dated 01.02.2006.

Bala ramulu, Ch (2000): *'Technology and Rural Development'*, Rawat Publications, *Jaipur.*

————(1999): *'International Organisations and Rural Employment Programs in India: Emerging Trends'*, Om Publishers Faridabad, New Delhi.

————(1993): *'Development Strategies in India: Emerging Trends'*, *(Co-Editor)* Khama Publishers, *New Delhi.*

———— (1991): *Public Policies: An Evaluation of Integrated Rural Development Programme*, Ajanta Publications, New Delhi.

————(1984): Administration on Anti-Poverty Programme (A study of SFDA), *Kakatiya School of Public Administration*, Warangal.

Mannuals/Circulars/GOs: Andhra Pradesh State Civil Supplies Corporation, Ltd, website: www.apscsc.gov.in.

(2013): 'Towards Holistic Panchayat Raj, 20th Anniversary Report of the Expert Committee on Leveraging Panchayats for Efficient Delivery of Public Goods and Services', Vol. 1. Policy Issues, National Panchayt Raj Day, April 24, Government of India.

Chapter–IV

Foodgrain Production, Procurement and Distribution System in Andhra Pradesh

The food security is a multi-dimensional concept consisting of agricultural production, procurement and distribution. Any discussion on food security policies should primarily focus on these aspects. In India, agriculture remains a very crucial sector for ensuring food security and inclusive and sustainable growth of Indian economy, as it employs 52.9 per cent of the total workforce (NSSO, 2011) and 46 per cent of the total geographical area. However, the growth rate in this sector, during the last six and a half decades, is less than four per cent. The decadal growth rates from 1950-51 to 2004-10 indicates that there are variations and it is low during the post-economic reforms period. The growth rate is negated due to high food inflation. Further, there are significant spatial and temporal differences in the performance of agriculture in different states. The States, which were doing very well before the reforms, are showing signs of stagnation or deceleration in the post-reform period, especially Haryana, Punjab, Tamil Nadu and Andhra Pradesh. The growth rate is quite low [1.90] during first phase of post period i.e., 1990-91 to 1999-2000 (Mahendra Dev, S and Vijay Laxmi Pandey, 2013). The share of agriculture and allied sectors in Gross Domestic Product (GDP) declined steadily from 38.8 per cent in 1980-81 to 14.2 per cent in 2010-11 (Ministry of Finance, Government of India, 2012).

However, gross production of foodgrains increased from 50.83 million tonnes in 1950-51 to 252 million tonnes in 2011-12, indicating five-fold increase, during the six decades of post-Independence period. During the Eleventh Plan Period, foodgrains production in the country recorded an increasing trend, except in 2009-10 when total foodgrains production declined in 218.1 million tonnes due to severe drought experienced in various parts of the country. However, during 2011-12, total foodgrains production reached an all-time high of 259.32 million tonnes and it is 250 million tonnes in 2012-13. The increase in output can mostly be attributed to the increase in yield per hectare rather than the expansion of area, though there has been a shift in area from foodgrains to non-foodgrain crops. The government instead of addressing the issue by initiating measures such as allocation of more budget to the agricultural sector and for enhancement of production, promote research, it is importing the foodgrains, especially pulses (red-gram dal and green-gram dal) from other countries. India imported about 62.18 lakh tonnes of foodgrains by spending Rs 24998 crore, during the 2012-13. Of this imports 40.19 lakh tonnes are pulses and government spent Rs 13,916 crore for the purpose. The estimates indicate that India need to produce/procure 330 million tonnes of foodgrains by 2020 to meet the required per capita availability to the people. Per capita net availability of foodgrains has been fluctuating around 440 grams per day, despite a huge build-up of stocks. Another concern is that the population growth rate is more than foodgrain production in the country.

The major challenges in enhancing the foodgrain production are climate change, change in the food habits/consumption of people, reduction in public investment in agricultural sector, conversion of agricultural land into non-agricultural sector or for production of non-foodgrain items, unfavourable weather conditions, scanty and erratic rainfall, MNCs control over seed production and least priority to the agricultural research, etc. Another major challenge is how to cope with foodgrain price inflation, which is increasing day by day. Unless, the Government of India and State Governments address these issues, it is difficult for implementation of NFS Act 2013 (Sreenivas, 2013). Against this background, in this chapter, an attempt is made to analyse the foodgrains production, procurement and distribution in

Andhra Pradesh, which are core concerns of the food security. The focus is more on the paddy, as the rice is major staple food of the people. The rice distribution constitute major component of the ration items under PDS in the State. This would give us deeper understanding on the strengths and weakness of the food security in the State.

Section -I

Profile of Andhra Pradesh

The Andhra Pradesh population, according to 2011 census, is 84.6 million i.e., 6.99 per cent of India's total population i.e. 1210 million. The geographical area of the State is 275.04 lakh hectares and accounts for 8.4 per cent of India's total geographical area and ranking fourth in terms of geographical area and fifth in terms of population among the Indian States. The density of population in the State is 308 per sq.km, which is lower than the density at all-India level i.e. 382 persons per sq.kms. The Scheduled Castes and Scheduled Tribes account for 16.2 per cent and 6.6 per cent of the total population, respectively, in the State. About one-third of the State population is living in urban areas and the rest is in the rural areas of the State. Rural Andhra Pradesh is predominantly agricultural with two-thirds of its work force engaged directly in agriculture sector. The poverty is reduced considerably from 30.1 per cent in 2004 to 9.27 per cent 2011. However, there are variations among the districts, in this regard. It is more in the districts of Rayalaseema and Andhra region, compared to Telangana region. The per capita income of the AP State is increasing year after year ranging Rs 15,507 in 1999-2000 to Rs 52814 in 2009-10 nearly three-fold increase in a span of nine years. There are disparities among the regions and districts. These trends reveals that basis for allocation of foodgrains to the districts should be on the per capita income and the districts which has less per capita income need to be given priority over the others in the State.

The total geographical area of the State is 275.04 lakh hectares. Out of this, 40.58 per cent is under net area sown (111.60 lakh hectares), 22.65 per cent under forest (62.30 lakh hectares), 8.26 per cent under current fallow lands (22.73 lakh hectares), 10.19 per cent under Land put non-agricultural uses (28.03 lakh hectares), 7.36 per cent under barren and uncultivated land (20.24 lakh hectares) and remaining

10.96 per cent (30.14 lakh hectares) is under other fallow land, cultivable waste, lands like permanent pastures and other grazing lands. The number of holdings has increased from 1.20 crore in 2005-06 to 1.32 crore in 2010-11. The total number of operational holdings in the State is found to be 131.75 lakhs covering an area of 142.93 lakh hectares, as against 120.45 lakh holdings. The average size of land holdings in the State was 1.20 hectares in 2005-06 and declined by 10 per cent to 1.08 hectares in 2010-11. The landholding size is, thus, unviable for household to get adequate foodgrains especially in the backward regions of the State. Rice, maize and cotton are the important crops, which occupy more than 60 per cent of total gross cropped area in the State. With respect to crop sector, there is a shift in the cropping pattern from food to non-food crops, particularly cotton, in the State. The spread of cotton in the areas with light textured soils very often result in unexpected crop failures and sometimes replacement of it with conventional crops such as jowar and castor (Government of AP, Department of Agriculture, and Action Plan 2013-14).

Agriculture and Allied Activities

Expansion of farm incomes continues to be an effective weapon for reducing poverty as more than half of the State's population remains depend on some form of farm activity for livelihoods. Rapid and sustainable growth in agriculture has been identified not only as a key driver for economic development but also for achieving self-sufficiency and ensuring food security to the people. Andhra Pradesh over the decades has witnessed gradual transformation of the agricultural sector. The nature of the transformation itself has undergone change overtime. During 1980s, there was a shift in agriculture from traditional cereal-based system towards commercial commodities such as oilseeds, cotton and sugarcane. By 1990s, even though the crop sector witnessed high volatility due to consecutive droughts and decelerating crop yields, the transformation continued towards high-value commodities such as fruits, vegetables, milk, meat, poultry and fish. In fact, high-value commodities performed impressively and rescued the agriculture sector largely (Government of AP, Department of Agriculture, and Action Plan, 2013-14).

Priority was accorded to the agricultural sector during 11th five-year plan period with the objective of shifting the excess labour force from the sector to other non-farm rural sectors such as rural industry through skill development to improve productivity. Ensuring food security and provision of gainful employment continues to be the essential premise of socio-economic development and employment guarantee schemes MGNREGS and other rural livelihoods programmes.

Improving farm incomes and ensuring sustainable growth in agriculture and allied sectors are of top priority for the State. In agriculture, the priority accorded to irrigation on one hand and the various farmer friendly initiatives put in place on the other have helped the State to achieve set growth targets during the 11th Plan. The State enjoys pre-eminence in crop production. With renewed focus on micro irrigation, System of Rice Intensification (SRI) cultivation, micronutrient application, development of dry land agriculture, farm mechanisation, increasing storage capacity and other agricultural related strategies. The State is set to scale new heights in agriculture during the 12th Five Year Plan.

Agriculture Extension Programmes Mission and Strategies

One of the major concerns of the State is to improve farm income both in absolute terms and as percentage of GSDP. The Department of Agriculture is, therefore, working with a mission of attaining sustainable agricultural production with minimum cultivation cost, which eventually will enhance return on investment to the farmer. The following strategies are being adopted for making the mission a reality.

- Re-engineering extension approach for effective extension reach;
- Empowering farmers with advanced agricultural practices;
- Capacity enhancement of departmental staff for efficient use of extension technology;
- Ensuring timely inputs and quality control;
- Soil test based fertilizer recommendation;
- Promotion of self reliance in seed production among farmers;
- Promotion of Integrated Crop Management through Integrated Nutrient Management (INM), Integrated Pest Management (IPM), efficient water management, etc.;

- Promotion of organic farming to meet the demands of World Market;
- Correcting micronutrient zinc deficiency;
- Reclamation of problematic soils to restore productivity;
- Natural Resource Management through watershed approach for development of agricultural land and environmental stability;
- Calamity management in the event of drought, floods, hailstorms etc.;
- Crop diversification programme;
- Promoting cultivation of low risk and low cost intensive crops;
- Farm mechanisation for item and cost effective farming practices;
- Promoting Farmers Organisation (Rythu Mitra Groups) for technical and monetary benefits in agriculture and allied activities;
- Facilitate agriculture Credit to farmers Women Empowerment and gender balance;
- Provide day-to-day information to farmer on crop production, input supply, and marketing through internet (AGRISNET).

The government has been organising several extension activities to increase productivity and reduce cost of cultivation, and improve quality and latest technology intervention in agriculture and allied activities. It also organised Rythu Chaitanya Yatras, Rythu Bata Programme, Monthly Workshops to educate farmers particularly small and marginal farmers at grassroot level. The focus of these Yatras was/ is on technology transfer, addressing the technology gaps identified in the village, creating awareness about government programmes for welfare of farmers ensuring timely credit delivery, effective input planning for kharif, agriculture mechanisation, crop diversification, water management, etc. In addition to these activities the Department also planned for Staff Trainings, Training Programmes to Farmers, Padi Pantalu Soil Testing, Online Soil Health Card Application; SEEDNET Application ; Nipunulanu Adigi Telusukondi ; SMS Alerts Application; Delivery of AGRISNET Services through Rajiv Citizen

Service Centres; Mee Seva Services; Kisan Call Centre; Farm Mechanisation Scheme; Crop Insurance; National Agricultural Insurance Scheme; Village as Insurance Unit Scheme; Agricultural Credit; Credit to New Non-loaned Farmers; The Andhra Pradesh Land Licensed Cultivators Act, 2011 (to provide loan and other benefits eligibility cards to land licensed cultivators); Pavala Vaddi Scheme on Crop Loans; Rythu Sri (Vaddileni Panta Runalu); Interest Waiver Scheme; etc, in the State. It also disseminated/ing the information through Agricultural Resources Information Systems Network – AGRISNET and General Information available in Portal, which contains information and recommendations on practices of 18 important crops grown, schemes, subsidies of department and other important information on agriculture.

Adarsha Rythu System

AP Government has introduced the Adarsha Rythu system in the year 2007-08. The main objective behind the identification of Adarsha Rythus is to create a nodal functionary between the farmers and extension staff of agriculture and other line departments to help bridge the gap between the scientific expertise and field level do-how. 49,161 Adarsha Rythus were deployed as against the target of 50,000 to strengthen extension services in the State. Adarsha Rythus assist extension staff in implementation of schemes like Polam Badi, Seed Village Programme, Organic farming, Rashtriya Krishi Vikasa Yojana, National Food Security Mission and the programmes mentioned above, etc. They are involved in day-to-day actions with regard to schemes and technology subsidized input availability and procedures to avail the same, the broad regulatory mechanism for inputs and steps to be taken in case of failure of a particular input. Adarsha Rythus are actively involved in mobilising farmers in special campaigns like Rythu Chaitanya Yatra, Rythu Sadassu, Prajapatham and Saguku Samayattam. However, after the division of the State both the State governments have abolished the Adarsha Rythu system in September 2014.

Extension Reforms

Agriculture Technology Management Agency: Government of India has introduced the "Support to State Extension Programmes for Extension – Reforms" (ATMA) Scheme from 1st June 2005 in a phased manner which is currently operational in 591 Districts of 29 States and 2 UTs. As a part of this scheme, the entire state of Andhra Pradesh except Urban district of Hyderabad is covered under ATMA with Central and State financial sharing being 90:10. The objectives of the Programme are:

- To develop an efficient, effective, demand driven, research integrated and financially sustainable public extension system.
- To revitalize Agricultural technology Generation Assessment refinement and Dissemination Systems.
- Reforming Public Sector Extension, Promoting private sector to effectively complement, supplement and wherever possible substitute public extension.
- Mainstreaming Gender concerns in Extension.
- Capacity Building/Skill up-gradation of farmers and extension functionaries.
- Enhance the quality and type of Technologies being disseminated by the Extension System.
- Strengthen Research-Extension Farmer (R.E.F.) Linkages.

Strategic Research and Extension Plan

One of the first tasks of ATMA is facilitation of the preparation of Strategic Research and Extension Plan (SREP) of the district. The SREP is prepared through participatory methodologies such as Participatory Rural Appraisal (PRA) involving all stakeholders and farmers. It also prioritizes research – extension strategies within the district. It becomes the basis for development of work plans at blocks/district level. All the 22 ATMA districts have developed their respective Strategic Research and Extension Plans. As the validity of SREPs is five years, the State has initiated revisiting of the SREPs of ATMA district.

Government of India Initiatives Rashtriya Krishi Vikasa Yojana

RKVY one of the flagship programmes of Government of India with 100 per cent central aid, is being implemented with an objective to achieve annual growth rate in excess of four per cent in agriculture sector during the XI Plan.

National Food Security Mission for Rice and Pulses

The National Food Security Mission for Rice is under implementation in the State since Rabi-2007-08 in 11 districts: Srikakulam, Vizianagaram, Visakhapatnam, Krishna, Guntur, Nellore, Medak, Mahabubnagar, Nalgonda, Khammam and Adilabad. While National Food Security Mission-Pulses is under implementation in 22 Districts: Srikakulam, Vizianagaram, Visakhapatnam, East Godavari, West Godavari, Krishna, Guntur, Prakasam, Nellore, Kurnool, Anantapur, Kadapa, Chittoor, Ranga Reddy, Nizamabad, Medak, Mahabubnagar, Nalgonda, Warangal, Khammam, Karimnagar, Adilabad. The objectives are increasing production of rice and pulses through area expansion and productivity enhancement in a sustainable manner in the identified districts; restoring soil fertility and productivity at the individual farm level; creation of employment opportunities, Enhancing farm level economy i.e., farm profits to restore confidence in farmers in the State.

Section-II

Area under Foodgrains in the State

All the above measures are undertaken to promote the agricultural production and its availability to the people, particularly to the target groups in the State. Here an attempt is made to present the area of production and output, during the past five decades in the State. An examination of Area under Foodgrains in Andhra Pradesh indicates that there is declined trend from an average of over eight million hectares, during the 1960's, to an average over seven million hectares in the decade (2001-2010). Area of foodgrains is also declined during all the decades except during 1961-70 when it exhibited a decadal growth of 3.4 per cent. Growth continued to decelerate after that period, with the most declines being observed during the decade of 1991-2010, followed by the decade of 1981-1991. This is mostly due to the economic reforms and giving priority to information technology and service sector and diversion of agricultural land for non-agricultural purposes in the State (see Table 4.1).

With regard to regional-wise analysis of area in foodgrains, the table shows that the State level trend is more or less similar across all the three regions in Andhra Pradesh. However, the deceleration in area is more observed in the Rayalaseema region, followed by Telangana. Area under foodgrains in the Rayalaseema region exhibited a continual decline right from the beginning observing a double-digit decline all through the decades. However, in Rayalaseema, during the last decade, there is considerable improvement in the area, which grew by 17.8 per cent. While in Telangana region the decline is observed from 1981 onwards and it continued even today. The rate of decline in area under foodgrains in Andhra region in all the decades is very less compared to other two regions. This indicates that the regional imbalances in terms of area under foodgrain are continued for the past four decades in the State (see Table 4.1).

Table 4.1: Area of Foodgrains, during the past five decades, in Andhra Pradesh

Period	*Andhra Region*		*Rayalaseema*		*Telangana*		*State*	
	Actual	*Per cent change*	*Actual*	*Per cent change*	*Actual*	*Per cent change*	*Actual*	*Per cent change*
Prior to 1960	3281358	N.A	2160432	N.A	3396943	N.A	8838733	N.A
1961-1970	3507045	6.88	1942188	-10.10	3697831	8.86	9147064	3.5
1971-1980	3427389	-2.27	1722991	-11.29	3901198	5.50	9051577	-1.0
1981-1990	3395069	-0.94	1160694	-32.63	3664444	-6.07	8220207	-9.2
1991-2000	3392928	-0.06	742877	-36.00	2973430	-18.86	7109234	-13.5
2001-2010	3201963	-5.63	875774	17.89	2960838	-0.42	7038575	-1.0

Source: Season and Crop reports, Govt of Andhra Pradesh.

The district-wise analysis discloses that area under foodgrain crops is declining in many districts; during the past, one and a half decades especially form 2001-2010 onwards. It is more in the Chittuor (-31.00 per cent), Visakhapatnam (-25.00 per cent), Adilabad (-22.98 per cent), Rangareddy (21.16), Vizianagaram (-13.67 per cent), Khammam (-13.65 per cent), and Krishna (-10.57 per cent) districts in the State. The Anantapur district, except 2011-2010 decade, in all the decades experienced the decline in the area under foodgrain crops. However, the area under foodgrain crops is more in Cuddapah (38.58 per cent), Kurnool (30.78 per cent), Mahabubnagar (14.39 per cent), Prakasam (13.48 per cent), Warangal (13.19 per cent) districts. These trends indicate that there are wide variations in the area of foodgrains and this would affect the foodgrain availability in the districts, which are experiencing declining trend in the State (see Table 4.2).

Table: 4. 2: Area of foodgrain crops (district-wise) in Andhra Pradesh 1955-2010 (hectares)

District	Prior to 1960		1961-1970		1971-1980		1981-1990		1991-2000		2001-2010	
	Actual	Per cent	Actual	Per cent	Actual	Per cent	Actual	Per cent	Actual	Per cent	Actual	Per cent
Srikakulam	372403	N.A	409297	9.91	361179	-11.76	272717	-24.49	304545	11.67	281617	-7.53
Vijayanagaram	0	N.A	0	N.A	41064	N.A	191934	367.4	222663	16.01	192221	-13.67
Vishakhapatnam	294534	N.A	363958	23.57	319993	-12.08	240605	-24.81	241969	0.57	180499	-25.40
East Godavari	402718	N.A	412999	2.55	420076	1.71	476661	13.47	538263	12.92	493159	-8.38
West Godavari	401050	N.A	417934	4.21	425164	1.73	484006	13.84	474997	-1.86	464976	-2.11
Krishna	502085	N.A	536186	6.79	557556	3.99	581315	4.26	543802	-6.45	486322	-10.57
Guntur	703123	N.A	701811	-0.19	541249	-22.88	492834	-8.94	523992	6.32	494302	-5.67
Prakasam	0	N.A	95029	N.A	454474	378.25	384553	-15.39	299721	-22.06	340114	13.48
Nellore	605446	N.A	569831	-5.88	306634	-46.19	270445	-11.80	242978	-10.16	268754	10.61
Andhra Region	3281358	N.A	3507045	6.88	3427389	-2.27	3395069	-0.94	3392928	-0.06	3201963	-5.63
YSR Kadapa	323295	N.A	292685	-9.47	270878	-7.45	180416	-33.40	107012	-40.69	148301	38.58
Chittor	311073	N.A	290922	-6.48	263233	-9.52	185726	-29.44	134799	-27.42	93005	-31.00
Kurnool	824736	N.A	734237	-10.97	643390	-12.37	495625	-22.97	337990	-31.81	442015	30.78
Ananthapur	701328	N.A	624344	-10.98	545490	-12.63	298927	-45.20	163076	-45.45	192453	18.01
Rayalaseema	2160432	N.A	1942188	-10.10	1722991	-11.29	1160694	-32.63	742877	-36.00	875774	17.89
Nizamabad	262729	N.A	276435	5.22	291752	5.54	290402	-0.46	257027	-11.49	279808	8.86
Karimnagar	391450	N.A	423161	8.10	459289	8.54	428106	-6.79	362828	-15.25	415025	14.39
Adilabad	373301	N.A	401670	7.60	440444	9.65	412073	-6.44	345687	-16.11	266259	-22.98
Medak	396452	N.A	407384	2.76	412564	1.27	403909	-2.10	376803	-6.71	399615	6.05
Warangal	392269	N.A	467184	19.10	465690	-0.32	399871	-14.13	284401	-28.88	321922	13.19
Khammam	280950	N.A	363542	29.40	378037	3.99	366749	-2.99	297986	-18.75	257302	-13.65
Rangareddy	0	N.A	0	N.A	79718	N.A	247873	210.94	216958	-12.47	171043	-21.16
Mahabubnagar	721750	N.A	744168	3.11	763624	2.61	605894	-20.66	441875	-27.07	473886	7.24
Nalgonda	578042	N.A	614286	6.27	610081	-0.68	509567	-16.48	389865	-23.49	375978	-3.56
Telangana	3396943	N.A	3697831	8.86	3901198	5.50	3664444	-6.07	2973430	-18.86	2960838	-0.42

Source: Season and Crop reports, Govt of Andhra Pradesh.

Output of Foodgrains in the State

Output of foodgrains recorded an uptick during all past five decades in Andhra Pradesh as it grew from an average of 5.8 million tonnes recorded during the decade prior to 1960 to over 16.1 million tonnes in the decade of 2001-2010. The growth rate has been positive and around 20.0 per cent during all the times. It is pertinent to note that though there is decline in the area under foodgrain, the output of foodgrains has increased considerably. This is mostly due to the adoption of modern technology in the agriculture sector (see Table 4.3).

However, when it comes to regional perspective, while Andhra and Telangana regions recorded growth during all the periods, Rayalaseema continued to exhibit deceleration in foodgrain output as it recorded negative growth in most of the periods, except 1971-80 (22.3 per cent) and 2001-2010 (32.8 per cent). The negative output in Rayalaseema region is in line with the trend as observed from the earlier table, which depicts a continued decline in area under foodgrains over period. During the last decade (2001-2010), the output is more in the Rayalaseema and Telangana compared to the Andhra region (see Table 4.3).

The average agricultural production, during 1955-56 to 2008-09, is 104.07 lakh tonnes in the State. However, the data on the foodgrain production indicates that there is four-fold increase in the Production i.e. from 55.33 lakh tonnes in 1955-56 to 204.21 lakh tonnes in 2008-09 in the State. The increase is more than the State average is mostly from 1988-89 onwards. In comparison to all-India level, its share is about seven. Six per cent of the total production in the country. There are variations, in this regard, the highest is 9.1 per cent and the lowest is 6.1 per cent (see Table 4.4).

Though there is variation in the information furnished by the Seasonal and Crop Reports, and Ministry of Agriculture, Government of Andhra Pradesh they do indicate the pattern of agricultural production in the State. What is important is that the State reflects the conditions prevailing in India at the macro level, with large stocks of surplus foodgrain and vast masses of population living under below poverty line. In Andhra Pradesh, the production of foodgrains and its availability is not uniform. Certain districts like West Godavari, East Godavari, Krishna, Guntur, Karimnagar, Warangal, and Nizamabad have surplus paddy/rice, while other drought prone districts like Chittur, Cudapha, Anantapur, Adilabad, and Nalgonda have deficit in paddy production. The State also has a large tribal population and drought prone areas within the districts. These trends justify the food security policy of TPDS in the state.

Table 4.3: Output of Foodgrains, during the past five decades, in Andhra Pradesh

(Tonnes)

	Andhra		*Rayalaseema*		*Telangana*		*State*	
	Actual	*Per cent*	*Actual*	*Per cent*	*Actual*	*Per cent*	*Actual*	*Per cent*
Prior to 1960	3009338	N.A	1000030	N.A	1792801	N.A	5802169	N.A
1961-1970	3332123	10.7	992612	-0.7	2385643	33.1	6710378	15.65
1971-1980	4120462	23.7	1214156	22.3	3146078	31.9	8480696	26.38
1981-1990	5885739	42.8	1138645	-6.2	3946769	25.5	10971153	29.37
1991-2000	6984622	18.7	1077020	-5.4	4684004	18.7	12745646	16.17
2001-2010	8286767	18.6	1430625	32.8	6416652	37.0	16134044	26.58

Source: Season and Crop reports, Govt of Andhra Pradesh.

Pl note: The output of food grains does not include here small Millets and Wheat. We do not have access to that data. However, contribution of these as two crops is very minute share in total output in the state.

Per capita Availability of Foodgrains

An examination of the per capita availability of foodgrains to the population in different decades (from 1961 to 2011, except 2011 decade) reveals that it is less than 200 kgs per year in the State. This works out to be less than 20 kgs per month per individual in the state (average is 16.6 kgs), indicating that there is shortage of foodgrains in the State. It is lowest during the decades of 1971 and 1991 (see Table 4.5).

Table 4.4: Output of Foodgrains (district-wise) in Andhra Pradesh

	Prior to 1960		*1961-70*		*1971-80*		*1981-90*		*1991-200*		*2001-2010*	
District	*Actual*	*Per cent*	*Actual*	*Per cent*	*Actual*	*Per cent*	*Actual*	*Per cent*	*Actual*	*Per cent*	*Actual*	*Per cent*
Srikakulam	321639	N.A	342138	6.4	360417	5.3	384895	6.8	446280	15.9	455877	2.2
Vijayanagaram	N.A	N.A	N.A	N.A	227594	N.A	244529	7.4	314329	28.5	326883	4.0
Vishakhapatnam	227872	N.A	246667	8.2	255389	3.5	217576	-14.8	244821	12.5	218885	-10.6
East Godavari	468516	N.A	516965	10.3	664649	28.6	956046	43.8	1142403	19.5	1421562	24.4
West Godavari	478284	N.A	614866	28.6	828499	34.7	1157539	39.7	1381985	19.4	1694501	22.6
Krishna	514010	N.A	580084	12.9	687774	18.6	1065720	55.0	1250618	17.3	1245620	-0.4
Guntur	408042	N.A	472247	15.7	635763	34.6	941335	48.1	1091355	15.9	1445646	32.5
Prakasam	222850	N.A	248280	11.4	299821	20.8	415019	38.4	512819	23.6	654672	27.7
Nellore	368126	N.A	310876	-15.6	365390	17.5	503081	37.7	600013	19.3	823121	37.2
Andhra region	3009338	N.A	3332123	10.7	4120462	23.7	5885739	42.8	6984622	18.7	8286767	18.6
Kadapa	174136	N.A	196130	12.6	232176	18.4	237870	2.5	205343	-13.7	217837	6.1
Chittor	299865	N.A	290737	-3.0	363469	25.0	274277	-24.5	243903	-11.1	185449	-24.0
Anantapur	268093	N.A	243002	-9.4	288912	18.9	237197	-17.9	211347	-10.9	266634	26.2
Kurnool	257936	N.A	262742	1.9	329600	25.4	389301	18.1	416427	7.0	760705	82.7
Rayalaseema	1000030		992612	-0.7	1214156	22.3	1138645	-6.2	1077020	-5.4	1430625	32.8
Nizamabad	193628	N.A	291584	50.6	367861	26.2	478743	30.1	541509	13.1	759329	40.2
Karimnagar	185538	N.A	293462	58.2	486562	65.8	728960	49.8	928360	27.4	1352040	45.6
Adilabad	198123	N.A	219961	11.0	250759	14.0	240859	-3.9	331056	37.4	383127	15.7
Medak	206991	N.A	267608	29.3	304029	13.6	380550	25.2	467952	23.0	656551	40.3
Warangal	196079	N.A	301575	53.8	396658	31.5	443015	11.7	524457	18.4	828777	58.0
Khammam	167789	N.A	216358	28.9	279895	29.4	394736	41.0	503109	27.5	630212	25.3
Ranga Reddy	123673	N.A	144371	16.7	183049	26.8	213305	16.5	223171	4.6	254231	13.9
Mehaboobnagar	261406	N.A	331392	26.8	390108	17.7	414668	6.3	432260	4.2	699855	61.9
Nalgonda	259574	N.A	319330	23.0	487157	52.6	651934	33.8	732131	12.3	852530	16.4
Telangana	1792801	N.A	2385643	33.1	3146078	31.9	3946769	25.5	4684004	18.7	6416652	37.0

Source: Season and Crop reports, Govt of Andhra Pradesh.

Table 4.5: The Population, Production, and per capita availability of foodgrains in Andhra Pradesh (decade-wise)

Year/ Decade	*Population (In lakhs)*	*Foodgrains (in lakh tonnes)*	*Per capita Availability of Foodgrains per year (in kgs)*	*Per capita Availability of Foodgrains per month (in kgs)*
1961	359.83	74.87	208	17.3
1971	435.04	72.90	167	13.9
1981	535.50	114.15	213	17.7
1991	665.08	117.15	176	14.6
2001	762.10	148.36	194	16.1
2011	845.81	203.14	240	20.0
Average			199.7	16.6

Source: Annual Report, Ministry of Agriculture, Government of AP and compilation from Season and Crop reports, Govt of Andhra Pradesh.

Section-III

The Procurement of Paddy/ Rice under Levy System in Andhra Pradesh

The players in the activity of procurement of paddy and rice are: FCI for setting targets to the state governments; state government functionaries and political executives who determine the levy policy-price and target; officials involved in implementation of levy policy; rice millers/traders who convert paddy into rice and obligated to levy of rice; the Self-help Groups or Agricultural Marketing Committees or Primary Agricultural Societies who purchase the paddy from the farmers; State Warehousing Corporations and Private agencies for constructing godowns for storing the rice; officials involved in storage and conservation of the procured rice; transport companies for transporting the paddy from the farmers/SHGs to the rice mills and transporting the rice from rice mills to the MLS points and FPSs; financial institutions for providing credit to the government for procuring the rice. Among these, the rice millers/traders and local officials, who are involved in procurement of rice, play crucial role in the implementation of the procurement policy.

Every year in August–September, the Government of India in consultation with the State governments decides the quantity of paddy that should procure in each State. The FCI is the nodal agency for procurement, distribution, and storage of foodgrains. Percentage of levy Rice to be delivered varies from State to State. However, the State governments have the autonomy to decide the mode of procurement i.e. imposing levy on paddy growers/farmers or rice mill point procurement/rice millers and traders. The Government of Andhra Pradesh has been procuring the paddy by adopting different strategies-through FCI; State Agencies; and regulated market yards through millers/traders. The procurement of paddy and rice, as per the guidelines of the State Government, take place based on the following conditions:

- Each miller/trader shall purchase paddy from farmers only at MSP and above price;
- Each miller/trader shall obtain the signature of the farmer in token of the amount from the miller/trader on the paddy voucher and that the said voucher should be countersigned by Sarpanch/ Panchhat Secretary/ Village Development Officer/ Ward member of Gram Panchayat;
- For delivery of rice as levy to FCI, each miller/trader shall produce the paddy purchase receipts obtained from the farmers as evidence that they have purchased paddy at MSP for issue of eligibility certificate permitting miller/trader to deliver rice as levy to FCI;
- The field staff has to verify 10 per cent of the paddy purchase receipts produced by the miller/trader, at random;
- The miller/trader who purchase Fair Average Quality (FAQ) paddy below the MSP, such miller/trader are not entitled to obtain eligibility certificates and liable for punishment under mill levy and other penal actions;
- As per the Andhra Pradesh government orders-Rice Procurement (levy) Order, 1984 each miller/trader is required to deliver three-fourths (the mill levy per cent is increased from 50 per cent to 75 per cent from 2004-2005 onwards) of the rice out of paddy purchased and milled by him/her as levy to the FCI. Thereafter the government gives permission/ release certificates to the latter for selling the remaining 25 per cent of rice within or outside the State at market rate.

The Civil Supplies Department fixes procurement of rice target for each district. The District administration in turn fixes the target for each mandal, per mill and per trader. The Tahasildar is responsible to send the note/order indicating the target to each mill/traders in the beginning of the levy season i.e. October/November. An analysis of the data on the procurement of rice, during 1996-97 to 2011-12, reveals that on an average the state government is procuring about 63,98,798 Metric tonnes of rice through different sources for distribution to the target group members and also other welfare programmes. However, there are variations in different years ranging from 2622678 Mts (in 2002-03) to 17363626 Mts (in 2011-12). The procurement of rice is more from 2002-03 onwards. It is important to note that there is also unprecedented increase in the number of ration cards i.e. 1981100 in 2005-06 to 2516900 in 2011-12 (see Table 4.6). The then government and the political leaders with a view to gain support of the people for the party encouraged the villagers to take the ration cards, especially White cards. There were informal instructions from the political executive to the officials to be liberal in granting the ration cards. This has given the opportunity to the non-poor to take White Cards and issue of bogus ration cards by the local authorities to the FPS dealers in the State, some of the officials maintained.

Procurement of Rice from 1996-97 to 2011-12 in AP

The analysis also reveals that the average procurement of rice per card /HH per year and per month is 254 kgs and 21 kgs, respectively. This works out to be five kgs of rice per person in the HH (assuming that the average size of the family is four) and it is hardly sufficient to meet the 10 days requirement of the family. The remaining days (20), the individual/family has to depend on the open market, where the price of the rice is beyond the reach of common person (Table 4.6).

Table 4.6: Procurement of Rice from 1996-97 to 2011-12 in AP (in Metric Tonnes)

S.No	*Year*	*Raw rice*	*Boiled rice*	*CMR(customi-zed rice)*	*Total rice*
1.	1996-97	2922641	1580945	0	4503586
2.	1997-98	2432166	1422365	0	3854531
3.	1998-99	949181	2089245	0	3038426
4.	1999-2000	3197381	2324515	0	5521896
5.	2000-01	4076742	3045846		7122588
6.	2001-02	4640714	1886157	139227	6666098

(Contd...)

7.	2002-03	1956402	659524	6752	2622678
8.	2003-04	2925341	1319580	118555	4363476
9.	2004-05	2643303	1248025	14543	3905871
10.	2005-06	2530839	2121719	246598	4899156
11.	2006-07	3190571	1661121	477180	5328872
12.	2007-08	4330330	2714078	376984	7421392
13.	2008-09	5263434	3035583	729894	9028911
14.	2009-10	4588365	2675891	287840	7552096
15.	2010-11	5559398	2409777	1218388	9187563
16.	2011-12 (on 15-9-2012)	4399977	1724808	11238841	17363626
	Total	55606785	31919179	14854802	102380766
	Average procurement per year	3475424	1994949	990320	6398798
	Average procurement of rice per cardholder per year (total cards in 2011, are 25169000)				254 kgs
	Average procurement of food grains per cardholder per month				21 kgs

Source: Office of AP Civil Supplies Commissioner, Government of AP.

The Procurement of Rice (district-wise)

The district and decade-wise analysis indicate that the Civil Supplies Corporation, during the past three decades (1983-84 to 2013-14), on an average procuring 31568454 Metric tonnes (all the districts) of rice for distribution to the ration cardholders and other target groups/ institutions, in the State. However, there are variations in the procurement of rice among the regions and districts. The analysis unfolds that the procurement of rice is more in Andhra region i.e. the average of all the districts of the region is 18926028 Metric tonnes, followed by Telangana region i.e. 12230206 Metric tonnes. It is very less in Rayalaseema region i.e. 412220 Metric tonnes (See table 4.7).

The procurement of rice in the districts (average of all the decades) is ranging between 23412 Metric tonnes to 5798714 Metric tonnes indicating the wide disparities among the districts. The lowest procurement of rice is in the districts such as Visakhapatnam (23412 Metric tonnes), Vijyanagaram (441347 Metric tonnes) in Andhra region; Chittur (45500 Metric tonnes) in Rayalaseema region and Hyderabad in Hyderabad (48565 Metric tonnes) and Rangareddy (344198 Metric tonnes) in Telengana region. While the highest procurement of rice is

Table 4.7: The procurement of Rice (district-wise) in Andhra Pradesh

Name of the District	*1983-84 to 1989-90*	*1990-91 to 2000-01*	*2001-02 to 2010-11*	*2011-12 to 2013-14*	*Total*	*Average of the all decades*
SRIKAKULAM	503868	1433282	2080973	792548	4810671	1202668
VIZIANAGARAM	171454	545020	670439	378474	1765387	441347
VISAKHAPATNAM	8322	21129	24853	39342	93646	23412
EAST GODAVARI	3271451	7932736	9660390	2330280	23194857	5798714
WEST GODAVARI	3518676	6960303	8822840	2001237	21303056	5325764
KRISHNA	2107660	4675786	610004	1366484	8759934	2189984
GUNTUR	1534738	3326396	2118736	482047	7461917	1865479
PRAKASAM	1005042	892335	646592	121814	2665783	666446
NELLORE	634119	1977181	2635497	402064	5648861	1412215
Andhra Region Total	12755330	27764168	27270324	7914290	75704112	18926028
CHITTOOR	15749	36417	86047	43788	182001	45500
CUDDAPAH	91490	265452	110680	30852	498474	124619
ANANTAPUR	3849	15071	47940	5346	72206	18052
KURNOOL	183178	299646	329838	83536	896198	224050
Rayalaseema Region Total	294266	616586	574505	163522	1648879	412220
MAHBUBNAGAR	486838	1073416	1125655	428576	3114485	778621
RANGA REDDY	198562	658034	397800	122395	1376791	344198
HYDERABAD	109115	83970	1174	0	194259	48565
MEDAK	953580	984584	1421271	562921	3922356	980589
NIZAMABAD	799902	1808722	4538769	1459663	8607056	2151764
ADILABAD	77847	149475	211457	59278	498057	124514
KARIMNAGAR	947851	3214751	4799314	796211	9758127	2439532
WARANGAL	670768	1919122	3747998	902710	7240598	1810150
KHAMMAM	442777	2180042	709573	127114	3459506	864877
NALGONDA	1361870	1073416	6639042	1675260	10749588	2687397
Telangana Region Total	6049110	13145532	23592053	6134128	48920823	12230206
ANDHRA PRADESH	19098706	41526286	51436882	14211940	126273814	31568454
Decade average of each district	830379	1805491	2236386	617910	5490166	1372541

Source: Office of AP Civil Supplies Commissioner, Government of AP.

more in the districts like East Godavari (5798714 Metric tonnes) and West Godavari (5325764 Metric tonnes) in Andhra region, followed by Nalgonda (2687397 Metric tonnes), Karimnagar (2439532 Metric tonnes) and Nizamabad (2151764 Metric tonnes) in Telangana region. In Rayalseema region the highest procurement of rice is more in Kurnool (224050 Metric tonnes) and Cuddapah (124619 Metric tonnes) (See Table 4.7).

Decentralised Procurement of Paddy and Rice Policy, 2012-13 in Andhra Pradesh

The FCI on behalf of the Government of India has been undertaking sale of wheat and rice at predetermined prices/reserve prices in the open market from time to time to enhance market supply of foodgrains to have a moderating influence on open market prices and to offload surplus stocks. A number of States, recently, have opted for implementation of the Decentralised Procurement Scheme (DCP), under which foodgrains are procured and distributed by State governments themselves. Under this scheme, the designated State government procure, store, and issue foodgrains under the TPDS and welfare schemes of the Government of India. The difference between the economic cost fixed for the state and the central issue price (CIP) is passed on to the State government as subsidy. The decentralised system of procurement, according the government, has the objectives of covering more farmers under Minimum Support Price (MSP) operations, improving efficiency of the PDS, providing foodgrains varieties suited to local tastes, and reducing transportation costs. Further, the government- both Central and State- continues to provide large and growing amounts of subsidy on foodgrains for distribution under the TPDS, other nutrition-based welfare schemes and open market operations.

The procurement of paddy and rice under centralised mechanism is causing for several problems such as delay in procurement, low price for the products to the farmers, high cost for transportation and supply of poor quality foodgrains, etc. In order to overcome some of these problems the Government of Andhra Pradesh is adopting the decentralised procurement (DCP) of Paddy/rice procure paddy directly from farmers through its agency viz. the AP State Civil Supplies

Corporation Ltd (APSCSCL) from Kharif Marketing Season (KMS) (G.O.Ms.No. 42, dt 03.10.2012) . This system has several advantages such as (a) State agencies ensures Minimum Support Price (MSP) and timely payment (within 48 hours) to farmers; eliminate the middlemen in procurement of paddy (b) motivate the farmers to produce more and (c) ensure smooth operation of procurement process and distribution. The salient features of the DCP are: (i) Procurement of Paddy from the farmers at MSP and rice from the rice millers/dealers at FCI procurement (Levy) rate under mill levy; (ii) Utilise the raw rice so procured for State's PDS and other schemes as per the allotment made by the Government of India; (iii) Deliver surplus rice, if any, to the FCI for Central Pool; (iv) Shortfall of raw rice, if any, for the State's PDS will be made available by the Government of India through FCI; (v) Government of India will reimburse the entire expenditure incurred by the State Government towards the procurement (acquisition) cost and distribution and also releases provisional subsidy based on 100 per cent of fixed items such as MSP, taxes and statutory levies including VAT, milling charges, drying (for raw rice) and at 95 per cent on the balance incidentals. The DCP initially introduced in seven districts namely (i) Karimnagar, (ii) Chittoor, (iii) Warangal, (iv) Nalgonda, (v) Guntur, (vi) Prakasham, (vii) Nellore. While in the remaining 16 districts, FCI accepts mill levy of raw rice and boiled rice from all districts of the state for central pool. The Telangana State government recently has decided to extend this method to two more districts viz, Nizamabad and Mahabubnagar from KMS, 2014.

Administrative Process for Procurement of Paddy and Rice in AP

AP State Civil Supplies Corporation Ltd is responsible for procurement of paddy and rice in coordination with the Joint Collectors of the District. The measures such as (i) giving wide publicity of the MSP for paddy for Common and Grade A along with the specifications prescribed for getting MSP through print and electronic media, and through pamphlets/leaflets, posters; (ii) identification of sub-agencies like Women Self-help Groups with support of Society of Elimination of Rural Poverty (SERP), Primary Agricultural Cooperative Societies (PACS), District Cooperative Marketing Societies, etc, for procurement of paddy; (iii) identification of areas for opening the exclusive Paddy

Purchase centres in addition to the AMCs; (iv) computerisation of all procurement points to be ensured before commencement of procurement; (v) availability of equipment like storage centres, Paddy Cleaners, Winnowing machines, sieves, moisture meters, callipers; (vi) coordinating and monitoring of the activities and assess the quantity of paddy likely to arrive at each of the purchase centre depending upon the neighbouring villages; (vii) storage arrangements at the purchase centre till paddy is moved to mills. The Corporation is promoting SHGs to purchase paddy from purchasing centres located in cluster of villages and transporting the paddy to the rice mills for milling and thereafter to the FPSs for distribution and if any excess is available transport to the godowns for future needs.

The Government Procurement Policy – Mana Biyyam – Manakosam

The State government launched Mana Biyyam – Manakosam policy in 2013, with a view to procure rice from local variety from local area to distribute to the cardholders. The FCI, instead of supplying the rice procured from our own state, it is supplying the rice procured from other states like Punjab, Chhattisgarh, Haryana, which are not in good quality and traditionally/culturally not suitable to our people. In fact, due to this, many BPL families, including APL families, sell the ration rice in the open market and thus the policy is giving scope for misuse of the PDS. This is in a way violating the right of 'Food Sovereignty' of the people. There are many instances, where target group members protesting against the supply of rice which is not culturally suitable to us. Therefore, the policy of Mana Biyyam Manakosam – our Rice for our Purpose assumes considerable importance (Eenadu, 15th November 2012). Initially this system is implemented in Nalgonda, Karimnagar, and Warangal, later extended to four more districts viz, Nalgonda, Chittur, Nellore, Guntur and Prakasam in the state. The Telangana state, recently, decided to extend this policy to Nizamabad and Mahabubunagar districts w.e.f. Khariff season 2014.

This policy, according to the government authorities, would not only ensure procurement of good quality of rice and supply the same to the target group, but also reduce the expenditure to the tune of nearly Rs 100 crore on the transportation of rice from FCI to the FPS and ensure MSP to the farmers. For the first time, the government announced the incentive price for eight varieties of the rice at Rs 1500 to encourage farmers to take up cultivation of fine variety of paddy and the bridge the demand-supply gap of the rice. Further, it also announced to open nearly 1779 paddy purchase centres close to the farmers and for about 100-paddy purchase centres would be set up only to purchase fine variety of paddy and hull it for distribution to the cardholders. The main aim of the policy, according to the government authorities, is to see that no farmer sells his/her produce at less than MSP. The farmers who do not get MSP could complain to toll number 18994252977.

Central Government Decision to Reduce the Procurement of Rice under Levy System

The present practice is that, the FCI procure 75 per cent of the total requirement of rice and distribute to the States every year. It is purchasing the rice at the rate of Rs 13.45 per kg and supplies it to the State governments to be supply to the BPL families at the rate of Rs 3 per kg. This means Central Government is spending Rs 10.45 as subsidy per kg. According to Ministry of Food Security, Government of India, it is going to incur Rs 1.37 lakh crore from the year 2014 towards the procurement of rice. The respective State government procures the remaining 25 per cent from the farmers/rice millers. The Central Government in order to reduce its burden on subsidy it has informed the State governments in 2013 that it would only procure 25 per cent of the foodgrains and the remaining 75 per cent of the requirement has to be procured by the respective State government. The State governments, including Andhra Pradesh pressurised the Central Government and saw that the same procedure continues in future also. The main argument is that the decision of the latter would be burden on the State governments to purchase the total rice from millers/farmers. The then UPA postphoned its decision up to August 2014, keeping in view the sixteenth Parliament elections scheduled in May 2014 and also issues related to the controversy on the bifurcation of the State.

The NDA Government, recently, informed the State government that it would procure only 25 per cent of rice under levy system from September 2014. This decision affects not only the implementation of

Re 1 per kg. rice scheme but also the farmers in getting remunerative prices for paddy. The rice millers/traders purchase the paddy and sometimes from the farmers at lower price below the MSP. Under these circumstances, the State government has to purchase the paddy from the farmers at MSP to meet the demand under PDS. However, the major problem is that the AP Civil Supplies Corporation has no adequate staff and other infrastructure to take up this job (Eenadu, July 22, 2014).

Issues in Procurement of Rice

No uniformity in fixation of district targets

The levy of rice policy has differentiating effects on millers and traders in the State. Several factors are contributing for this. Firstly, lack of uniformity in fixation of district targets i.e. procurement of rice. Based on average cultivable land and costs of production, the State government, every year, fixes the price and targets for each district for procurement of rice. However, the district targets are not fixed on any scientific method. The district officials either over emphasis or underestimate the production of Paddy and the price is also usually lower than the market prices, which is giving scope for the rice millers/ traders to evade of levy. In order to overcome the levy of rice, millers locate or set up new venture or relocate the mills in the districts/talukas/ mandals, where the low level of paddy is grown and low targets for levy of paddy/rice. They import the paddy from other districts, hull it, and make profits by selling the rice in the open market. Thus, variations in the fixation of targets is causing scope for the traders to relocate their entrepreneurship in the backward areas and evading levy of rice to the government.

Secondly, the millers/traders supply less profitable (take away rate) rice to the FCI/ procuring agency to fulfil their obligation under levy system and sell more profitable rice in the open market. The FCI, based on the length-breadth ratio, classify the rice as superfine, fine and common and determine differential price system. The farmers in Andhra Pradesh, during the past six to seven years, are growing modern variety i.e. 10010 or 10016 or JJ paddy, which is giving more output compared to other varieties, in spite of odds such as lack of adequate water and bad weather conditions. However, the breadth of it is more solid/ rock-hard, tasteless and hard to digest and thus, less demand for it in the market. The millers/traders prefer to offer such varieties to the FCI and the same is allotted to the States for distribution under PDS. The millers/traders obtain the clearance certificate from the authorities concerned and sell the better quality of rice in the open market or export it outside the state and earn profits. In fact, one of the small traders commented that the levy system has become more profitable to the traders, especially the big mill owners/traders, and a source of income.

Thirdly, the traders are mostly come from dominant communities (upper caste and upper class), enjoy the political support and influence the procurement policy of the government. They also establish rapport with the officials-local and higher levels- and try to evade levy of rice. Further the Rice Millers/Traders Association (at all levels from state to mandal) establishes direct rapport with the policy-makers and opposition and influence the policy and its implementation and turn out the most powerful instrument in determining or intervening the state levy policy, as it finances the political parties in the elections.

Procurement Policy to Benefit the Rice Millers

Under the decentralised procurement policy, the State government has proposed to purchase about 30 lakh tonnes of paddy, during the year 2012. Subsequently the government withdrew its decision and decided to purchase the 11-lakh tonnes of rice from millers to distribute it to the target group. The critics argue that the government yielded to the pressure of rice traders and changed its decision to benefit the latter. The traders, under one other pretext, are paying less than MSP to the farmers for the purchase of paddy. They usually adopt the techniques such as quality of paddy is not good, power shortage to hull the paddy, giving assurance that they would give advance amount for cultivation for the next year, etc, and compelling the farmers to dispose the products at lower price. Further, the commission agents are farming a group/ring and stick on to pay the particular amount – generally less than MSP, etc. The concerned officials of the Corporation also feel convenient to continue this practice, as the paddy purchase from the farmers is a burden and do not have the adequate/ required infrastructure and personnel to do the task. Further, it is also easy to mediate with the millers for their personal benefits rather than with the farmers. The critics also maintain that the quality of rice supplied by the millers is not good (Eenadu, October 9, 2012). However, the Corporation officials claim that the reason for withdrawal of the decision to purchase the paddy from the farmers is due to the decline of Finance Department to grant loan to the corporation for the above said purpose. The Finance Department kept the file pending for months together. These factors indicates that the State government took the decision without taking into account of the financial resources, availability of infrastructure to purchase, transport and store the purchased paddy, above all, the pressure of paddy/rice traders/millers, etc.

Prohibition to Export the Quality Rice (2014-15)

The Telangana state government has announced its policy on the procurement of paddy and rice for the year 2014-15 w.e.f. kariff season. It has banned the export of quality rice such as Sona masuri, Samba masuri, Vijaya masuri, Tella masuri, Gidda masuri, BPT, Jillakar, etc, which are in greater demand in the State. The rice traders/millers have to sell it in the markets located within the State. Further, the rice traders/ millers are allowed to sell 75 per cent of the rice procured/hulled in the open market (within the state) only after fulfilling the levy of rice to the extent of 25 per cent of their business to the government for distribution under PDS. This is also subject to the permission of Joint Collector of the respective district. The government has also warned the rice traders/ millers to pay the MSP to the farmers while procuring the paddy. It also has decided to establish Control Room in every district to take the complaints from the farmers and monitor the rice trading activity in the district. For this purpose the government also allotted toll free numbers-1967 or 1800 425 0082.

Depositing the Paddy Sale Amount in Farmers' Bank Account

As per the State government norm, the paddy-purchasing agency has to reimburse the amount to the farmer within three days of the transaction. However, the farmers, who sell their products in the government market yard has to wait for more than a month to get the amount/ cheque/ demand draft and, in this regard, sometimes they have to give bribe to the authorities concerned. In order to overcome this problem, the government has decided to credit/transfer the amount to the farmer's account through online on the same day or within 48 hours of sale of product. This method is implemented in districts i.e. Medak and Nizamabad districts as an experimental basis. The response of the farmers to this method, according to the officials, is quite satisfactory. The Telangana State government, recently, has decided to extend this method to all the districts, except Hyderabad, in a phased manner. The government is planning to implement this in four districts- Nalgonda, Khammam, Karimnagar and Warangal, during the year 2014 khariff marketing season onwards. However, some of the farmers are not showing interest in the depositing the amount through online method. Their fear is that the bankers would deduct the amount towards payment of loan amount, if any. The official sources indicate that the government is firm to implement the online transfer of the amount to the farmers, who are coming forward to avail this facility.

However, the real problem of transfer of money lies in the process evolved for payment and inaction of the government officials to complete the procedure. The Civil Supplies Department/Corporation has to transfer the amount first to the concerned District Offices, which are engaged in the purchase the paddy from the farmers. The district officials in turn transfer the amount to its field level office and then latter transfer the amount/or give the cheque to the seller of the product. For instance, the Civil Supplies Department transfers the amount to the District Cooperative Department and the later in-turn transfer to the District Cooperative Marketing Society (DCMS). The District Society disburses the amount to its field level offices, which are actually engaged in purchase of paddy from the farmers. The entire process is causing for the delay in payment of amount to the farmers. This indicates that online mode for payment is not the solution except simplifying the procedure and real concern of the higher officials to take decisions immediately.

Section IV

Storage Capacity in the Country

Proper storage facilities for the operations of agricultural marketing – purchase and sale of foodgrains is paramount for implementation of

National Food Security. In India, 21 crore tonnes of wheat is becoming wastage every year, due to the lack of proper storage facilities. Further, the bad climate conditions are also contributing for this situation. This situation is posing a serious problem not only to meet the needs of growing population but also distribution of foodgrains to the target group under PDS. In this context, it is appropriate to note the observations made by AD Gorwala Committee (1954). The Committee point out that we could save about 10 per cent of total production, if we have adequate space and proper facilities for storage of production and practice of scientific management methods to preserve the stored foodgrains. In many States, the procured foodgrains are covered with plastic sheets/covers or stored in open place. These methods are unsafe and unscientific in managing the foodgrains storage. The S.L. Guru Committee (2001) suggested that the government should advance loans to the farmers to store the foodgrains properly. The government also appointed task force committee to examine the implementation of the proposals of the committee. However, there is not much progress, in this regard.

To meet the requirement of all-time high stock levels of 823.17 lakh tonnes achieved in 2012, the FCI restored to short-term hiring of storage facility to efficiently manage the stocks. In order to incentivising the creation of storage capacity in the country, the government initiated the Private Entrepreneurs Guarantee (PEG) Scheme that aims to construct storage godowns through private entrepreneurs. Under the PEG Scheme, the FCI guarantees 10-year usage of storage capacities to private investors and nine years to the Central Warehousing Corporation (CWC), and State Warehousing Corporations (SWC). The government decided to construct godowns in 19 States with a total capacity of 197 lakh tonnes and of this, a capacity of 132.73 lakh tonnes has been approved and released orders for construction. These measures are expected to address the shortage of covered godown space largely.

Enhancing the Foodgrain Storage Capacity of Godowns under PPP in the State

The situation in Andhra Pradesh is no different. In AP the Mohankanda Committee point out that the farmers are not getting proper remuneration for their product due to the lack of storage facilities in the State. The existing godown facilities are not sufficient to store one-fourth of the total production. The AMC is collecting one per cent of sale amount from farmers as marketing fee and the total amount accumulated by 2011-12 was about Rs 520 crore and it may increase year after year. In addition to this, crores of amounts are accumulated with the Marketing and State Warehouse Corporation for this purpose.

However, the State government is showing some interest in procuring the foodgrains; it is not showing the same enthusiasm in increasing storage capacity and practicing scientific methods to manage it. For instance, the Government of India, during the financial year 2011-12 allocated the thousands crores for construction of new godowns in the entire country but the Andhra Pradesh government could not avail this facility. What is lacking is the political will to increase the storage capacity in the State (Sreenivas, M, 2012).

The Andhra Pradesh Civil Supplies Corporation is having 436 MLS points in the State for storage of stocks. Out of these, the Corporation manages 29 MLS points are being handled by Grijan Cooperative Societies (GCC) and the remaining of them (408). It is hiring the godowns depending on the requirement in the districts. The existing storage capacity managed by both government and private agencies is 10.87 crore tonnes. The government estimates indicates that by the end of March, 2017 the storage capacity requirement would be 14.50 crore tonnes. Therefore, during the 12th Plan Period 2012-17 the government is proposing to construct the gowdowns which can store 3.50 crore tonnes of foodgrains. This is also quite inadequate to store the procured foodgrains.

The Civil Supplies Department is contemplating to store the foodgrains in each godowns located at mandal level sufficient to supply it for four months to the cardholders. This would reduce the cost of transporting the foodgrain to the tune of Rs 50 crore every year in the State. The AMC would get Rs 20 crore as rent on godowns. For this purposc thc Dcpartment/Corporation, recently, decided to enhance the foodgrain storage capacity to distribute in the State. The Civil Supplies Department/ Corporation has requested the Agricultural Marketing Department to provide/construct about 439 godowns spread over in the State on hiring basis to store 11.37 lakh tonnes of foodgrains. The later has agreed to give the existing available godowns and construct new godowns for the said purpose. This would not only benefit the Corporation to store and supply quality foodgrains to the target group, but also benefit the AMC by way of getting rent amount.

Section -V

Distribution of Foodgrains

The food security policy generally has several dimensions. One, the policy is a welfare measure as it involves distribution of subsidised foodgrains to the needy and eliminate malnutrition; two, an instrument for influence the foodgrain market and means to promote foodgrain production; three, contribute to economic redistribution. Foodgrain distribution includes: (i) Subsidised rice to BPL families of White cardholders at the rate of 4 kg per head subject to a maximum of 20 kg. per family per month at Rs 2 per kg. (The Telangana State Government has recently announced that it would supply six kgs rice per month per individual, irrespective of the number of persons in the family); (ii) Subsidised rice to AAY families @ 35 kg. per month at Rs 2 per kg, irrespective of number of members in the card. The cost of subsidised rice is reduced i.e. Rs two to Re one from 2013 onwards; (iii) Annapurna beneficiaries is being re-allotted @ 10 kgs. per beneficiary per month, free of cost; (iv) infirm/ crippled weavers @ 25 kgs per month per beneficiary free of cost w.e.f. January 2006; (v) other rice subsidy schemes such as Social Welfare Hostels, and National Child Labour Project and Residential Bridge Courses; (vi) wheat distribution to the BPL/APL/AAY card holders of urban areas up to a maximum of 10 kgs. per family per month @ Rs 12 per kg. i.e. on economic cost without incurring any subsidy; (vii) "Mana Biyyam" (our Rice) scheme on 16.1.2013 (initially introduced in three districts i.e., Warangal, Karimnagar, Nalgonda); (viii) scheme of Amma Hastam i.e providing nine essential commodities at a cost of Rs 185 to the White card holders.

The State has a long history in public distribution system. The experience with the rice, wheat and other essential commodities distribution at subsidised rate is more than three decades. Every successive government has introduced reforms in the distribution system to suit to its political gains. Indrakanth (1987), Olsen (1989), Venugopal (1992), Indrakanth (1997; 2000), Krishna Rao (1993), Parthasarathy (1995), Radhakrishna, *et.al* (1997), World Bank (1997), Dutta and Ramaswamy (2001), Indrakanth and Harikishan (2003), Sambi Reddy (2004), Surjit Deb (2009) etc., have examined the performance of the impact of the PDS on the living conditions of the poor in the State. Here an attempt is made to analyse the Subsidised Rice Scheme (SRS), which would give the insights on the phenomena.

'Two-Rupees-a-kilo Rice' as Political Commodity

The supply of Subsidised Rice Scheme (SRS), which is popularly known as 1 kg rice at Rs 2 to the poor has a long history and every political party used it as political commodity to come into power. The government (Congress Party) keeping in view ensuing State Assembly elections in November 1982, announced that it would supply the subsidised rice at Rs 1.90 kg. Rs 2.10 kg. and Rs 2.15 kgs. three varieties i.e., common, fine and superfine rice, respectively, through PDS from December 1982. Nevertheless, the party lost majority in the Assembly elections and the regional political party – Telugu Desam Party (TDP) came into power. The TDP gave electoral promise that it would supply five kgs rice to the people at Rs 2 per kg. in addition, this has influenced the voters significantly and voted for the party with massive mandate in 1983. This policy statement made the regional political party to come into power by overthrowing the Congress – the national party, which ruled the State uninterruptedly for over two and a half decades (1956-1982). The TDP Government introduced the policy of supply of rice at subsidised rate. Subsequently, every successive government continued the supply of 1 Kg rice at Rs 2 and less than that, with modifications in the supply of quantity and governance and to meet the political compulsions. This policy has become a 'model' for other States. The scheme in reality served dual purposes. One, distribution of subsidised rice to the needy and eliminate hunger and malnutrition in the State, two, the desire of government in power to seek legitimacy for its rule (Krishna Rao, IYR, 1993).

The TDP Government introduced the SRS popularity known as Two-Rupees-a-kilo Rice, in 1983, for the benefit of poor. The circumstances that motivated/compelled the then government for initiating SRS were: the prevalence of drought conditions during early 1980's; unrest among the poor due to the failure of the public policies to reach the poor; continuous price rise of foodgrains; widening of disparities between the better endowed areas and backward areas; failure of PAP to tide over unrest in the rural areas; announcement of State Assembly elections in the first week of January 1983; emergence of new regional political party – Telugu Desam Party (TDP) and aspiring political power; and failure of the then government (Congress Party) in addressing the issues of the poor and backward areas, etc. the problems of poor, particularly food insecurity remained unresolved.

The subsequent governments have changed the price and quantity of rice supplied under SRS. From 1st November 1990, the government supplied the rice at Rs 1.90 per kg. in addition, latter i.e., in 1991 the Government has enhanced the price from Rs 1.90 to Rs 3 per kg. with a reduced entitlement of 4 kgs per head per month. From January 27, 1992, again the price of rice per kg. was raised to Rs 3.50, with a reduced entitlement i.e., a maximum of 16 kgs per family (Krishna Rao, 1993). The reports from the field reveal that greater quantity of foodgrains supplied under PDS were utilised by urban households and neglecting the poor households. For instance, of the total allocation 36,410 tonnes of grains per month (allotted the Government of India) the State Government allocated 35 per cent (12,865 tonnes) only two urban districts viz., Hyderabad and Visakhapatnam. The remaining quantity of grain was distributed to 21 districts through PDS (Venugopal, K.R., 1992).

The TDP Government in its second term in 1995 restored the original policy i.e., supply of rice at Rs 2 per kg. with 5 kgs per head per month to a maximum of 25 kgs per family. The same political party with the change in the leadership i.e., Nara Chandrababu Naidu in August 1996 hiked the price from Rs 2 per kg to 3.50 per kg with reduced entitlement (Sambireddy, 2004) and in 2000-01 it reached Rs 5.25 per kg. (Surajit Deb, 2009).

The World Bank (1997) was of the view that the largest of the welfare schemes in terms of cost is the rice subsidy scheme. It has grown faster than all other components of welfare programmes and accounts for more than half the cost of all welfare programmes and covers about 85 per cent of the population. The major challenge for the government was to reverse the expenditure trends, especially on subsidies. Considering the fiscal constraints of Andhra Pradesh the Bank suggested an 'effective anti-poverty strategy':

- Promotion of rapid, sustained, labour-intensive growth to provide employment and income to a large part of the population below the poverty line;
- Effective provision of basic social services such as universal primary education and basic healthcare to the poor on a widespread basis to enable them to better participate in the growth process;
- Smaller and self-targeted transfer programmes for the poor.

Against this strategy, the Bank suggested that: "it is cost effective to replace the rice scheme with another subsidy programme, which would provide the same level of subsidy per family and also serve a social objective. An improved and effective Mid-day Meal scheme and other incentives to achieve universal primary education would be good alternatives to the rice scheme. If the rice scheme has to kept, it needs to be modified on the following lines: (a) replace the good quality rice with cheaper foodgrains to deter the higher income groups from taking advantage of the programme— this measure would facilitate self-targeting and improve efficiency of the programme; (b) reduce the number of ration cards in three years so that the scheme covers only the population below the poverty line; (c) link the issue price to the cost of programme, with subsidy not exceeding 50 per cent of the cost to the government; and (d) discourage the use of ration cards as ID cards." However, except (a) all the governments due to political compulsions and failure of implementing agencies dishonour the suggested modifications. In fact, the numbers of cards are increasing year after year and the APL families also withdrawing the rice (even if the rice is lower quality) and selling it in the open market or to intermediaries at higher price.

The Congress government under the leadership of Y. Rajashekar Reddy has reduced the price of the rice i.e., Rs 2 per kg. in 2008 keeping in view the ensuing State Assembly elections in 2009. In 2013, the Congress government under the leadership of N. Kiran Kumar Reddy further reduced the price of rice to Rs 1 per kg, with 4 kgs per head per month to a maximum of 20 kgs per BPL HH. The Telangana state government is contemplating to enhance the supply the rice to 6 kgs per person per month irrespective of the number of persons in the HH (November, 2014)

Thus, the price and quantity of the rice per kg supplied under PDS has undergone changes mostly based on the political considerations and partly to limit the subsidy expenditure on the scheme. Food inflation, increase in the agricultural wages and agricultural production and availability of foodgrains in the open market influenced the subsidised rice policy.

The Issues and Challenges in the Distribution of Foodgrains in Andhra Pradesh

The above presentation reveals that every successive government is modifying the norms of the PDS and treated it as 'vote security' programme, without taking into account the problems involved in the implementation. In fact, the numbers of cards are increasing year after year. The APL families also withdraw the rice (even if the rice is lower quality) and selling it in the open market or to intermediaries at higher price. In fact, it is described as one of the most corrupt sectors of the government. Here an attempt is made to analyse the issues involved in the implementation of PDS in the State.

Distribution of Fair Price Shops and Ration Cards and Percentage of Households Possessing Cards in 2001 and 2011

The number of households in Andhra Pradesh, according to 2001 and 2011 census was 17004305, and 2,10,24,534, respectively. Similarly, the number of FPSs was 40130 in 2001 and 44769 in 2011. An examination of distribution FPS unfolds that each FPS is catering 424 HHs/ ration cards in 2001 and it has increased to 470 in 2011 in the State (see Table 4.8).

With regard to the distribution of ration cards, in 2001, the analysis reveals that of the HHs (17004305 in the State) 99 per cent (16850450 HHs- both APL and BPL HHS) HHs obtained ration cards. The BPL HHs account for 69.57 per cent (11723290 HHs) of the total ration cards in the State. The APL HHs accounts for 30.43 per cent (5127160) of the total ration cards in the state (see Table 4.8). However, there are variations in the distribution of ration cards among the regions and districts. In Andhra region more than 100 per cent HHs (100 per cent) have obtained ration cards, followed by Telengana (98 per cent) and Rayalaseema (96 per cent). Similarly, there are variations among the districts. The highest is in Hyderabad (118 per cent HHs) and the lowest is Khammam, Chittur and Rangareddy (92 per cent HHs). With regard to the distribution of ration cards to the BPL HHs, (69.57 per cent) Andhra and Rayalaseema regions account for more than State average number of HHS i.e. 71 per cent and 70 per cent, respectively, while Telengana region account for less than State average i.e 63 per cent of the total HHs. There are also variations among the districts ranging 32 per cent to 81 per cent of the HHs. The highest number of BPL cards are in Vizianagaram (81per cent HHs) and Srikakulam (80 per cent HHs) and the lowest number of BPL cards are in Hyderabad (32 per cent HHs)*, Rangareddy (57 per cent HHs) and Nizamabad (61 per cent HHs)

In 2011, of the total number of HHs (2,10,24, and 534) more than hundered per cent (119 per cent i.e. 25259063 HHs) obtained the ration cards, indicating that the ration cards are more than the HHs in the State. The number of HHs obtained BPL/ white cards and APL/pink cards are 22264634 HHs and 2994429 HHs, accounting 106 per cent and 14 per cent of the total HHS, respectively, in the State. The region-wise analysis reveals that it is almost reflecting the State average in all the regions. The highest percentage of ration cards distribution to the total hhs of the respective district is in Hyderabad 150.7 per cent of the total HHs), Vizaianagaram (119.6 per cent of the total hhs), East Godadavari (117.5 per cent of the total hhs). These trends indicate that majority of the non-poor obtained the ration cards, especially BPL cards. Recognising this fact in 2010, the government has directed the officials to eliminate the bogus cards by conducting Gram Sabah's throughout the State. Despite this the number of ration cards have increased in the subsequent years and the total number of ration cards, as on 31.5.2014, are 263.18 lakhs and of this 233.24 lakhs (88.6 per cent) are BPL/White cards and 29.94 lakhs (11.3 per cent) are APL/Pink cards. Thus, the administrative machinery failed to arrest the malpractices (see Table 4.8).

Table 4.8: No. of Households and distribution of Ration Cards in 2001 and 2011 in Andhra Pradesh

Items	*2001*	*2011*
HHs	17004305	2, 10, 24,534
No. of Fair Price Shops in the State	40130	44,769
Average number of HH for each FPSs	424	470
HHs obtained ration cards	16850450	2, 52, 59,063
Percentage of HHs obtained ration cards to the total HHs in the State	99 per cent	120 per cent
BPL HHs obtained ration cards	11723290	22264634
Percentage of BPL HHs obtained ration cards to the total HHs in the State	69.57 per cent	106 per cent
Percentage of BPL HHs obtained ration cards to the total HHs in Andhra region	71 per cent	105 per cent
Percentage of BPL HHs obtained ration cards to the total HHs Rayalseema region	70 per cent,	109 per cent
Percentage of BPL HHs obtained ration cards to the total HHs Telangana region	63 per cent	105 per cent
The per centage of poverty in 2004-05* and 2011-12	30.01 per cent	9.27 per cent
APL HHs obtained ration cards	5127160	2994429
Percentage of APL HHs obtained ration cards to the total HHs	30. 43 per cent	14 per cent

Source; Complied from Statistical Abstract, AP, Directorate of Economics and Statistics, Govt of AP and AP Civil Supplies Department/Corporation, Government of AP.

*Source: estimated from unit level data 61st & 68th NSS, respectively.

Distribution of Ration Cards in the AP during 1998-99 to 2012- 13

The data on the ration cards (BPL, APL and others/temporary) unfolds that the Andhra Pradesh government, during 1998-99 to 2012-13, on an average granted 8,99,887 ration cards to the BPL and APL HHs in the State. The analysis unfolds that of the total cards, 74.0 per cent, 21.5 per cent and 9 per cent are white card holders (6,63,123) APL card holders (193348) and temporary cardholders (81067), respectively (see Tables 4.9 to 4.12). However, there are variations in the distribution of ration cards in different years and among regions and districts. There is a gradual increase in granting the cards from 1998-99 to 2005-06 and it is very high from 2006-07 onwards. The variations range between 7,16,448 cards (4,92,403 white cards) in 1998-99 to 11,13,195 cards (9,11,220 white cards) in 2010-11 and then slightly declined to 1067878 cards in 2012-13 in the State. This is mostly due to the then government 'vote security' approach.

Region-wise analysis reveals that ration cards distribution (average during 1998-99 to 2012-13) is more in Andhra region (9, 80,449 cards of this 728888 are white cards) and higher than State average, followed by Rayalaseema (859530 cards of this 669765 are white cards) and Telangana (843251 cards of this 601278 cards are white cards) regions (see Tables 4.9 to 4.12). The districts which has more than the State average number of cards (average during 1998-99 to 2012-13) are: East Godavari (13,84,065 of this 9,93,070 are White cards), Guntur (12,92,434 of this 9,27,533 are white cards), Krishna (11,69,982 of this 8,23,002 are white cards), West Godavari (10,84,180 of this 8,04,268 are white cards) and Visakhapatnam (10,88,343 of this 7,71,435) in Andhra region; while it is Warangal (11,02,549 of this 9,10,926 are white cards), Hyderabad (10,43,603 of this 4,28,051 are white cards), Rangareddy (10,33,570 of this 6,61,295 are white cards) and Karimnagar (9,64,162 of this 6,68,678 are white cards) districts in Telangana region. In Rayalaseema region, Chittor (9, 61,250 of this 7,18,509 are white cards) and Anantapur (9,31,584 of this 7,54,980 are white cards) districts received the highest number of ration cards (see Tables 4.9 to 4.13).

In Andhra region, the distribution of ration cards is lowest (less than the State average) are in Vijayanagaram (5,56,379 of this 4,37,518 are white cards) and Srikakulam (6,90,510 and of this 5,57,878 are white cards), Nellore (7,63,934 of this 5,78,521 are white cards) and Prakasam (7,94,211 of this 5,83,839 are white cards). In Rayalaseema region, the lowest number is in Cuddapah (6,73,213 of this 5,22,085 are white cards) and Kurnool (8,44,116 of this 6,53,884 are white cards). In Telangana region, it is in the districts i.e Nizamabad (5,84,452 of this 4,20,022 are white cards) Adilabad (6,40,210 of this 4,94,236 are white cards), Khammam (6,71,972 of this 4,86,869 are white cards), and Medak (6,67,585 of this 5,06,634 are white cards), Nalgonda (8,51,734 of this 6,47,499 are white cards) and Mahabubnagar 8,75,418 of this 7,00,088 are white cards) see Tables 4.9 to 4.13).

Table 4. 9. Distribution of Ration cards (White/Pink & Temporary) (District & year wise) in UAP during 1998-99 to 2012-13

District	1998-99	1999-2000	2000-2001	2001-2002	2002-2003	2003-2004	2004-2005	2005-2006	2006-2007	2007-2008	2008-2009	2009-2010	2010-2011	2011-12	2012-13	AVG
SRIKAKULAM	575,071	575071	580047	583148	576556	641579	631343	685338.5	739334	752443.5	765553	777183	826080	834064	814844	690,510
VIZIANAGARAM	511,073	511073	516137	519169	501114	567553	157718	394786.5	631855	640289.5	648724	648894	709187	702477	685633	556,379
VISAKHAPATNAM	883,568	883568	885058	889323	874661	998646	982628	1082630	1182632	1193446.5	1204261	1261487	1368444	1337913	1296872	1,088,343
EAST GODAVARI	1,170,220	1170220	1201338	1205843	1099519	1314652	1296643	1384208.5	1471774	1474354	1476934	1455703	1707817	1678653	1653100	1,384,065
WEST GODAVARI	933,996	933996	945022	948989	915453	1056675	1042443	1085566	1128689	1140800	1152911	1135442	1298199	1309276	1235237	1,084,180
KRISHNA	1,035,779	1035779	1061691	1065770	978693	1131032	1115413	1165879.5	1216346	1243614.5	1270883	1267153	1335709	1306008	1319983	1,169,982
GUNTUR	1,088,167	1088167	1096051	1100556	1026841	1227981	1210269	1282303	1354337	1386607.5	1418878	1404863	1605645	1576547	1519303	1,292,434
PRAKASAM	678,462	678462	685111	689216	667109	723834	710233	760106	809979	854666.5	899354	875249	979735	960548	941100	794,211
NELLORE	629,613	629613	631636	635053	601741	682458	671662	753439	835216	838419.5	841623	920053	953269	941536	893677	763,934
Andhra Region	**7,505,949**	**7505949**	**7602091**	**7637067**	**7241687**	**8344410**	**7818352**	**8,594,257**	**9370162**	**9,524,642**	**9679121**	**9746027**	**10784085**	**10647022**	**10359749**	**8,824,038**
Average	**833,994**	**833,994**	**844,677**	**848,563**	**804,632**	**927,157**	**868,706**	**954,917**	**1,041,129**	**1,058,294**	**1,075,458**	**1,082,892**	**1,198,232**	**1,183,002**	**1,151,083**	**980,449**
CHITTOOR	775,164	775164	778509	782726	764062	877213	861799	954430	1047061	1092605	1138149	1136127	1154917	1151916	1128902	961,250
CUDDAPAH	557,436	557436	557436	560448	520948	609568	598698	665081.5	731465	733419.5	735374	818277	825679	822276	804654	673,213
ANANTAPUR	748,406	748406	803389	807189	779706	894253	879580	954954.5	1030329	1075158	1119987	1122965	1146275	1147823	1134718	959,543
KURNOOL	630,953	630953	634666	638610	562791	678713	664905	806066.5	947228	962219	977210	1033662	1177756	1170190	1145811	844,116
Rayalaseema Region	**2,711,959**	**2711959**	**2774000**	**2788973**	**2627507**	**3059747**	**3004982**	**3,380,533**	**3756083**	**3,863,402**	**3970720**	**4111031**	**4304627**	**4292205**	**4214085**	**3,438,121**
Average	**677,990**	**677,990**	**693,500**	**697,243**	**656,877**	**764,937**	**751,246**	**845,133**	**939,021**	**965,850**	**992,680**	**1,027,758**	**1,076,157**	**1,073,051**	**1,053,521**	**859,530**
MAHBUBNAGAR	646,101	646101	650373	655033	646686	790937	776146	904581.5	1033017	1033164	1033311	1077398	1093307	1079332	1065783	875,418
RANGA REDDY	637,590	637590	678518	682883	637144	879126	865868	1067907.5	1269947	1285527	1301107	1317261	1491853	1417308	1333924	1,033,570
HYDERABAD	792,584	792584	816776	821242	787900	977463	970246	1057713	1145180	1183555	1221930	1276094	1302403	1272479	1235899	1,043,603
MEDAK	524,048	524048	524185	528161	515598	616202	606686	682618	758550	759245.5	759941	758501	827064	828904	800020	667,585
NIZAMABAD	454,308	454308	454308	457597	446353	558831	550465	587246.5	624028	635713	647398	657418	781641	744699	712461	584,452
ADILABAD	523,729	523729	532243	536903	508693	611251	600960	647123.5	693287	703101.5	712916	718438	775023	769050	746698	640,210
KARIMNAGAR	813,896	813896	813205	817552	798882	889954	874339	950337.5	1026336	1062093.5	1097851	1100672	1150094	1143608	1109710	964,162
WARANGAL	660,233	660233	675620	680280	4496364	701626	687910	788052	888194	937565.5	986937	1042323	1128511	1119052	1085327	1,102,549
KHAMMAM	535,919	535919	548749	553143	503252	601104	589738	661294.5	732851	750544	768237	764571	862485	847092	824686	671,972
NALGONDA	671,985	671985	687182	691616	659647	753578	739437	827187.5	914938	930135	945332	1009376	1102399	1098312	1072857	851,731
Telangana Region	**6,260,393**	**6260393**	**6381159**	**6424410**	**10000519**	**7380072**	**7261795**	**8,174,062**	**9086328**	**9,280,644**	**9474960**	**9722052**	**10514780**	**10319836**	**9987365**	**8,435,251**
Average	**626,039**	**626,039**	**638,116**	**642,441**	**1,000,052**	**738,007**	**726,180**	**817,406**	**908,633**	**928,064**	**947,496**	**972,205**	**1,051,478**	**1,031,984**	**998,737**	**843,525**
ANDHRA PRADESH	16,478,301	16478301	16757250	16850450	19869713	18784229	18085129	20,148,851	22212573	22,668,687	23124801	23579110	25603492	25259063	24561199	
Average of total AP	**716,448**	**716,448**	**728,576**	**732,628**	**863,901**	**816,706**	**786,310**	**876,037**	**965,764**	**985,595**	**1,005,426**	**1,025,179**	**1,113,195**	**1,098,220**	**1,067,878**	**899,887**

Source: Complied from Statistical Abstract, AP, Directorate of Economics and Statistics, Govt of AP & AP Civil Supplies Department/Corporation, Government of AP.

Table - 4.10. Distribution of White and AAY/AP Ration cards (District & year wise) in UAP during 1998-99 to 2012-13

District	1998-99	1999-2000	2000-2001	2001-2002	2002-2003	2003-2004	2004-2005	2005-2006	2006-2007	2007-2008	2008-2009	2009-2010	2010-2011	AVERAGE
SRIKAKULAM	463,062	463062	460173	463274	456682	518137	507901	586067	664233	674851	685469	718847	707888	566,896
VIZIANAGARAM	416,287	416287	413838	416870	398815	459802	49967	312571	575175	583239.5	591304	603814	608117	449,699
VISAKHAPATNAM	602,829	602829	601535	605800	591138	701691	685673	819739	953805	963000	972195	1047881	1073318	786,264
EAST GODAVARI	778,608	778608	774961	779466	673142	869438	851429	1036286	1221143	1223723	1226303	1286936	1460842	996,991
WEST GODAVAR	650,505	650505	651085	655052	621516	762488	748256	857132	966007	978076.5	990146	1022312	1049836	815,609
KRISHNA	680,160	680160	680285	684364	597287	738734	723115	841661	960206	984923.5	1009641	1098654	1147000	832,784
GUNTUR	711,813	711813	716309	720814	647099	827171	809459	952657	1095855	1136540	1177225	1255110	1347834	931,515
PRAKASAM	475,818	475818	477682	481787	459680	505815	492214	576294	660374	709195.5	758017	789991	821879	591,120
NELLORE	473,335	473335	474046	477463	444151	514788	503992	601887	699782	702447.5	705113	808550	779550	589,111
Andhra Region	**5,252,417**	**5,252,417**	**5,249,914**	**5,284,890**	**4,889,510**	**5,898,064**	**5,372,006**	**6584293**	**7796580**	**7955997**	**8,115,413**	**8,632,095**	**8,996,264**	**6,559,989**
Average	**583,602**	**583,602**	**583,324**	**587,210**	**543,279**	**655,340**	**596,890**	**731,588**	**866,287**	**884,000**	**901,713**	**959,122**	**999,585**	**728,888**
CHITTOOR	551,649	551649	552284	556501	537837	637337	621923	757511	893098	931935	970772	1000313	935726	730,657
CUDDAPAH	419,498	419498	419498	422510	383010	464513	453643	549138	644633	647013	649393	740201	687997	530,811
ANANTAPUR	580,883	580883	583567	587367	559884	667513	652840	791898	930955	973091	1015227	1040502	982930	765,195
KURNOOL	463,347	463347	465733	469677	393858	502500	488692	666309	843925	858261	872597	959957	1032939	652,396
Rayalaseema Region	**2,015,377**	**2,015,377**	**2,021,082**	**2,036,055**	**1,874,589**	**2,271,863**	**2,217,098**	**2764855**	**3312611**	**3410300**	**3,507,989**	**3,740,973**	**3,639,592**	**2,679,059**
Average	**503,844**	**503,844**	**505,271**	**509,014**	**468,647**	**567,966**	**554,275**	**691,214**	**828,153**	**852,575**	**876,997**	**935,243**	**909,898**	**669,765**
MAHBUBNAGAR	496,651	496651	499521	504181	495834	636964	622173	776887	931600	931747	931894	1010296	943069	713,651
RANGA REDDY	404,775	404775	416369	420734	374995	516525	503267	701760	900252	915832	931412	1024947	1127384	664,848
HYDERABAD	221,298	221298	220931	225397	192055	223575	216358	425402	634446	648694	662942	733515	723513	411,494
MEDAK	369,248	369248	369299	373275	360712	448643	439127	548248	657369	670284	683199	693469	698913	513,926
NIZAMABAD	291,416	291416	291416	294705	283461	362328	353962	445875	537788	544449	551110	596498	668767	424,092
ADILABAD	402,805	402805	396269	400929	372719	468216	457925	534575	611225	621039.5	630854	648217	633283	506,220
KARIMNAGAR	509,665	509655	508633	512980	494310	573810	558195	672440	786685	821102.5	855520	1000452	967299	674,673
WARANGAL	496,431	496431	506464	511124	4327208	531948	518232	649541	780850	827388	873926	945479	954454	955,344
KHAMMAM	376,675	376675	377123	381517	331626	415728	404362	510214	616065	630457	644849	681513	710782	496,737
NALGONDA	488,522	488522	503069	507503	475534	564265	550124	669605	789086	803217	817348	921737	894743	651,790
Telangana Region	**4,057,486**	**4,057,476**	**4,089,094**	**4,132,345**	**7,708,454**	**4,742,002**	**4,623,725**	**5,934,546**	**7,245,366**	**7,414,210**	**7,583,054**	**8,256,123**	**8,322,207**	**6,012,776**
Average	**405,749**	**405,748**	**408,909**	**413,235**	**770,845**	**474,200**	**462,373**	**593,455**	**724,537**	**741,421**	**758,305**	**825,612**	**832,221**	**601,278**
ANDHRA PRADESH	11,325,280	11,325,270	11,360,090	11,453,290	14,472,553	12,911,929	12,212,829	15,283,693	18,354,557	18,780,507	19,206,456	20,629,191	20,958,063	15,251,824
Average of total AP	**492,403**	**492,403**	**493,917**	**497,969**	**629,241**	**561,388**	**530,993**	**664,508**	**798,024**	**816,544**	**835,063**	**896,921**	**911,220**	**663,123**

Source: Complied from Statistical Abstract, AP, Directorate of Economics and Statistics, Govt of AP & AP Civil Supplies Department/Corporation, Government of AP.

Table 4.11. Distribution of White ration cards (District & year wise) in UAP during 1998-99 to 2012-13

DISTRICT	1998-99	1999-2000	2000-2001	2001-2002	2002-2003	2003-2004	2004-2005	2005-2006	2006-2007	2007-2008	2008-2009	2009-2010	2010-2011	2011-12	2012-13	Average
SRIKAKULAM	463,062	463,062	460173	463,274	456682	518,137	507901	557,140	606378	616,133	625888	658,991	634755	634413	702175	557,878
VIZIANAGARAM	416,287	416,287	413838	416,870	398815	459,802	49967	286,125	522282	528,963	535644	547,879	528796	491984	549227	437,518
VISAKHAPATNAM	602,829	602,829	601535	605,800	591138	701,691	685673	780,213	874752	882,152	889551	965,237	892360	890580	1005183	771,435
EAST GODAVARI	778,608	778,608	774961	779,466	673142	869,438	851429	992,427	1133425	1,133,425	1133425	1,194,058	1203345	1202960	1397338	993,070
WEST GODAVARI	650,505	650,505	651085	655,052	621516	762,488	748256	820,953	893649	901,480	909311	941,477	905593	905372	1046773	804,268
KRISHNA	680,160	680,160	680285	684,364	597287	738,734	723115	809,977	896838	912,304	927769	1,023,073	959563	949534	1081869	823,002
GUNTUR	711,813	711,813	716309	720,814	647099	827,171	809459	909,508	1009557	1,047,971	1086385	1,164,270	1134881	1134380	1281568	927,533
PRAKASAM	475,818	475,818	477682	481,787	459680	505,815	492214	550,843	609471	648,437	687402	719,376	686315	686167	800764	583,839
NELLORE	473,335	473,335	474046	477,463	444151	514,788	503992	574,132	644271	643,584	642897	746,334	675613	674870	715003	578,521
Andhra Region	**5,252,417**	**5,252,417**	**5249914**	**5,284,890**	**4889510**	**5,898,064**	**5372006**	**6,281,315**	**7190623**	**7,314,448**	**7438272**	**7,960,695**	**7621221**	**7570260**	**8579900**	**6,477,063**
Average	**583,602**	**583,602**	**583,324**	**587,210**	**543,279**	**655,340**	**596,890**	**697,924**	**798,958**	**812,716**	**826,475**	**884,522**	**846,802**	**841,140**	**953,322**	**719,674**
CHITTOOR	551,649	551,649	552284	556,501	537837	637,337	621923	716,397	810871	849,133	887395	916,936	852846	834450	900433	718,509
CUDDAPAH	419,498	419,498	419498	422,510	383010	464,513	453643	523,120	592596	591,192	589787	680,593	610897	597786	663129	522,085
ANANTAPUR	580,883	580,883	583567	587,367	559884	667,513	652840	756,266	859692	897,019	934345	959,620	902723	863552	938543	754,980
KURNOOL	463,347	463,347	465733	469,677	393858	502,500	488692	632,179	775666	788,576	801485	888,845	832364	832321	1009675	653,884
Rayalaseema Region	**2,015,377**	**2,015,377**	**2021082**	**2,036,055**	**1874589**	**2,271,863**	**2217098**	**2,627,962**	**3038825**	**3,125,919**	**3213012**	**3,445,994**	**3198830**	**3128109**	**3511780**	**2,649,458**
Average	**503,844**	**503,844**	**505,271**	**509,014**	**468,647**	**567,966**	**554,275**	**656,990**	**759,706**	**781,480**	**803,253**	**861,499**	**799,708**	**782,027**	**877,945**	**662,365**
MAHBUBNAGAR	496,651	496,651	499521	504,181	495834	636,964	622173	735,627	849080	849,080	849080	927,160	877202	806575	855545	700,088
RANGA REDDY	404,775	404,775	416369	420,734	374995	516,525	503267	667,527	831787	845,522	859257	952,792	878966	870070	972060	661,295
HYDERABAD	221,298	221,298	220931	225,397	192055	223,575	216358	414,093	611827	619,229	626631	697,204	628851	628283	673731	428,051
MEDAK	369,248	369,248	369299	373,275	360712	448,643	439127	518,240	597353	608,744	620135	630,405	611487	613710	669877	506,634
NIZAMABAD	291,416	291,416	291416	294,705	283461	362,328	353962	424,044	494126	496,641	499156	544,544	536432	529937	606740	420,022
ADILABAD	402,805	402,805	396269	400,929	372719	468,216	457925	503,173	548420	553,877	559334	576,697	585476	577066	607829	494,236
KARIMNAGAR	509,665	509,655	508633	512,980	494310	573,810	558195	635,024	711852	744,971	778089	917,877	856595	856425	862089	668,678
WARANGAL	496,431	496,431	506464	511,124	4327208	531,948	518232	615,947	713661	755,212	796763	868,316	816671	804603	904881	910,926
KHAMMAM	376,675	376,675	377123	381,517	331626	415,728	404362	480,460	556558	566,388	576218	612,882	586405	581455	678963	486,869
NALGONDA	488,522	488,522	503069	507,503	475534	564,265	550124	635,737	721349	730,429	739509	843,623	798406	798172	867723	647,499
Telangana Region	**4,057,486**	**4,057,476**	**4089094**	**4,132,345**	**7708454**	**4,742,002**	**4623725**	**5,629,869**	**6636013**	**6,770,093**	**6904172**	**7,571,500**	**7176491**	**7066296**	**7699438**	**5,924,297**
Average	**405,749**	**405,748**	**408,909**	**413,235**	**770,845**	**474,200**	**462,373**	**562,987**	**663,601**	**677,009**	**690,417**	**757,150**	**717,649**	**706,630**	**769,944**	**592,430**
ANDHRA PRADESH	**11,325,280**	**11,325,270**	**11,360,090**	**11,453,290**	**14,472,553**	**12,911,929**	**12,212,829**	**14,539,145**	**16,865,461**	**17,210,459**	**17555456**	**18978189**	**17996542**	**17764665**	**19791118**	**15,050,818**
Average of total AP	**492,403**	**492,403**	**493,917**	**497,969**	**629,241**	**561,388**	**530,993**	**632,137**	**733,281**	**748,281**	**763,281**	**825,139**	**782,458**	**772,377**	**860,483**	**654,383**

Source: Complied from Statistical Abstract, AP, Directorate of Economics and Statistics, Govt of AP & AP Civil Supplies Department/Corporation, Government of AP.

Table 4.12. Disatribution of PINK Ration cards (District & year wise) in UAP during 1998-99 to 2012-13

DISTRICT	1998-99	1999-2000	2000-2001	2001-2002	2002-2003	2003-2004	2004-2005	2005-2006	2006-2007	2007-2008	2008-2009	2009-2010	2010-2011	2011-12	2012-13	AVG
SRIKAKULAM	112,009	112,009	119874	119,874	119874	123,442	123442	99,272	75101	77,593	80084	58,336	58336	58336	58409	93,066
VIZIANAGARAM	94,786	94,786	102299	102,299	102299	107,751	107751	82,216	56680	57,050	57420	45,080	45135	45135	44975	76,377
VISAKHAPATNAM	280,739	280,739	283523	283,523	283523	296,955	296955	262,891	228827	230,447	232066	213,606	212482	212482	212805	254,104
EAST GODAVARI	391,612	391,612	426377	426,377	426377	445,214	445214	347,923	250631	250,631	250631	168,767	154097	154097	167476	313,136
WEST GODAVARI	283,491	283,491	293937	293,937	293937	294,187	294187	228,435	162682	162,724	162765	113,130	167528	167528	113178	221,009
KRISHNA	355,691	355,619	381406	381,406	381406	392,298	392298	324,219	256140	258,691	261242	168,499	113128	113128	167306	286,832
GUNTUR	376,354	376,354	379742	379,742	379742	400,810	400810	329,646	258482	250,068	241653	149,753	166971	166971	154126	294,082
PRAKASAM	202,644	202,644	207429	207,429	207429	218,019	218019	183,812	149605	145,471	141337	85,258	87241	87241	87143	162,048
NELLORE	156,278	156,278	157590	157,590	157590	167,670	167670	151,552	135434	135,972	136510	111,503	111503	111503	111473	141,741
Andhra Region	**2,253,604**	**2,253,532**	**2352177**	**2,352,177**	**2352177**	**2,446,346**	**2446346**	**2,009,964**	**1573582**	**1,568,645**	**1563708**	**1,113,932**	**1116421**	**1116421**	**1116891**	**1842395**
Average	**250,400**	**250,392**	**261,353**	**261,353**	**261,353**	**271,816**	**271,816**	**223,329**	**174,842**	**174,294**	**173,745**	**123,770**	**124,047**	**124,047**	**124,099**	**204,711**
CHITTOOR	223,515	223,515	226225	226,225	226225	239,876	239876	196,920	153963	160,670	167377	135,814	135814	135814	135827	188510
CUDDAPAH	137,938	137,938	137938	137,938	137938	145,055	145055	115,944	86832	86,407	85981	78,076	78076	78076	78057	111150
ANANTAPUR	167,523	167,523	219822	219,822	219822	226,740	226740	163,057	99374	102,067	104760	82,463	82463	82463	82390	149802
KURNOOL	167,606	167,606	168933	168,933	168933	176,213	176213	139,758	103303	103,958	104613	73,705	73705	73705	73679	129391
Rayalaseema Region	**696,582**	**696,582**	**752918**	**752,918**	**752918**	**787,884**	**787884**	**615,678**	**443472**	**453,102**	**462731**	**370,058**	**370058**	**370058**	**369953**	**610983**
Average	**174,146**	**174,146**	**188,230**	**188,230**	**188,230**	**196,971**	**196,971**	**153,920**	**110,868**	**113,275**	**115,683**	**92,515**	**92,515**	**92,515**	**92,488**	**144,713**
MAHBUBNAGAR	149,450	149,450	150852	150,852	150852	153,973	153973	127,695	101417	101,417	101417	67,102	67102	67102	67048	117313
RANGA REDDY	232,815	232,815	262149	262,149	262149	362,601	362601	366,148	369695	369,695	369695	292,314	292314	292314	294167	308241
HYDERABAD	571,286	571,286	595845	595,845	595845	753,888	753888	632,311	510734	534,861	558988	542,579	542579	542579	541078	589573
MEDAK	154,800	154,800	154886	154,886	154886	167,559	167559	134,370	101181	88,962	76742	65,032	65087	65087	65062	118060
NIZAMABAD	162,892	162,892	162892	162,892	162892	196,503	196503	141,372	86240	91,264	96288	60,920	60920	60920	60848	124416
ADILABAD	120,924	120,924	135974	135,974	135974	143,035	143035	112,549	82062	82,062	82062	70,221	70220	70220	70077	105021
KARIMNAGAR	304,241	304,241	304572	304,572	304572	316,144	316144	277,898	239651	240,991	242331	100,220	100220	100220	100195	237081
WARANGAL	163,802	163,802	169156	169,156	169156	169,678	169678	138,511	107344	110,178	113011	96,844	96894	96894	96787	135393
KHAMMAM	159,244	159,244	171626	171,626	171626	185,376	185376	151,081	116786	120,087	123388	83,058	83072	83072	82913	136505
NALGONDA	183,463	183,463	184113	184,113	184113	189,313	189313	157,583	125852	126,918	127984	87,639	129542	129542	129420	154158
Telangana Region	**2,202,917**	**2,202,917**	**2292065**	**2,292,065**	**2292065**	**2,638,070**	**2638070**	**2,239,516**	**1840962**	**1,866,434**	**1891906**	**1,465,929**	**1507950**	**1507950**	**1507595**	**2105451**
Average	220,292	220,292	229,207	229,207	229,207	263,807	263,807	223,952	184,096	186,643	189,191	146,593	150,795	150,795	150,760	202,576
ANDHRA PRADESH	**5,153,103**	**5,153,031**	**5,397,160**	**5,397,160**	**5,397,160**	**5,872,300**	**5,872,300**	**4,865,158**	**3,858,016**	**3,888,181**	**3918345**	**2949919**	**2994429**	**2994429**	**2994439**	**4447009**
Average of total AP	224,048	224,045	234,659	234,659	234,659	255,317	255,317	211,529	167,740	169,051	170,363	128,257	130,193	130,193	130,193	193,348

Source: Complied from Statistical Abstract, AP, Directorate of Economics and Statistics, Govt of AP & AP Civil Supplies Department/Corporation, Government of AP.

Table 4.13 DistributionTemporary Ration cards (District & year wise) in UAP during 1998-99 to 2010-11

District	1998-99	1999-2000	2000-2001	2001-2002	2002-2003	2003-2004	2004-2005	2005-2006	2006-2007	2007-2008	2008-2009	2009-2010	2010-2011	AVERAGE
SRIKAKULAM									57855	58718	59581	59856	73133	61,829
VIZIANAGARAM									52893	54276.5	55660	55935	79321	59,617
VISAKHAPATNAM									79053	80848.5	82644	82644	180958	101,230
EAST GODAVARI									87718	90298	92878	92878	257497	124,254
WEST GODAVARI									72358	76596.5	80835	80835	144243	90,974
KRISHNA									63368	72620	81872	75581	187437	96,176
GUNTUR									86298	88569	90840	90840	212953	113,900
PRAKASAM									50903	60759	70615	70615	135564	77,691
NELLORE									55511	58863.5	62216	62216	103937	68,549
Andhra Region									**605957**	**641,549**	**677141**	**671400**	**1375043**	**794,218**
Average									**67,329**	**71,283**	**75,238**	**74,600**	**152,783**	**88,246**
CHITTOOR									82227	82802	83377	83377	82880	82,933
CUDDAPAH									52037	55821.5	59606	59608	77100	60,835
ANANTAPUR									71263	76072.5	80882	80882	80207	77,861
KURNOOL									68259	69685.5	71112	71112	200575	96,149
Rayalaseema Region									**273786**	**284,382**	**294977**	**294979**	**440762**	**317,777**
Average									**68,447**	**71,095**	**73,744**	**73,745**	**110,191**	**79,444**
MAHBUBNAGAR									82520	82667	82814	83136	65867	79,401
RANGA REDDY									68465	70310	72155	72155	248418	106,301
HYDERABAD									22619	29465	36311	36311	94662	43,874
MEDAK									60016	61540	63064	63064	87426	67,022
NIZAMABAD									43662	47808	51954	51954	132335	65,543
ADILABAD									62805	67162.5	71520	71520	47807	64,163
KARIMNAGAR									74833	76132	77431	82575	110704	84,335
WARANGAL									67189	72176	77163	77163	137783	86,295
KHAMMAM									59507	64069	68631	68631	124377	77,043
NALGONDA									67737	72788	77839	78114	96337	78,563
Telangana Region									**609353**	**644,118**	**678882**	**684623**	**1145716**	**752,538**
Average									**60,935**	**64,412**	**67,888**	**68,462**	**114,572**	**75,254**
ANDHRA PRADESH									1489096	1,570,048	1651000	1651002	2961521	1,864,533
Average of total AP									**64,743**	**68,263**	**71,783**	**71,783**	**128,762**	**81,067**

Source: Complied from Statistical Abstract, AP, Directorate of Economics and Statistics, Govt of AP & AP Civil Supplies Department/Corporation, Government of AP.

The System of Foodgrain Distribution

The government is responsible for distribution of foodgrain in the state. For this purpose, it depends on both public institutions and private agencies. The Andhra Pradesh Civil Supplies Corporation is biggest wholesaler, which purchase the foodgrains from the FCI (rice and wheat), factories (sugar) and private traders and sell through 45116 outlets/Fair Price Shops/ Cooperative Societies/Non-Governmental Organisations at subsidised rates. The State government conditions the terms and references for selling the foodgrains both by the public and private agencies.

The Requirement, Allocation, and Issue Price of Rice

The State government distributes the rice to the different categories of people every month. The requirement, allocation and distribution of commodities to each of the category during the month of January 2014 are presented below, which would give us clue to understand the distribution process. The total requirement of rice per month is 3.63 lakh metric tonnes and it varies from month to month. The large part of the rice is distributed to the BPL families at Rs 1 per kg up to a maximum of 20 kgs to each hh. For instance, the requirement of rice under PDS to be distributed to BPL families in the State is about 341486.116 Mts per month. Of this, the Government of India is allotting 87674 Mts i.e. 25.6 per cent of the requirement at the rate of Rs 565 per qtl to the state government. For the remaining requirement the State government lifts the APL rice allocated by Central government at the rate of Rs 830 per qtl (see Table 4.14). The following table presents the issue prices of commodities-rice, wheat, etc, Government of India and consumer price of the commodity supplied by the State government to the different target groups under different schemes.

Distribution of Foodgrains to the Cardholders

The total population and total HHs of the state, according to 2011 census, is 8,45,80,777 and 2,10,24,534, respectively. The Civil Supplies Corporation has distributed 2,52,59,063 ration cards and out of this 2,22,64,634 (88.14 per cent) white cards were issued to the BPL families in 2011-12 in the State. It has distributed 3168969 tonnes (3168969000 kgs) of foodgrains to the cardholders in the state.

Table 4.14: Price and quantity of commodities distribution to the Cardholders/institutions in Andhra Pradesh (as on May 2014)

Category	*GoI Allocation of Rice to the State government (monthly average allotment in 2013, Qty. in Mts).*	*GoI Issue Prices (per qtl (in Rs)*	*End Consumer Prices of Commodity (Price per kg in Rs) supplied by State Govt)*	*Quantity of supply (in Kg/lit) per cardholder per month by the state Govt*	*Remarks*
APL	131334	Rs 830.00	Rs 9.00	30 kgs	Non-subsidy
BPL	87674	Rs 565.00	Rs 1.00	4 kgs per head a maximum of 20kgs per cardholder	The total requirement of rice pm 3.63 lakh MTs. The remaining requirement the state government lifts the APL rice @ Rs 830 per Qtl
Social Welfare Institutions	5722	Rs 565.00	Rs 1.00	17839.618 Mts (varies from month to month)	All hostels, Residential schools and colleges of SC/ST&BC and others
Antyodaya Anna Yojana	54524	Rs 300.00	Rs 1.00	35 kgs per cardholder	Poorest of the poor identified by Dist Collector.
Annapurna	932	Rs 565.00	Free of cost	10 kgs per head	Senior citizens who are not getting pension
NPNSPE (MDM)	10674.103	Free of cost	Free of cost	——	Rice will be released to DWCRA women & they in turn supply the cooked food to the students
WBNP	9440 Mts	Rs 565.00	Rs 4.00	9440 Mts	It is for 3 months to 88 ICDS projects
SABALA	3596 1st quarter	Rs 565.00	Rs 400 per qtl (govt releases it to the WDCW	6 kgs for each adolescent girl for 3 months	Initially the program was implemented in 7 districts. From july 2013 it is extended to all the 23 districts-.
Wheat	No allocation for BPL families	Rs 610.00	Rs 7.00	1 kg pocket to be supplied under Amma Hastam	State govt not opted for it under BPL.
Levy sugar	9731.800From June 2013 decontrolled, the state govt has to purchase from open market.	—	Rs 13.50	½ kg	

(Contd...)

Amma Hastham - w.e.f.11-4-2013		State government meet the expenditure from its budget		The state government supplies of 9 items a total of Rs 185 pm. wef. 11-4-2013. A non-woven carry bag costing Rs 11.50 will be given to the all the BPL beneficiaries as one time measure
Palmlein oil	—	Rs 40 (per lit)	1 lit	
Red gram dal			Rs 50.00 (1.kg)	1 kg
Sugar	—	Rs 6.75 (1 kg)	1 kg	
Wheat	—	Rs 7.00 (1.kg)	1 kg	
Atta	—	Rs 16.50 (1 kg)	1 kg	
Iodized Salt	—	Rs 5.00. (1 kg)	1 kg	
Tamarind	—	Rs 30.00 (500 grams)	500 grams	
Red Chilli Powder	—	Rs 20. (250 grams)	250 grams	
Turmeric Powder	—	Rs 12.00 (100 grams)	100 grams	

NPNSPE=National Programme of Nutritional Support to Primary Education
WBNP=Wheat Based Nutrition Programme
SABALA=Scheme for Empowerment of Adolescent Girls
Source: the Office of Commissioner of Civil Supplies, Government of AP.

If we distribute it to the total population, it works out to be 37.45 kgs and 3.12 kgs per person per year and per month, respectively. The distribution of foodgrains per hh per year and per month works out to be 150.72 kgs per year and 12. 56 kgs per month, respectively in the State (see Table 4.14). If we compute the foodgrain distribution, it would work out 150.72 kgs and 12.56 kgs per cardholder HH per year and per month, respectively. The average foodgrain distribution to the BPL cardholders was less than the above i.e. 142.33 kgs per year 11.86 kgs per month. It is pertinent to mention here that the computation is on the assumption that (a) PDS foodgrains are distributed equally among the whole hhs/ population in the state, and (b) that no diversion of foodgrains from PDS to the open market.

If the foodgrain requirement were taken as 450 g per person per day, the foodgrains supplied under PDS would provide on average foodgrains for six days and seven days in a month to the total cardholders and White cardholders, respectively, in the State. In other words, PDS contributed to about 20 per cent of the total foodgrain requirement of the HHs. For the remaining 24/23 days (80 per cent) he/she has to depend on the open market or self produced, (see Table 4.15). This shows that ensuring food security to the poor through public policies is very marginal in the State.

Table 4.15: Food Distribution and Food Security to the HHs/Persons in AP in 2011-12

Population (2011) in AP	8,45,80,777
Households (2011) in AP	2,10,24,534
Ration cards (2011) in AP	2,52,59,063
No. of BPL/White ration cards in 2011 in AP	2,22,64,634
Foodgrains distributed (rice and wheat) in 2011-12 under PDS	3168969 Metric tonnes (3168969000 kgs)
Distribution of foodgrains to the total population per year and per month	37.46 kgs per year or 3.12 kgs per month
Distribution of foodgrains per hhs per year and per month	150.72 kgs per year12.56 kgs per month
Distribution of foodgrains per cardholder hhs per year and per month	125.45 kgs per year 10.45 kgs per month

(Contd...)

Distribution of food grains per person of the cardholder hh per month (average size of the family 4 members in 2011 in AP	2. 61 kgs
Meeting foodgrain requirement per person of a hh in a month (450 grams per day)	6 days
Contribution to the total requirement of foodgrain to the person/hh in a month	20 per cent
Dependence of the person/ hh on the open market or own production	80 per cent
Distribution of foodgrains per BPL hhs per year and per month	142.33 kgs per year 11.86 kgs per month
Distribution of foodgrains per person of the BPL cardholder hh per month (average size of the family in 2011 in AP is 4 members	3 days
Meeting foodgrain requirement per person of a BPL hh per month (450 grams per day)	7 days

Source: Complied from Statistical Abstract, AP, Directorate of Economics and Statistics, Govt of AP & AP Civil Supplies Department/Corporation, Government of AP.

Distribution of Rice during 1998-99 to 2012-13 in AP

The data on the distribution of rice (subsidised and non=subsidized), during one and a half decades (1998-99 to 2012-13), discloses that the Andhra Pradesh government on an average distributed 1,77,972 quintals (qls) of rice to the BPL and APL HHs and the social welfare institutions. The analysis unfolds that of the total distributed rice, 91.4 per cent is distributed to White cardholders, including AAY and Annapurna (average quantity of rice distribution, during 1998-99 to 2012-13 is 1, 62,706 qls) and the remaining of it (7.5 per cent) is distributed to APL cardholders (see Tables 4.15 and 4.16). However, there are variations in the distribution of rice in different years and among regions and districts. The variations range between 71,923 qls to 9,59,562 qls rice. This is mostly due to the variations in the granting of ration cards and allotment of the quantity of rice for distribution to different categories/groups/institutions in the State. However, there is enormous increase in the allotment of rice to the districts higher than the state average during the years 2004-05 and 2009-10 in which State Assembly elections were held. This indicates that the ruling party considered the PDS as 'vote security programme'.

Region-wise analysis reveals that rice distribution is more in Andhra region 1,88,192 qls (1,72,567 qls for White card holders), followed by Rayalaseema 1,82,932 qls (1,66,799 qls for White card holders) higher than State average. While in Telangana region, 1, 66,790 qls (1, 52,193 qls of rice is distributed to White cardholders) (see Tables 4.15, 4.16). The districts which received highest number of quintals of rice i.e. more than the State average are: East Godavari (2,52,428 qls of this 2,28,582 qls allotted to White card holders), Guntur (2,35,483 qls of this 2,15,562 qls allotted to White card holders), West Godavari (2,09,379 qls of this 1,92,193 qls allotted to White card holders) and Visakhapatnam (2,09,619 qls of this 1,91,782 qls allotted to White card holders), Krishna (2,02,109 qls of this 1,85,014 qls allotted to White card holders), in Andhra region; while it is Warangal (2,57,845 qls of this 2,41,650 qls allotted to White card holders), Mahabubnagar 1,94,942 qls of this 1,77,673 qls allotted to White card holders), Rangareddy (1,87,678 qls of this 1,67,988 qls allotted to White card holders) and Karimnagar (1,82,642 qls of this 1,65,929 qls allotted to White card holders) districts in Telangana region. In Rayalaseema region Chittor (1,98,628 qls of this 1,81,526 qls allotted to White card holders) and Ananatapur (2,17,026 qls of this 1,97,738 qls allotted to White card holders) districts received the highest quantity of rice (see tables 4.16, 4.17).

The districts which received lowest quantity of rice (less than the State average) are: Vizianagaram (1,29,859 qls of this 1,19,806 qls allotted to White card holders) and Srikakulam (1,48,884 qls of this 1,37,004 qls allotted to White card holders), Nellore (1,48,193 qls of this 1,37,036 qls allotted to White card holders) and Prakasam (1,57,773 qls of this 1,46,177 qls allotted to White card holders) districts in Andhra region; Cuddapah (1,40,532 qls of this 1,30,278 qls allotted to White card holders) and Kurnool (1,75,543 of this 1,57,654 qls allotted to White card holders) in Rayalaseema region; Nizamabad (1,15,949 qls of this 1,04,992 qls allotted to White card holders), Khammam (1,31,885 qls of this 1,19,756 qls allotted to White card holders), Adilabad (1,39,247 qls of this 1,27,989 qls allotted to White card holders), Hyderabad (1,40,378 qls of this 1,27,221 qls allotted to White card holders), Medak (1,15,949 qls of this 1,33,144 qls allotted to White card holders) and Nalgonda (1,70,894 qls of this 1,55,578 qls allotted to White card holders) districts in Telangana region (see Tables 4.16, 4.17).

District	Table. 4.16 Distribution of Rice to White, AAY,AP, & APL Card holders & NS (District & year wise) under PDS in UAP during 1998-99 to 2012-13 (Quantity in Metric tonnes)														
	1998-99	1999-2000	2000-2001	2001-2002	2002-2003	2003-2004	2004-2005	2005-2006	2006-2007	2007-2008	2008-2009	2009-2010	2010-2011	2011-12	2012-13	AVERAGE
SRIKAKULAM	91,169	86107	83025	77922	76309	82389	770280	114321	123478	125803	128127	125773	122659	111762	114140	148,884
VIZIANAGARAM	82,215	74460	70210	64526	62820	70204	680328	99636	107830	112026	116222	112369	110647	95455	88940	129,859
VISAKHAPATNAM	124,438	103800	126054	94579	80747	92972	1155766	155873	167494	179152	190810	183045	172521	159818	157214	209,619
EAST GODAVARI	147,162	124344	116569	102118	92695	113009	1502385	167943	194692	200688	206683	223869	215541	195277	183438	252,428
WEST GODAVARI	136,409	110187	105022	97713	93313	104816	1228337	156995	162758	155754	148750	171376	175744	150987	142530	209,379
KRISHNA	135,802	11793	102979	10338	96088	97252	1289145	154715	162674	161837	160999	168571	173364	154529	151549	202,109
GUNTUR	132,220	121449	105719	86156	94953	110002	1405004	172806	175447	182692	189937	197892	199988	184193	173795	235,483
PRAKASAM	93,022	90047	84104	77567	71235	83504	859552	144471	116727	122927	129127	132713	128797	120611	112190	157,773
NELLORE	87,027	83870	76115	66768	65831	72661	803533	130106	115864	120520	125176	128229	124375	116750	106077	148,193
Andhra Region	**1,029,464**	**806,057**	**869,797**	**677,687**	**733,991**	**826,809**	**9,694,330**	**1296865**	**1326964**	**1361397**	**1,395,831**	**1,443,837**	**1,423,636**	**1,289,382**	**1,229,873**	**1,693,728**
Average	**114,385**	**89,562**	**96,644**	**75,299**	**81,555**	**91,868**	**1,077,148**	**144,096**	**147,440**	**151,266**	**155,092**	**160,426**	**158,182**	**143,265**	**136,653**	**188,192**
CHITTOOR	118,737	107305	102431	93365	56362	103478	1048623	167143	164426	176097	187768	182879	172872	161056	136876	198,628
CUDDAPAH	87,489	83703	72194	70108	57553	74681	730113	128265	117473	120929	124385	126188	119488	102950	92467	140,532
ANANTAPUR	124,466	116884	102369	106016	104567	115334	1075970	208886	175540	191452	207364	202337	190692	171151	162366	217,026
KURNOOL	96,142	94359	83540	81071	75186	87831	829281	145506	147501	159847	172192	174423	172827	159213	154219	175,543
Rayalaseema Region	**426,834**	**402,251**	**360,534**	**350,560**	**293,668**	**381,324**	**3,683,987**	**649799**	**604941**	**648325**	**691,709**	**685,827**	**655,879**	**594,370**	**545,928**	**731,729**
Average	**106,709**	**100,563**	**90,134**	**87,640**	**73,417**	**95,331**	**920,997**	**162,450**	**151,235**	**162,081**	**172,927**	**171,457**	**163,970**	**148,593**	**136,482**	**182,932**
MAHBUBNAGAR	103,921	99811	98035	90325	82627	100429	964258	164549	161907	176887	191866	193522	184118	164745	147128	194,942
RANGA REDDY	94,417	84788	74675	72020	68462	77463	1026071	147494	155995	163911	171827	182679	179706	158980	156684	187,678
HYDERABAD	79,490	43764	42299	37128	37622	36958	1042260	54870	85400	98411	111422	122137	118995	99669	95246	140,378
MEDAK	81,315	75951	71254	64179	61607	69314	745815	122591	122108	131171	140233	139424	137693	125008	109403	146,471
NIZAMABAD	63,835	56211	53724	4973	49248	56438	659821	86400	96749	101853	106956	110374	108234	96548	87871	115,949
ADILABAD	89,249	76265	74687	66804	60428	71680	741691	110980	111959	119263	126568	124322	116046	100417	98344	139,247
KARIMNAGAR	98,689	87828	81566	77611	73033	83058	1032366	149061	136269	144467	152665	169029	164080	144818	145094	182,642
WARANGAL	108,514	101023	98043	81543	74562	90045	854322	145948	141126	153678	166230	1406477	160548	149453	136169	257,845
KHAMMAM	78,592	73580	61278	55211	48090	61871	722993	98874	107825	112518	117212	115931	119785	107115	96949	131,855
NALGONDA	92,974	91440	85590	76188	73627	85507	902012	134040	139476	147879	156283	152326	156162	138464	131442	170,894
Telangana Region	**890,996**	**790,661**	**741,151**	**625,987**	**629,306**	**732,763**	**8,691,608**	**1,214,807**	**1,258,813**	**1,350,038**	**1,441,262**	**2,716,221**	**1,445,367**	**1,285,217**	**1,204,330**	**1,667,902**
Average	**89,100**	**79,066**	**74,115**	**62,599**	**62,931**	**73,276**	**869,161**	**121,481**	**125,881**	**135,004**	**144,126**	**271,622**	**144,537**	**128,522**	**120,433**	**166,790**
ANDHRA PRADESH	2,347,294	1,998,969	1,971,482	1,654,234	1,656,965	1,940,896	22,069,926	3,161,472	3,190,718	3,359,760	3,528,802	4,845,885	3,524,882	3,168,969	2,980,131	4,093,359
Average of total AP	**102,056**	**86,912**	**85,717**	**71,923**	**72,042**	**84,387**	**959,562**	**137,455**	**138,727**	**146,077**	**153,426**	**210,691**	**153,256**	**137,781**	**129,571**	**177,972**

Source: Compiled from Statistical Abstract, AP, Directorate of Economics and Statistics, Govt of AP & AP Civil Supplies Department/Corporation, Government of AP.

Table 4. 17. Distribution of Rice to BPL, AAY, AP Ration Card holders (District & year wise)under PDS in UAP during 1998-99 to 2012-13 (Quantity in Metric tonnes)

District	1998-99	1999-2000	2000-2001	2001-2002	2002-2003	2003-2004	2004-2005	2005-2006	2006-2007	2007-2008	2008-2009	2009-2010	2010-2011	2011-12	2012-13	AVERAGE
SRIKAKULAM	86,110	86107	83025	77922	76309	82389	677914	114321	120054	124091	128127	125773	122651	75132	75132	137,004
VIZIANAGARAM	74,100	74460	70210	64526	62820	70204	601833	99636	107761	111992	116222	112369	110609	60172	60172	119,806
VISAKHAPATNAM	104,553	103800	126054	94579	80747	92972	1047654	155873	166890	178850	190810	183045	172109	89396	89396	191,782
EAST GODAVARI	125,873	124344	116569	102118	92695	113009	1367691	167943	191988	199236	206483	223869	209908	93505	93505	228,582
WEST GODAVARI	111,503	110187	105022	97713	93313	104816	1104133	156995	161510	154880	148250	171376	175268	92060	95060	192,139
KRISHNA	118,394	11793	102979	10338	96088	97252	1178737	154715	156380	158590	160799	168571	171099	93237	96237	185,014
GUNTUR	121,328	121449	105719	86156	94953	110002	1280340	172806	171228	180532	189837	197892	199816	101189	100189	215,562
PRAKASAM	90,359	90047	84104	77567	71235	83504	768148	144471	114052	121590	129127	132713	128649	78541	78541	146,177
NELLORE	82,129	83870	76115	66768	65831	72661	720952	130106	114626	119901	125176	128229	124264	72458	72458	137,036
Andhra Region	**914,349**	**806,057**	**869,797**	**677,687**	**733,991**	**826,809**	**8,747,402**	**1296865**	**1304490**	**1349660**	**1,394,831**	**1,443,837**	**1,414,373**	**755,690**	**760,690**	**1,553,102**
Average	**101,594**	**89,562**	**96,644**	**75,299**	**81,555**	**91,868**	**971,934**	**144,096**	**144,943**	**149,962**	**154,981**	**160,426**	**157,153**	**83,966**	**84,521**	**172,567**
CHITTOOR	107,405	107305	102431	93365	56362	103478	929173	167143	164396	176082	187768	182879	172856	86126	86126	181,526
CUDDAPAH	86,355	83703	72194	70108	57553	74681	646641	128265	117407	120896	124385	126188	119237	63277	63277	130,278
ANANTAPUR	119,381	116884	102369	106016	104567	115334	943702	208886	175365	191365	207364	202337	190571	88767	93168	197,738
KURNOOL	95,031	94359	83540	81071	75186	87831	723498	145506	147498	159845	172192	174423	171855	76989	75992	157,654
Rayalaseema Region	**408,172**	**402,251**	**360,534**	**350,560**	**293,668**	**381,324**	**3,243,014**	**649799**	**604666**	**648188**	**691,709**	**685,827**	**654,519**	**315,159**	**318,563**	**667,197**
Average	**102,043**	**100,563**	**90,134**	**87,640**	**73,417**	**95,331**	**810,754**	**162,450**	**151,167**	**162,047**	**172,927**	**171,457**	**163,630**	**78,790**	**79,641**	**166,799**
MAHBUBNAGAR	101,054	99811	98035	90325	82627	100429	842968	164549	161815	176840	191866	193522	184047	88603	88603	177,673
RANGA REDDY	84,535	84788	74675	72020	68462	77463	925054	147494	155729	163728	171727	182679	179167	66224	66224	167,998
HYDERABAD	48,890	43764	42299	37128	37622	36958	1000943	54870	85063	98142	111222	122137	118890	36196	34196	127,221
MEDAK	76,289	75951	71254	64179	61607	69314	658485	122591	122003	131068	140133	139424	137669	63597	63597	133,144
NIZAMABAD	57,105	56211	53724	4978	49248	56438	593321	86400	96428	101692	106956	110374	108163	46919	46919	104,992
ADILABAD	77,167	76265	74687	66804	60428	71680	660624	110980	111525	118947	126368	124322	116045	61999	61999	127,989
KARIMNAGAR	88,197	87828	81566	77611	73033	83058	937362	149061	136056	144311	152565	169029	163506	73874	71874	165,929
WARANGAL	97,624	101023	98043	81543	74562	90045	751717	145948	140538	153334	166130	1406477	160548	78607	78607	241,650
KHAMMAM	71,145	73580	61278	55211	48090	61871	647931	98874	106331	111671	117012	115931	119297	54059	54059	119,756
NALGONDA	89,229	91440	85590	76188	73627	85507	803108	134040	138559	147421	156283	152326	155884	72232	72232	155,578
Telangana Region	**791,235**	**790,661**	**741,151**	**625,987**	**629,306**	**732,763**	**7,821,513**	**1,214,807**	**1,254,046**	**1,347,154**	**1,440,262**	**2,716,221**	**1,443,216**	**642,310**	**638,310**	**1,521,929**
Average	**79,124**	**79,066**	**74,115**	**62,599**	**62,931**	**73,276**	**782,151**	**121,481**	**125,405**	**134,715**	**144,026**	**271,622**	**144,322**	**64,231**	**63,831**	**152,193**
ANDHRA PRADESH	2,113,756	1,998,969	1,971,482	1,654,234	1,656,965	1,940,896	19,811,929	3,161,472	3,163,202	3,345,002	3,526,802	4,845,885	3,512,108	1,713,159	1,717,563	3,742,228
Average of total AP	**91,902**	**86,912**	**85,717**	**71,923**	**72,042**	**84,387**	**861,388**	**137,455**	**137,531**	**145,435**	**153,339**	**210,691**	**152,700**	**74,485**	**74,677**	**162,706**

Source: Compiled from Statistical Abstract, AP, Directorate of Economics and Statistics, Govt of AP & AP Civil Supplies Department/Corporation, Government of AP.

Distribution of Wheat

An examination of the distribution of wheat, during 1998-99 to 2012-13, reveals that on an average, 1,797 tonnes is distributed to the cardholders in the State. If we share this to the total White cardholders/hhs (22264634), it works out to be eight kgs and 0.66 kgs per cardholder per year and per month. There are variations in the distribution of wheat in different years and among regions and districts. The distribution of wheat during 1998-99 and 1999-2000 was 5851 tonnes and 4377 tonnes, respectively, and it was reduced to 199 tonnes in 2004-05. Subsequent years it was enhanced to around the state average (see Table 4.18). This is mostly due to the policy change in the allotment of foodgrains to different categories/ groups/ institutions. Prior to 1997 the State government used to procure wheat from Central Government for distribution to APL/BPL cardholders, but the government subsequently gave priority to the Subsidised Rice Scheme (SRS) to the target group and social welfare institutions. Region-wise analysis reveals that wheat distribution is more in Telangana region (24382 qls), followed by Rayalaseema (1518 qls) and Andhra regions (1174 qls). The highest allocation is made to the urban districts such as Hyderabad (13,506 tonnes), Rangareddy (4978 tonnes) and Visakhapatnam (3851 tonnes), higher than the State average. The lowest allocation is to the districts such as Nizamabad (417 tonnes), Adilabad (520 tonnes), West Godavari (592 tonnes), East Godavari (696 tonnes) which is less than the State average, (see Table 4.18).

Distribution of Sugar

With regard to the distribution of sugar, during 1998-99 to 2012-13 the data reveals that on an average, 6,578 tonnes is distributed to the cardholders in the State. If we compute this to the total White cardholders/hhs (22264634) in the State, it works out to be 29.54 kgs and 2.5 kgs per cardholder per year and per month. However, there are variations in the distribution of Sugar in different years and among regions and districts. The variations range between 1075 tonnes to 15,399 tonnes in the State. There is considerable decrease in the allocation in the years 2003-04 and 2004-05 (see Table 4.19).

Region-wise analysis reveals that Sugar distribution is more in Andhra region (7,277 tonnes) followed by Rayalaseema region

Ttable . 4.18. Distribution of WHEAT to Ration Card holders (District & year wise) under PDS in UAP during 1998-99 to 2012-13 (Quantity in Metric tonnes)

SL.NO	DISTRICT	1998-99	1999-2000	2000-2001	2001-2002	2002-2003	2003-2004	2004-2005	2005-2006	2006-2007	2007-2008	2008-2009	2009-2010	2010-2011	2011-12	2012-13	AVG
1	SRIKAKULAM	1,352	567	3	9	20	-	-	1,080	1079.682	741	402	816	1230	790	790	683
2	VIZIANAGARAM	1,637	672	278	120	128	257	-	1,135	1135.205	974	813	887	960	1130	1130	804
3	VISAKHAPATNAM	6,111	4,750	426	1,127	1470	1,343	-	6,857	6856.959	4,988	3119	3,710	4300	4430	4430	3,851
4	EAST GODAVARI	2,584	807	54	-	-	-	-		-		-	300	300	760	760	696
5	WEST GODAVARI	1,156	418	36	110	2	-	-	1,085	1085.247	832	579	590	600	600	600	592
6	KRISHNA	2,888	1,698	223	-	311	50	-	2,622	2621.528	1,840	1058	1,109	1160	880	880	1,239
7	GUNTUR	2,852	1,945	23	212	-	84	52.99	1,291	2529.68	1,815	1100	1,030	960	640	640	1,084
8	PRAKASAM	1,572	797	126	73	18	2	-	1,379	1379.358	990	600	785	970	480	480	689
9	NELLORE	1,853	1,108	117	83	17	-	-	2,128	2127.516	1,427	726	783	840	419.6	419.6	927
	Andhra Region	**22,005**	**12,762**	**1286**	**1,734**	**1966**	**1,736**	**52.99**	**17,577**	**18815.175**	**13,606**	**8397**	**10,009**	**11320**	**10129.6**	**10129.6**	**9435**
	Average	**2,445**	**1,418**	**143**	**193**	**281**	**347**	**53**	**2,197**	**2,352**	**1,701**	**1,050**	**1,112**	**1,258**	**1,126**	**1,126**	**1,174**
10	CHITTOOR	3,612	1,380	639	317	18	559	12.271	1,009	2004.772	1,625	1245	1,925	2604	2864.3	2864.3	1512
11	CUDDAPAH	1,336	1,049	135	557	210	16	-	1,984	1983.666	1,574	1164	1,732	2300	1746	1746	1252
12	ANANTAPUR	6,420	4,250	58	-	340	347	-	2,790	2789.81	2,062	1335	1,388	1440	2140	2140	1964
13	KURNOOL	3,212	1,927	147	289	382	6	-	2,307	2306.589	1,578	849	1,478	2106	1103.4	1103.4	1342
	Rayalaseema Region	**14,580**	**8,606**	**979**	**1,163**	**950**	**928**	**12.271**	**8,089**	**9084.837**	**6,839**	**4593**	**6,522**	**8450**	**7853.7**	**7853.7**	**5767**
	Average	**3,645**	**2,152**	**245**	**291**	**238**	**232**	**12**	**2,022**	**2,271**	**1,710**	**1,148**	**1,630**	**2,113**	**1,963**	**1,963**	**1,518**
14	MAHBUBNAGAR	3,706	2,184	167	155	23	218	-	1,759	1758.725	1,385	1012	956	900	1197.4	1197.4	1187
15	RANGA REDDY	15,082	14,944	1089	1,397	848	1,388	32.5	2,903	5773.745	4,526	3278	5,671	8064	4834.1	4834.1	4978
16	HYDERABAD	57,867	50,676	2752	3,633	4088	6,862	1444.98	6,674	11903.526	9,712	7520	8,920	10320	10109.9	10109.9	13506
17	MEDAK	4,267	2,446	96	24	1	530	67.6	446	824.957	725	625	1,223	1820	843	843	985
18	NIZAMABAD	3,545	1,691	160	4	-	200	41.55	23	4.245	16	28	29	30	30	30	417
19	ADILABAD	1,780	1,252	21	-	5	25	10.51	260	509.786	555	600	660	720	703.7	703.7	520
20	KARIMNAGAR	2,695	1,249	56	50	-	-	0.2	792	1582.928	1,084	585	593	600	450	450	784
21	WARANGAL	3,980	1,957	185	127	1	461	128.336	839	1549.292	990	430	813	1196	650	650	930
22	KHAMMAM	2,196	1,297	173	6	37	151	-	1,188	1188.154	807	426	573	720	720	720	729
23	NALGONDA	2,875	1,610	127	46	156	138	-	224	223.582	127	30	700	1369	730	730	649
	Telangana Region	**97,993**	**79,306**	**4826**	**5,442**	**5159**	**9,973**	**1725.676**	**15,108**	**25318.94**	**19,926**	**14534**	**20,137**	**25739**	**20268.1**	**20268.1**	**24382**
	Average	**9,799**	**7,931**	**483**	**544**	**645**	**1,108**	**247**	**1,511**	**2,532**	**1,993**	**1,453**	**2,014**	**2,574**	**2,027**	**2,027**	**2,468**
	ANDHRA PRADESH	**134,578**	**100,674**	**7091**	**8,339**	**8075**	**12,637**	**1790.937**	**40,773**	**53218.952**	**40,371**	**27524**	**20,137**	**45509**	**38251.4**	**38251.4**	38,481
	Average of total AP	**5,851**	**4,377**	**308**	**363**	**425**	**702**	**199**	**1,853**	**2,419**	**1,835**	**1,251**	**1,594**	**1,979**	**1,663**	**1,663**	**1,797**

Source: Compiled from Statistical Abstract, AP, Directorate of Economics and Statistics, Govt of AP & AP Civil Supplies Department/Corporation, Government of AP.

Table . 4.19. Distribution of Sugar to ration card holders (District & year wise) under PDS in UAP during 1998-99 to 2012-13 (Quantity in Metric tonnes)

DISTRICT	1998-99	1999-2000	2000-2001	2001-2002	2002-2003	2003-2004	2004-2005	2005-2006	2006-2007	2007-2008	2008-2009	2009-2010	2010-2011	2011-12	2012-13	AVG
SRIKAKULAM	9,503	10,236	11154	6,298	5196	1,716	500	3,063	5626.773	6,149	6671	2,858	4493	3884.6	4684.5	5,469
VIZIANAGARAM	9,705	9,630	9512	4,506	3656	722	407.793	2,640	4871.367	5,133	5394	2,966	3948	3457.8	4107.4	4,710
VISAKHAPATNAM	17,206	18,001	14774	7,156	6116	3,362	2700	5,018	7336.159	8,338	9339	5,547	6475	5855.8	6817.7	8,269
EAST GODAVARI	21,892	22,772	23664	8,650	6731	1,603	203.522	4,204	8205.073	8,403	8600	5,709	8560	7897.9	8833.3	9,729
WEST GODAVARI	18,948	18,620	22138	6,573	6869	2,110	410	4,263	8116.717	8,861	9606	5,384	6594	6114.9	6819.4	8,762
KRISHNA	18,991	19,032	18653	6,150	6480	1,741	640	3,949	7258.222	7,698	8137	5,901	7021	6435.1	7485.9	8,371
GUNTUR	20,469	18,997	18312	9,016	5179	1,050	2560.016	5,470	8379.26	8,160	7941	6,729	7379	7352	8331.3	9,021
PRAKASAM	12,582	12,253	11439	5,118	3889	378	1724.987	3,361	4996.288	4,753	4510	4,251	4874	4599.1	5554.9	5,619
NELLORE	13,019	12,830	11143	5,022	3645	1,174	999.968	3,139	5278.837	4,916	4553	3,797	4488	4263.3	4835.8	5,540
Andhra Region	**142,315**	**142,371**	**140789**	**58,489**	**47761**	**13,856**	**10146.286**	**35,107**	**60069**	**62,410**	**64751**	**43,132**	**53832**	**49860.5**	**57470.2**	**65,491**
Average	**15,813**	**15,819**	**15,643**	**6,499**	**5,307**	**1,540**	**1,127**	**3,901**	**6,674**	**6,934**	**7,195**	**4,792**	**5,981**	**5,540**	**6,386**	**7,277**
CHITTOOR	16,799	15,685	16163	6,030	4798	1,410	1298.525	3,500	5700.854	5,785	5870	4,973	5742	5353.9	6645	7,050
CUDDAPAH	11,904	11,842	11575	5,324	3733	399	1770	3,576	5382.686	5,292	5202	3,515	3989	3893.6	4726.2	5,475
ANANTAPUR	15,572	14,732	13833	7,678	5446	1,091	2780	4,246	5712.32	5,232	4752	5,923	6600	5913.5	6673.9	7,079
KURNOOL	13,108	13,047	12126	5,456	4007	314	1230	2,800	4370.562	3,950	3530	4,576	5272	4739.6	6316.1	5,656
Rayalaseema Region	**57,383**	**55,306**	**53697**	**24,488**	**17984**	**3,214**	**7078.525**	**14,122**	**21166**	**20,260**	**19354**	**18,987**	**21603**	**19500.6**	**24361.2**	**25,260**
Average	**14,346**	**13,827**	**13,424**	**6,122**	**4,496**	**804**	**1,770**	**3,531**	**5,292**	**5,065**	**4,839**	**4,747**	**5,401**	**4,975**	**6,090**	**6,315**
MAHBUBNAGAR	13,768	13,050	12595	4,919	2631	273	1007.273	2,321	3635.089	3,695	3754	4,460	6013	5029	6566.6	5,581
RANGA REDDY	18,555	18,656	16695	3,677	3893	1,081	2812.181	4,107	5401.528	5,578	5755	6,736	5837	5890.9	6729.2	7,427
HYDERABAD	36,769	35,650	30728	1,860	1714	509	5576.413	4,300	3023.073	3,809	4595	7,023	3579	3766.3	4479.9	9,825
MEDAK	10,124	9,530	13486	5,093	3010	855	890	2,323	3755.056	3,887	4019	3,628	4242	3871.3	4449.8	4,878
NIZAMABAD	11,624	11,612	18238	3,904	2337	257	500	1,701	2902.78	2,757	2611	2,715	3513	3363.4	4096.8	4,809
ADILABAD	9,654	9,672	9908	4,630	3755	589	284.732	2,199	4113.134	4,041	3968	2,906	3893	3273.8	3783.7	4,445
KARIMNAGAR	15,853	16,582	16628	6,303	4309	841	1122.394	3,272	5422.013	4,811	4199	3,831	5447	5111	5283.7	6,601
WARANGAL	14,210	14,641	12120	5,379	3088	456	1570	3,195	4820.135	4,657	4494	4,206	5548	4762.5	5686.6	5,922
KHAMMAM	10,702	10,575	10155	6,806	3594	1,322	700	2,716	4732.157	4,758	4784	3,883	3755	4057.5	4612.9	5,144
NALGONDA	13,227	12,664	11052	5,769	4652	1,478	762	2,952	5142.48	5,294	5446	3,851	5608	4853.1	5991.2	5,916
Telangana Region	**154,486**	**152,632**	**151605**	**48,340**	**32983**	**7,661**	**15225**	**29086**	**42947**	**43,286**	**43625**	**43,239**	**47435**	**43978.8**	**51680.4**	**60,547**
Average	**15,449**	**15,263**	**15,161**	**4,834**	**3,298**	**766**	**1,522**	**2,909**	**4,295**	**4,329**	**4,363**	**4,324**	**4,744**	**4,398**	**5,168**	**6,055**
ANDHRA PRADESH	**354,184**	**350,309**	**346091**	**131,317**	**98728**	**24,731**	**32450**	**78316**	**124183**	**125,956**	**127729**	**105,358**	**122870**	**113739.9**	**133511.8**	**151,298**
Average of total AP	**15,399**	**15,231**	**15,047**	**5,709**	**4,293**	**1,075**	**1,411**	**3,405**	**5,399**	**5,476**	**5,553**	**4,581**	**5,342**	**4,945**	**5,805**	**6,578**

Source: Complied from Statistical Abstract, AP, Directorate of Economics and Statistics, Govt of AP & AP Civil Supplies Department/Corporation, Government of AP.

(6,315 tonnes) and Telangana region (6,055) tonnes. The districts, which received sugar higher than the State average, are East Godavari (9,729 tonnes), Guntur (9,021 tonnes), West Godavari (8,762 tonnes), Krishna (8,371 tonnes) and Visakhapatnam (8,269 tonnes) in Andhra region. Anantapur (7079 tonnes) and Chittur (7,050 tonnes) in Rayalasemma region: and Hyderabad (9,825 tonnes), Rangareddy (7427 tonnes) and Karimnagar (6,601 tonnes) in Telangana region (see Table 4.19).

The districts which received less than the State average are: Adilabad (4,445 tonnes), Nizamabad (4,809 tonnes), Medak (4,878 tonnes), Khammam (5,144 tonnes), Mahabubnagar (5,581 tonnes), Nalgonda (5,916 tonnes) and Warangal (5,922 tonnes) in Telangana region; Vizianagaram (4,710 tonnes), Srikakulam (5,469 tonnes), Nellore (5,540 tonnes) and Prakasam (5,619 tonnes) in Andhra region; and Cuddapah (5,475 tonnes) and Kurnool (5,656 tonnes) (see Table 4.19).

Summing Up

The Andhra Pradesh consists of three regions-Andhra, Rayalaseema and Telangana- and they vary in terms of physical and human resources and socio-economic conditions of people. The Andhra region has better endowed resources compared to other two regions. The State is predominantly agricultural with two-thirds of its work force engaged directly in agricultural sector. The land inequalities exist in the State. The average size of land holdings, in 2010-11, is 1.08 hectares, which is unviable to generate adequate employment and income to the HH, especially in the backward regions of the State. However, agriculture sector over the decades is transforming from traditional cereal-based system towards commercial commodities- such as cotton, chilly, oil seeds, sugarcane - and high value commodities – such as fruits, vegetables, milk, meat, and poultry. The work force is gradually shifting from agriculture sector to non-agriculture sector and people are migrating to urban areas in search of livelihood and services. Further, agricultural land is diverted for non-agricultural purposes, particularly during the post-economic reforms period. The State has acquired the character of being one of the leading States in promoting service sector-IT sector- and creating employment opportunities to the skilled workforce. Though State reflects the conditions prevailing elsewhere in India at the macro level with large stocks of surplus foodgrains production, its availability is not adequate in all the districts. The State also has a large tribal population and drought-prone areas within the districts. The unemployment and poverty is more in these areas.

An examination of cultivable area and agricultural production in the State reveals that though the cultivable area is declining, there is four-fold increase in foodgrains production i.e. from 55.33 lakh tonnes in 1955-56 to 204.21 lakh tonnes in 2008-09. In comparison to all India level, its share is about eight per cent of the total production in the country. This is mostly due to the adoption of modern technology in the agriculture sector. An examination of area under foodgrains over the decades reveals that it has declined from an average of over eight million hectares during 1960s to an average over seven million hectares in the decade 2001-200. Growth continued to decelerate, especially during the decade of 1991-2010, the economic reforms period. During this period, the State has given priority to the IT, service sector, and added to it agricultural land is diverted to non-agricultural purposes. The analysis also reveals that the regional imbalances in terms of area under production (deceleration in area under foodgrains is more in Rayalaseema region, followed by Telangana region) are continued for the past four decades in the State.

The output of foodgrains recorded an increase during all the past six decades in the State as it grew from an average of 5.8 million tonnes prior to 1960 to over 16.1 million tonnes in the decade of 2001-2011. The growth rate has been positive and around 20 per cent during all the decades. This is mostly due to adoption of modern technology in the agriculture sector. However, there are regional variations in the output particularly Rayalaseema experienced negative growth rate in most of the decades.

The analysis indicates that multiple players- Central, and State governments, traders/millers, transporters, SHGs/NGOs are involved in the procurement of foodgrains-paddy and rice. The State government is gearing its administrative machinery for decentralised procurement partly due to the Central Government decision to procure only

25 per cent of requirement and partly to give priority to Mana Biyyam Manakosam (Our Rice for Our Purpose) policy and provide remunerative price to the farmers and delivery of foodgrains to the beneficiaries. The Central Government is also insisting on the decentralised procurement to reduce its burden on subsidy on procurement of paddy and rice.

An examination of the procurement of rice during 1996-97 to 2011-12 unfolds that an average the State government is procuring 6398798 Metric tonnes of rice through different agencies for distribution to the target groups and welfare institutions. The analysis also reveals that the average procurement of rice per card HH per year and per month is 254 kgs and 21 kgs, respectively. This works out to be 5 kgs of rice per person in the HH (the average size of the family, according to 2011 census, in the State is 4) and it is hardly sufficient to meet the 10 days requirement and the remaining days (20) the individual/family has to depend on the open market, where the price of the rice is beyond the reach of a common man. However, there are variations in procurement of rice among the regions and districts, indicating the disparities in the State.

The analysis reveals that procurement of paddy and rice under levy system either under centralised or decentralised system is subjected to several problems, which seriously affect the food security policies in the State. The major concerns of the governance are: no scientific method and delay in fixing the price for the products; no logical/precise method in fixing the targets per district/mandal/mill/trader by the administration; favouring or disfavouring the traders in releasing certificates/permission letter to traders to sell the rice in the open market; harassing the traders for non-compliance of documents for verification; non-conformity of administrative procedures with legal regulations; taking the advantage of the provision i.e. exemption of levy of rice to the farmers for own consumption (rice traders/millers are claiming that they are farmers while selling the rice in the open market or exporting to other states and escaping from the levy of rice); fixing the price of the levy rice lower than the market price; unhealthy competition between the big firm traders and small firm traders and the former make use all the provisions which are advantages of the policy with the support of the officials; delay in the issue of voucher and transport permission to the traders by the officials for selling the rice in the open market or export it; frequent transfers of officials, specially the district officials who play crucial role in solving the issues involved in the levy system; lack of coordination between the government departments or overlap in the activities as several departments are involved in the task; pressure from the officials to get posting in the levy enforce wing/department as it is a lucrative opportunity; politicians pressure on the enforcing authorities for mobilisation of funds for elections; occasional threats from the media for money for not exposing the offenses committed by the officials, etc; promoting PPP mode for construction of godowns for storage of foodgrains. All these factors are collectively or individually influencing the functioning the governance of food security policies in the State.

The millers/traders viewpoint is that paying bribes to officials/ politicians at various levels is costing nearly Rs twenty to thirty thousand per miller/trader per year. They also classified the bribing system as annual, seasonal and occasional. The government departments connected to this process include: revenue, civil supplies, pollution control board, labour, factories, commercial tax office, road transport authority (check posts), electricity board, police and the political executives starting from Gram Panchayat to Minister of the State. This is the common feature in all the regimes in the State. It is impossible to run the business without giving bribe to the officials and politicians and others, they maintained.

Thus, the enforcing authority and rice millers/traders collectively are defeating the very purpose of levy system. The enforcing authority interest in procurement of rice is to legitimize its responsibility and partly for personal benefits, while the traders/millers interest in free market is for earning more profits. However, both the parties manipulate or violate official rule system in order to get more benefits out of them. How to reconcile the interests of these groups is the major challenge of food security programmes in the State. The organisational structures and the functionaries have failed to alter the prevailing situation in the civil supplies department and on the other hand, they succumbed to the existing socio-economic systems i.e. powerful trade/ millers and political set up.

The analysis indicates that the supply of SRS to the poor was (commenced 1983) nearly one and a half decades ahead of other States (commenced from 1997) and became a model State for others in the country. Since three decades, the SRS has become an electoral promise and a 'vote security scheme' for political parties in the State. In fact, a regional political party- TDP came into power by overthrowing the National political party, which ruled the State for several decades in the State. Every successive government has reformed/altered or floated the norms of SRS (eligibility criterion for identification of target groups and supply of quantity of foodgrains to cardholders, etc) either before the State Assembly elections or on the first day or immediately after taking charge of the government. Recently both State Governments - Telangana and AP- are trying to introduce new schemes such as opening food centres for supply of cooked food to the poor at subsidised rate, especially in the urban areas. All these efforts of the government appear to be to divert the attention of poor on the real problems-unemployment, poverty and inequalities in the society.

The most pertinent observation in this study is that despite the decrease in the per centage of poverty decade after decade in the State (poverty in 2004-05 was 30.01 percent and it reduced to 9.27 per cent in 2011-12), the percentage of ration cards granted to the HHs are strangely increased from 69.5 per cent in 2001 to 105 per cent in 2011 of the total HHs. The percentage of HHs obtained White ration cards, during the same period, has increased enormously from 99 per cent to 119 per cent of the total HHs in the State. These trends indicate that a large number of ration cards are bogus and the governance has failed to control the malpractices. Further, it is clearly indicating that SRS has become political commodity for the ruling class and profitable venture for traders/millers, FPS dealers, bureaucracy and non-poor in the State.

The analysis confirm the fact that food security policies are only incremental in nature as the distribution of foodgrains per cardholder per year, per month and per person of the cardholder HH is 141.86 kgs, 11.82 kgs and 2.95 kgs, respectively. The foodgrains supplied under TPDS is sufficient for six days (20 per cent of the requirement) in a month and for the remaining 24 days (80 per cent), they have to depend on the open market, where the cost of the foodgrain price is beyond the reach of poor. Thus, SRS has not made significant positive impact on the food security of the poor.

References

Dutta, B and Ramaswamy (2001): Targeting and Efficiency in Public Distribution of System: the Case of Andhra Pradesh and Maharashtra', *Economic and Political Weekly, 36.*

Gajendra Singh, and Boghal, TS, (2006): 'Food Security: Key Issues and Strategies for Andhra Pradesh', *The Asian Economic Review*, Journal of Indian Institute of Economics, Hyderabad, no. 48.

G.O. Ms. No. 470, dated 10.11.1995; G.O. Ms. No. 495, dated 16.12.1995 and vide G.O. No.54 dated 10.08.2004, Food & Civil Supplies (CS-IV) Department).

G.O. Ms.No. 24 CA, F & CS (CS.I) Dept. dt. 3.10.2011. Food & Civil Supplies (CS-IV) Department).

Indrakanth, S (1992): 'Public Distribution System in Andhra Pradesh' with Special Reference to Rice', *Indian Journal of Economics* 72 (286).

———— (1997): 'Coverage and Leakeges in PDS in Andhra Pradesh', *Economic and Political Weekly, 32.*

———— (2000): 'Food Security and Public Support: a Study of Andhra Pradesh' in N. Krishnaji and TN Krishna (ed) Public Support for Food Security, Sage Publication, New Delhi.

Indrakanth, S and Harikishan (2003): 'Food Security in Andhra Pradesh in Retrospective and Prospective in Mahendra Dev , S, Kannaan KP and Nira Ramchandran (ed), Towards Food Secure India, Issues and Policies, Manohar Publications, New Delhi.

Krishna Rao, IYR, (1993): 'Andhra Pradesh; An Experiment in Food Security' *Economic and Political Weekly*, 28.

Lr.No. 16(13)/2010-Py.I dated 9.8.2012 of the Joint Director, Movement, Dept. of Food and Public Distribution, *Ministry of Consumer Affairs, Food and Public Distribution,* New Delhi.

Lr.No.16 (13)/2010 – PY.I dated 20.9.2012 of the Dept. of Food and Public Distribution, *Ministry of Consumer Affairs, Food and Public Distribution,* New Delhi.

Lr.No.16 (13)/2010 – PY.I dated 26.9.2012 of the Dept. of Food and Public Distribution, *Ministry of Consumer Affairs, Food and Public Distribution,* New Delhi.

Olsen, WK, (1989): 'Eat Now, Pay Later, Impact of 2/kg Scheme' *Economic and Political Weekly*, 24.

Pardhasardhy, G, (1995): 'Public Intervention and Rural poverty: Case of Non Sustainable Reduction in Andhra Pradesh, *Economic and Political Weekly,* 30.

Parthasarathy, G and Nirmala KA (1997): 'Lakadawala Estimate of poverty and targeted PDS- Injustice to Andhra Pradesh, *Economic and Political Weekly,* 32, no. 16.

Radhakrishna, R, (2005), 'Food and Nutrition Security of the Poor- Emerging Perspectives and Policy Issues', *Economic and Political Weekly,* April 30, pp. 1817-1821.

Radhakrishna, R and S. Indrakanth (1987): 'Effects of Rice Market Inervention Policies in India, The Case Study of Andhra Pradesh' in JK Johnson (ed) Evaluation of Rice Market Intervention Policies: Some Asian Examples (Manala, Asian Development Bank).

Radhakrishna, R and Indrakanth, S (1991): 'Foodgrain Sector: Growth, Equity and Market intervention', in MV Nadkarni, AS Seetaramulu and Abudul Aziz (ed), *India: the Emerging Challenges,* Sage publications, New Delhi.

Radhakrishna, R and Hanumantha Rao, K (1994): 'Food Security, Public Distribution and Price Policy', Centre for Economic and Social Studies, *Working paper, 26*, Hyderabad.

Radhakrishna, R, Subba Rao, K, S. Indrakanth and Ravi, C (1997): 'India's Public Distribution System: A National and International Perspective', *World Bank Discussion Paper* no. 380, (Washington DC- The World Bank).

Sambi Reddy, B (2004): 'Food Security in Regional Perspective: The Case of Andhra Pradesh' *Journal of Rural Development*, National Institute of Rural Development, Hyderabad.

Sreenivas, M, 2012, 23rd October, *Eenadu,* Hyderabad edition.

Sreenivas, M 2013, 1st August, *Eenadu,* Hyderabad edition.

Surjit Deb (2009): 'Public Distribution of Rice in Andhra Pradesh': Efficiency and Reform Options, *Economic and Political Weekly,* Vol. 44, No. 51, December.

The Consumer Affairs, Food and Civil Supplies Department, Andhra Pradesh, Hyderabad on 1st June 2009 Material submitted to Justice Wadwa Committee.

The A.P. Rice Procurement (Levy) Order, 1984 issued in G.O. Ms. No. 28, F and A (CS.I) Dept., dt. 25-1-1984.

Venugopal, KR, (1992): 'Deliverance from Hunger: the Public Distribution System in India', Sage publications, New Delhi.

World Bank (1997): 'India, Andhra Pradesh: Agenda, Economic Reforms, Report no. 15901-In (Washington DC- Industry and Finance Division (South Asian Region).

Chapter - V

Governance of PDS in Nalgonda District

For a proper understanding of the administrative behaviour and its performance, it is necessary to know the environmental factors like the people, place, socio-economic structure etc., for they considerably influence the administrative structure and process (Riggs, F.W. 1961). Rigs observe that the ecology of organisation/administration is as much a limiting factor as is the ecology of biological species. The interaction between the environment and administration is very relevant at the lower levels as it would enable us to understand the dynamics that influence the process of governance. In this context, the brief profile of the Nalgonda district and villages under study is presented. The attempt has twin objectives; one, to give a descriptive sketch of the ecology the influence of which can be perceived throughout the study; two, to examine the impact of some of the ecological variables on the working of the civil supplies department/corporation as experienced in the implementation of PDS.

Section- I

Profile of the Study Area

Nalgonda is predominantly an agricultural district of Telangana State. As per 2011 Census, an overwhelming percentage (81.1 per cent) of people live in the rural areas, while nearly one fourth of people (18.9 per cent) live in the urban areas. The total population of the district, as per 2011 Census, is 3488809 of which male and female account for 50.44 per cent (17, 59,772) and 49.56 per cent (17, 29,037), respectively. The population growth rate is declining over the decade of 2001 to 2011 (13.88 per cent in 2001 and 7.4 per cent in 2011). However, the density of population has increased from 228 in 2001 per sq.km. to 245 per sq.km. in 2011. This is less than the state average i.e., 275. The average literacy rate of the district is 64.20 per cent, which is less than the state average i.e., 67.66 per cent in 2011. The district rank, in this regard, is 13 of 23 districts. The literacy rate among the male is more (74.10 per cent) compared to female (54.9 per cent) indicating the discrimination to the female literacy. It is also evident from the fact that the district has a sex ratio of 982 females for every 1000 males.

The geographical area of the district is 1424000 hectares. For the purpose of administrative convenience, the district is divided into five revenue divisions (viz., Nalgonda, Suryapet, Miryalguda, Bhuvnagiri and Devarakonda), 59 mandals; 20 towns; 1161 revenue villages; and 1178 gram panchayats. The land utilisation of the district reveals that 46.78 per cent the total geographical area is under cultivation. The area sown more than once, as per 2010-2011 Agricultural Censuses, is 14.4 of the total geographical area, indicating the backwardness of the district.

Nearly half of the geographical area is uncultivated (fallow lands, cultivate wastelands). The land put to non-agricultural purpose is 8.9 per cent of the geographical area. An insignificant percentage of geographical area is under forest (i.e., 5.86 per cent). The nature of land is loamy stands (dubba) and red soil, which are unfertile. The fertile black cotton soil forms only nine per cent of geographical area. The average rainfall of the district is 752 mm, which is less than state average i.e., 940 mm. Though the rivers Krishna, Musi, Aleru, Peddavagu, Dindi and Paleru flow through Nalgonda district, only few mandals – Myriyalaguda, Huzurnagar, Kodad have assured irrigation facilities, while other mandals have to depend on monsoon, which is scanty and irregular, for cultivation in the district. The major crops grown in the district are paddy, pulses, millets, oil seeds and mousambi (lime fruit). The per capita income of the individual in the district in 2008-09 is Rs 46345, which equals to the State average. However, during 1999-2000 to 2007-08 it is less than state average. The increase is mostly due to the expansion of service sector and infrastructural facilities in urbanisation areas, especially surrounding areas of State Capital.

The economy of Nalgonda district indicates that it is one of the most backward districts of the state both in unified Andhra Pradesh and Telangana State. It is the country's 250 poorest districts, out of 640 districts (Government of India, Ministry of PR, Sept. 8, 2009 – A note on the BRGFP). The district is covered under BRGF – Centrally sponsored scheme – since 2006. All the mandals, except a few are declared as drought prone areas. Due to drought, poor peasants and agricultural labourers, who belong to the backward and less developed mandals, migrate to the developed blocks or to the cities in search of livelihood opportunities. Large-scale migration is observed during the agricultural operation period. The total landholdings (2010-11) in the district are 757188 accounting 904256.01 hectares and the average size of the land is 1.19 hectares, which is slightly higher than the State average i.e. 1.08 hectares. The analysis reveals that the marginal farmers and small farmers though possess for 58 per cent and 25 per cent of the total holdings, they account for 23 per cent and 30 per cent of the total land, respectively.

As mentioned earlier, from each revenue division one mandal is selected i.e., Aleru, Chityal, Gurampode, Munagala and Kodad for the study. These mandals have certain common features and variations in terms of population, rural-urban matrix, landholding pattern etc., of the five mandals, three are rural and backward (Aleru, Gurrampodu, Munagala) while the other two (Chityal and Kodad) are relatively better off and possess urban characteristics. The average geographical area of the mandals is 24135.6 hectares, with an average population of 59044. Except Kodad mandal, the average rainfall of mandals is less than the district average. There are variations in the irrigated area, net area irrigated, area irrigated more than once and the productivity across the mandals. The area irrigated more than once in Kodad is (7342 hectares), which is quite high (more than three times) to the district average (2293 hectares). The situation in other four mandals is below the district average. With regard to the gross irrigated area and net irrigated area, similar situation is prevailing in all the mandals. Area under the principal crop i.e., paddy in the four mandals is quite low to the district average (5266 hectares). These trends indicate that except Kodad mandal all the other mandals are backward in terms of cultivable area and food-grain production. However, the Chitiyal mandal geographically is close to Hyderabad.

Unlike Kodad, in all other mandals the farmers grow jowar, bajra, maize, groundnut, green-gram, and red-gram. Nevertheless, the productivity of these crops is not high, as the farmers, especially marginal and small farmers depend on the traditional seeds even to date. The raising of commercial crops especially chillies, cotton is also very less in the district and mandals compared to other districts/ mandals in the State. The average size of landholdings in the district is 1.41 hectares. In the case of selected mandals, the land holding size in three mandals is very small and unviable per a family to depend on agriculture.

The characteristics of the district and mandals, under study reveal that the district and mandals (except Kodad mandal) they are subjected to drought and productivity of the land is also very low. The land is also concentrated in the hands of a few and the land holding size of the marginal and small farmers is unviable to generate adequate employment, foodgrains and income to the household members. Further, clean drinking water supply to the people is the most important challenge of district administration. Of the 1178 gram panchayats, nearly 500 villages in the district are affected by the high fluorine content in water. It is estimated that nearly one million people are affected by fluoridise in the district. This causes health-hazardous to the people and many young people are subjected to serious health problems, especially belong to the poor households.

All these trends call for launching of public policies for ensuring food security, including supply of safe drinking water to the people. The Government of India and State Government have launched several policies/programmes for this purpose (the details are discussed in the Chapter-II). In order to understand the governance of the food security programmes and their impact on the living conditions of the poor, an in-depth study is undertaken in five villages, selecting one village from each selected mandals, are selected. The villages are Gundala-gudem (Aleru mandal), Urumadla (Chityal mandal), Thenarpally (Gurrampodu mandal), Kokkirani (Mungaala mandal) and Gudibanda (Kodad

Mandal). These villages are selected by giving weightage to the size of population, proximity to the mandal headquarters, literacy rate and number of social security schemes, etc. The detailed data is collected on physical and social capital infrastructure, sources of drinking water and sanction facilities, land utilisation, crop cultivation, services available, marketing services etc.

The villages under study possess certain representative characteristics of the region in social, economic and political aspects. Socially they are multi-caste and multi-religion villages representing most of major castes and religions. Most of people in these villages depend on agriculture. However, the youth in the backward mandals are taking up non-agricultural jobs and supporting the family income. All the political parties are very active and elite of the villagers are affiliated to one or the other political parties. Thus, the households of the villages are neither too small, where the phenomena cannot be studied in all its dimensions, nor is it too big and unwieldy for an individual investigator to work. The household is number ranging from 836 to 1071 of the villages. In each village, the social security schemes such as old-age pensions, widow pensioners, PHC beneficiary's, mid-day meal beneficiaries, Anganwadi centres, assistance to freedom fighters etc, are in operation.

The crops raised in the villages are paddy, red-gram and vegetables. The farmers, in the recent past, are raising the commercial crops- cotton crop. The farmers, except in Kodad, depend on bore-well for irrigation purposes. However, there are some variations between villages, especially in the access to physical and social capital infrastructure (schools, hospitals/medical facilities) and drinking water and sanitation facilities, transport and marketing services. Except Gudibanda (two FPSs), each village has one fair price shop (FPS). The number of ration cards – BPL, Annapurna, AAP, and APL also vary from village to village. A detailed survey of these villages on the implementation of PDS would provide deeper insight into the phenomena. For this purpose 100 respondents (20 respondents from each village), Six FPS dealers are selected and administered a structured questionnaire. The data is also collected through informal discussions with elite of the villages and the officials concerned.

Section-II

Area under Foodgrains and Output in the District

Here an attempt is made to present the area of production and output, during the past five decades in the district. An examination of Area under Foodgrains indicates that there is declined trend from an average of over 614286 hectares, during the 1960's, to an average over 33887 hectares in the decade (2011-2012). Area of foodgrains is also declined during all the decades with the most declines being observed during the decade of 1991-2010 (-23.49 per cent), followed by the decade of 1981-1991 (-1648 per cent). This is mostly due to the economic reforms giving priority to information technology and service sectors and diversion of agricultural land for non-agricultural purposes in the State (see Table 5.1).

Table 5.1: Area of Foodgrain Crops and Output of Foodgrains in Nalgonda District during 1955-2011-12

	Nalgonda District				*Andhra Pradesh State*			
	Area of foodgrain crops (in Hectares)		*Output of Foodgrains (in Metric tonnes)*		*Area of foodgrain crops (in Hectares)*		*Output of Foodgrains (in Metric tonnes)*	
Year/Decade	*Actual*	*Per cent*	*Actual*	*Per cent*	*Actual*	*Per cent*	*Actual*	*Per cent*
Prior to 1960	578042	NA	259574	N.A	8838733	N.A	5802169	NA
1961-1970	614286	6.27	319330	23.0	9147064	3.5	6710378	15.65
1971-80	610081	-0.68	487157	52.6	9051577	-1.0	8480696	26.38
1981-90	509567	-16.48	651934	33.8	8220207	-9.2	10971153	29.37
1991-2000	389865	-23.49	732131	12.3	7109234	-13.5	12745646	16.17
2001-2010	375978	-3.56	852530	16.4	7038575	-1.0	16134044	26.58
2011-12	33887		973281					

Source: Compiled from Statistical Abstract, AP, Directorate of Economics and Statistics, Govt of AP & AP Civil Supplies Department/Corporation, Government of AP.

With regard to output of foodgrains the district has experienced high growth rate in all the decades and it grew from an average of 3,19,330 tonnes recorded during the decade 1961-70 to over 8,52,530 tonnes in the decade of 2001-2010. The growth rate was very high during 1971-80 (52.6 per cent) and 1991-2000 (33.8 per cent) periods. There is four-fold increase in the Production i.e. from 259574 tonnes during 1955-56 to 1960 to 852530 tonnes in 2001-2010 decade in the district. The growth rate is more than the region and state average (see Table 5.1). It is pertinent to note that though there is decline in the area under food grain, the output of foodgrains has increased considerably. This is mostly due to the adoption of modern technology in the agriculture sector.

Per capita Availability of Foodgrains

An examination of the per capita availability of foodgrains to the population in different decades (1961 to 2011, except 1971 and 2001 decades) reveals that it is more than the 260 kgs per year in the district. This works out to be more than 20 kgs per month per individual in the district (state average is 16.6 kgs). It is highest in 2011 i.e. 396.37 kgs and 33 kgs per year and per month respectively. It is lowest during the decades of 1971 and 2001 (see Table 5.2).

Table 5.2: The Population, Production, and Per capita Availability of Foodgrain in Nalgonda District

Year/ Decade	*Population (In persons)*	*Foodgrains production (in lakh tonnes)*	*Per capita availability of foodgrains per year (in kgs)*	*Per capita availability of foodgrains per month (in kgs)*
1971	1819738	358221	197.00	16.41
1981	2279685	593197	260.21	21.68
1991	2852092	740592	259.66	21.63
2001	3245400	640414	197.32	16.44
2011	3483648	1380821	396.37	33.00

Source: Annual Report, Ministry of Agriculture, Government of AP and compilation from *Season and Crop reports, Govt of Andhra Pradesh.*

The Procurement of Rice

The analysis indicate that the Civil Supplies Corporation, during the past three decades (1983-84 to 2013-14), on an average, procure 26,87,397 Metric tonnes of rice for distribution to the ration card holders and other target groups/ institutions, in the district. However, there are variations in the procurement of rice in different decades. The analysis unfolds that the procurement of rice is more during 2001-02 to 2010-11 (6639042 Metric tonnes) (see Table 5.3).

Table 5.3. Procurement of Rice from 1983-2013-14 (Metric tonnes)

Year/ Decade	*District*	*Telangana region*	*State*
1983-84 to 1989-90	1361870	6049110	19098706
1990-91 to 2000-01	1073416	13145532	41526286
2001-02 to 2010-11	6639042	23592053	51436882
2011-12 to 2013-14	1675260	6134128	14211940
Total	10749588	48920823	126273814
Average of the all decades	26,87,397	1,22,30,206	3,15,68,454

Source: Annual Report, Ministry of Agriculture, Government of AP and compilation from *Season and Crop reports, Govt of Andhra Pradesh.*

Distribution of Fair Price Shops and Ration Cards and Percentage of Households Possessing Cards in 2001 and 2011

The population according to 2001 and 2011 census was 3245400 and 3483648 respectively, and number of households during the same period was 723015 and 87539, respectively, in the district. Similarly, the number of FPSs were 1801in 2001 and 2021 in 2011. On an average, each FPS is catering 401 HHs/ ration card in 2001 and it has increased to 423 in 2011 in the district (see Table 5.4).

With regard to the distribution of ration cards, in 2001, the analysis reveals that of the HHs (723015) 95.65 per cent of the HHs (691616 HHs- both APL and BPL) obtained ration cards. The BPL hhs account for 70.19 per cent (507503 HHs) of the total ration cards in the district. The APL hhs accounts for 25.46 per cent (184113) of the total ration cards. A negligible percentage (4 per cent) of the hhs received temporary cards, during the Rachhabanda programme (see Table 5.4). While in 2011, of the total number of hhs (87,539) the concerned authorities issued 968770 White ration cards, which are more than the total households (110.59 per cent) are. The APL hhs account for 14.78 per cent (129542 hhs) of the total hhs in the district. Thus, the administrative machinery failed to arrest the malpractices (see Table 5.4).

Foodgrins Distribution and Security to the People

The Civil Supplies Corporation has distributed 76234 tonnes (76234000 kgs) of foodgrains to the cardholders in the district.

If we distribute it to the total population, it works out to be 23.48 kgs and 1.95 kgs per person per year and per month, respectively. The distribution of foodgrains per hh per year and per month works out to be 105.43 kgs per year and 8.78 kgs per month, respectively. The distribution of foodgrains per cardholder per year and per month works out to be 110.22 kgs and 9.18 kgs, respectively. Distribution of foodgrains per person of the cardholder hh per month (average size of the family is five members in 2001) works out to be 1.83 kgs (see Table 5.4).

The average foodgrain distribution to the BPL cardholders was 150.21 kgs per year 12.51 kgs per month. It would meet the 2.5 days requirement per person of the BPL cardholder/ hh per month (average size of the family is five members in 2001). It is pertinent to mention here that the computation is on the assumption that (a) PDS foodgrains are distributed equally among the whole hhs/ population in the state, and (b) that no diversion of foodgrains from PDS to the open market.

If the foodgrain requirement is taken as 450 g per person per day, the foodgrains under PDS would be sufficient for two and a half days and seven days in a month to the per person of the card holders and White card holders, respectively, in the district. In other words PDS contributed to less one-fourth (7 days 23.3 per cent) of the total foodgrain requirement of the HHs and for the remaining three-fourths (23 days or 78.7 per cent) he/she has to depend on the open market or self produced, (see Table 5.4). This shows that ensuring food security to the poor through public policies is very marginal in the district.

The analysis reveals that there is only marginal improvement in the food security situation in 2011, compared to 2001 decade. The authorities concerned have distributed 1,38,464 tonnes (1,38,464,000) kgs to the cardholders/hhs. Distribution of foodgrains to the total population per year and per month works out to be 39.74 kgs per year and 3.31 kgs, respectively. Distribution of foodgrains per hhs per year and per month comes to 158.07 and 13.16 kgs. Distribution of foodgrains per cardholder/ hhs per year and per month would be 126.06 kgs and 10.50 kgs respectively. The average size of the family in 2011 is four members in the district and if we share to each member of the family, it will be sufficient for about 2.6 days.

Table 5.4: Distribution of Ration Cards, Foodgrains, and Food Security to the HHs/Persons in Nalgonda in 2011-12

Items	*2001*	*2011*
Distribution of Ration Cards in the District		
Population (in persons)	3245400	3483648
Households	723015	875939
No. of Fair Price Shops	1801	2021
Average number of HH for each FPSs	401	433
HHs obtained Ration cards	691616	1098312
Percentage of HHs obtained ration cards to the total HHs in the district	95.65	125.3
BPL HHs obtained ration cards in the district	507503	968770
Percentage of BPL HHs obtained ration cards to the total HHs	70.19	110.59
The per centage of poverty in 2004-05* & 2011-12	20.46	12.51
APL HHs obtained ration cards	184113	129542
Percentage of APL HHs obtained ration cards to the total HHs	25.46	14.78
Foodgrains distribution and Security to the People		
Foodgrains distributed (rice and wheat) in under PDS	76,234 tonnes (76234000 kgs)	1,38,464 tonnes (138464000 kgs)
Distribution of food grains to the total population per year and per month	23.48 kgs per year 1.95 kgs per month	39.74 kgs per year or 3.31 kgs per month
Distribution of foodgrains per hhs per year and per month	105.43 kgs per year 8.78 kgs per month	158. 07 kgs per year 13.16 kgs per month
Distribution of food grains per cardholder hhs per year and per month	110.22 kgs per year 9.18 kgs per month	126.06 kgs per year 10.50 kgs per month
Distribution of foodgrains per person of the cardholder hh per month (average size of the family 5 members in 2001 and 4 members in 2011	1.83 kgs per month	2.6 Kgs per month
Meeting foodgrain requirement per person of a hh in a month (450 grams per day)	5 days	6 days
Contribution to the total requirement of foodgrain to the person/hh in a month	16 per cent	20 per cent
Dependence of the person/ hh on the open market or own production	84 per cent	80 per cent

(Contd...)

Distribution of foodgrains per BPL hhs per year and per month	150.21 kgs per year 12.51 kgs per month	142.33 kgs per year 11.86 kgs per month
Distribution of food grains per person of the BPL cardholder hh per month (average size of the family 5 members in 2001 and 4 members In 2011	2.5 days	3 days
Meeting foodgrain requirement per person of a BPL hh per month (450 grams per day)	6.5 days	7 days

Source: Compiled from Statistical Abstract, AP, Directorate of Economics and Statistics, Govt of AP & AP Civil Supplies Department/Corporation, Government of AP.

**Source*: estimated from unit level data 61st and 68th NSS, respectively.

The distribution of ration cards during the 1988-89 to 2012-13 reveals that an average 851731 cards were distributed in the district. Of this 647499, 154158 and 78563 were white cards, pink/APL and temporary cards, respectively. The distribution of foodgrains during the same period was 170894 qls, 155578 qls, 649 qls and 5916 qls of rice, rice to BPL hhs, wheat and sugar, respectively (see Table 5.5).

Section -III

Socio-economic Background of the Respondents

To start with, an attempt is made to understand the socio-economic background of the respondents such as age, caste, education, land, family size, earning members and income of the households etc., to find out who they are- whether belong to the BPL families or APL families (the data is presented in table form and they are accessible at the end of the chapter). The gender particulars of the respondents reveal that nearly three-fourths (72 per cent) of them are male, while a little over one-fourth (28 per cent) are female (see Table 5.6). This indicates that the ration cards are mostly issued in the name of male members of household members. In this context, the recent decision of Telangana State Government to issue ration cards in the name of female members of the household is a positive measure towards the process of empowerment of women.

The caste-wise analysis reveals that there is no discrimination in granting the ration cards as the respondents belong to all the castes with equal representation (see Table 5.7). The age particulars of the respondents reveal that more than half of them (54 per cent) come from middle age group, while a little over one-fourth (27 per cent) are

Table 5.5: Distribution of Ration Cards and Foodgrains in Nalgonda District during 1988-89 to 2012-13

Year	*Distribution of ration cards*				*Distribution of foodgrains (in tonnes)*			
	Total	*White*	*Pink*	*Temporary*	*Rice*	*Rice to BPL hhs*	*Wheat*	*Sugar*
1998-99	671,985	488,522	183,463	-	92,974	89,229	2,875	13227
1999-2000	671985	488,522	183,463	-	91440	91440	1,610	12664
2000-01	687182	503069	184113	-	85590	85590	127	11052
2001-02	691616	507,503	184,113	-	76188	76188	46	5769
2002-03	659647	475534	184113	-	73627	73627	156	4652
2003-04	753578	564,265	189,313	-	85507	85507	138	1478
2004-05	739437	550124	189313	-	902012	803108	-	762
2005-06	827187.5	635,737	157,583	-	134040	134040	224	2952
2006-07	914938	721349	125852	67737	139476	138559	223.582	5142.48
2008-08	930135	730,429	126,918	72788	147879	147421	127	5294
2008-09	945332	739509	127984	77839	156283	156283	30	5446
2009-10	1009376	843,623	87,639	78114	152326	152326	700	3851
2010-11	1102399	798406	129542	96337	156162	155884	1369	5608
2011-12	1098312	798172	129542	-	138464	72232	730	4853.1
2012-13	1072857	867723	129420	-	131442	72232	730	5991.2
*District	8,51,731	647499	154158	78563	170894	155578	649	5916
** Region	8,43,525	592430	202576	75254	166790	152193	2468	6055
***State	8,99,887	654383	193348	81067	177972	162706	1797	6578

*District Average (1998-99 to 2012-13); **Telangana region Average (1998-99 to 2012-13); ***State Average (1998-99 to 2012-13) Source; Compiled from Statistical Abstract, AP, Directorate of Economics and Statistics, Govt of AP & AP Civil Supplies Department/Corporation, Government of AP

Table 5.6: Gender particulars of the respondents (village wise)

Village and gender/ Caste	Gudibandatotal						Gundlagudem						Kokkireni					
	Male		Female		Total		Male		Female		Total		Male		Female		Total	
	No.	Per cent	No.	Per cent	No.	Per cent	No.	Per cent	No.	Per cent	No.	Per cent	No.	Per cent	No.	Per cent	No.	Per cent
OC	4	30.8	1	14.3	5	25.0	4	28.6	1	16.7	5	25.0	4	28.6	1	16.7	5	25.0
SC	3	23.1	2	28.6	5	25.0	3	21.4	2	33.3	5	25.0	3	21.4	2	33.3	5	25.0
ST	3	23.1	2	28.6	5	25.0	4	28.6	1	16.7	5	25.0	4	28.6	1	16.7	5	25.0
OBC	3	23.1	2	28.6	5	25.0	3	21.4	2	33.3	5	25.0	3	21.4	2	33.3	5	
Total	**13**	**100**	**7**	**100**	**20**	**100**	**14**	**100.0**	**6**	**100.0**	**20**	**100.0**	**14**	**100**	**6**	**100**	**20**	**100**

Continued

Village and gender/ Caste	Urumadla						Thenepally						All					
	Male		Female		Total		Male		Female		Total		Male		Female		Total	
	No.	Per cent	No.	Per cent	No.	Per cent	No.	Per cent	No.	Per cent	No.	Per cent	No.	Per cent	No.	Per cent	No.	Per cent
OC	3	18.8	2	50.0	5	25.0	3	18.8	2	50.0	5	25.0	18	25.0	8	28.6	26	26
SC	3	18.8	2	50.0	5	25.0	5	31.3		0.0	5	25.0	17	23.6	8	28.6	25	25
ST	5	31.3	0	0.0	5	25.0	4	25.0	1	25.0	5	25.0	19	26.4	6	21.4	25	25
OBC	5	31.3	0	0.0	5	25.0	4	25.0	1	25.0	5	25.0	18	25.0	6	21.4	24	24
Total	**16**	**100**	**4**	**100**	**20**	**100**	**16**	**100**	**4**	**100**	**20**	**100**	**72**	**100**	**28**	**100**	**100**	**100**

from young age group. About one-fifth of the respondents (17 per cent) belong to old age group. The respondents, who belong to less than 25 years, is very negligible (two per cent) (See Table 2). The average age of the respondents is 45 years. The marital status of the respondents reveals that all most all of them (96 per cent) are married, while an insignificant of them (Four per cent) are unmarried. Among the married, about 16 per cent of them are either divorced or living separately. This situation is more among the upper castes compared to other castes (Table 5.8). Almost all the respondents, except four, are Hindus. An insignificant percentage of the respondents belong Muslim (two per cent) and Christian Communities.

Table 5.7: Age Particulars of Respondents

Age/ Caste	*Age in Years*									
	<25		*20-35*		*36-59*		*60 and Above*		*Total*	
	Actual	*Per cent*	*Actual*	*Per cent*	*Actual*	*Per cent*	*Actual*	*Per cent*	*Actual*	*Per cent*
OC	0	0.0	5	18.5	16	29.6	5	29.4	26	26.0
SC	0	0.0	9	33.3	11	20.4	5	29.4	25	25.0
ST	1	50.0	7	25.9	14	25.9	3	17.6	25	25.0
OBC	1	50.0	6	22.2	13	24.1	4	23.5	24	24.0
Total	2	100.0	27	100.0	54	100.0	17	100.0	100	100.0
Total	2	2.0	27	27.0	54	54.0	17	17.0	100	100.0

The education levels of the respondents show that considerable percentage of them (30 per cent) is illiterate. About 14, 21, and 18 per cent of the respondents have completed their primary/upper primary, high school education, respectively. A negligible percentage of them have obtained intermediate (Seven per cent), Graduation (Seven per cent), Diploma education (two per cent) and Post Graduate (one per cent) degree. The representation of the respondents, who have completed high school and higher education, is slightly more among the upper castes and backward castes (see Table 5.9).

The occupation particulars of the respondents are presented in Table 5.10. It shows that 32 per cent, 36 per cent and 14 per cent of respondents' primary profession is agriculture, agricultural labour and non-agricultural labour, respectively. A negligible percentage of the respondents' occupation is government employment (two per cent), private employment (four per cent), self-employed (eight per cent)

Table 5.8: Marital Status of the Respondents

Marital Status/Caste	Married	Per cent	Unmarried	Per cent	Divorced	Per cent	Separated	Per cent	Total	Per cent
OC	20	24.1	1	25.0	4	40.0	1	33.3	G1	26.0
SC	19	22.9	1	25.0	3	30.0	2	66.7	25	25.0
ST	22	26.5	2	50.0	1	10.0	0	0.0	25	25.0
OBC	22	26.5	0	0.0	2	20.0	0	0.0	24	24.0
Total	83	100	4	100	10	100.0	3	100.0	100	100.0
Total	83	83.0	4	4.0	10	10.0	3	3.0	100	100.0

Table 5.9: Education Particulars of the Respondents

Education	Illiterate		Primary		Upper		SSC		Intermediate		Graduate		Diploma		Post Graduate			
levels/ Caste	No.	Per cent	No.	Per cent	No.	Per cent	No.	Per cent	No.	Per cent	No.	Per cent	No.	Per cent	No.	Per cent	No.	Per cent
OC	2	6.7	3	21.4	8	38.1	9	50.0	1	14.3	2	28.6	1	50.0	0	0.0	26	26.0
SC	10	33.3	4	28.6	4	19.0	3	16.7	2	28.6	2	28.6	0	0.0	0	0.0	25	25.0
ST	11	36.7	3	21.4	6	28.6	2	11.1	2	28.6	0	0.0	0	0.0	1	100	25	25.0
OBC	7	23.3	4	28.6	3	14.3	4	22.2	2	28.6	3	42.9	1	50.0	0	0.0	24	24.0
Total	**30**	**100**	**14**	**100**	**21**	**100**	**18**	**100**	**7**	**100**	**7**	**100**	**2**	**100**	**1**	**1.0**	**100**	**100**

and others (four per cent). The caste-wise analysis reveals that among the agricultural profession, the forward caste and backward classes constitute major chunk and the lowest percentage is the Scheduled Castes. While among the agricultural labour and non-agricultural labour profession, majority of the respondents belong to the scheduled castes and scheduled tribes. These trends indicate the economic reforms, or rural-poverty programmes have not contributed much for change in the professions of the castes. The same old situation is prevailing in the district.

The land particulars of the respondents reveals that majority of them are land-holding class, especially marginal farmers (34 per cent) and small farmers (34 per cent) categories. A negligible percentage of them belong to medium farmers (eight per cent) and large farmers (four per cent) categories, who are not eligible to get white cards. However, one-fifth of the total respondents (20 per cent) are landless in the district. The average land holding of the respondents is 3.58 acres. The caste-wise analysis unfolds that scheduled castes and tribes mostly belong to the landless and marginal farmers' categories, while the backward classes and forward castes mostly belong to small farmers and medium and large farmers, respectively. This indicates that the land inequalities still exist among the castes. The forward caste continues to possess more land compared to other communities (see Table 5.11). The average number of earning members/working population of the respondent household is three. However, the percentage of earning members is more among the male compared to female earning members of the family. There are variations between male and female in employment opportunities and income earnings. It is pertinent to note that in addition to the household work, female members are forced to work outside and earn money to meet the family expenditure (Table 5.12).

During the field survey a great majority of the respondents (71 per cent) reported that they are incurring an amount of Rs 5001 to 10,000 per month on the foodgrains and another one-fifth of them (20 per cent) are incurring Rs 1001 to Rs 5000. The average expenditure per household per month works out to be Rs 5955. More than half their income is spent on foodgrains. The respondents, who are spending Rs 1001 to Rs 2000 on foodgrain are mostly belonging to forward

Table 5.10: Occupation Particulars of the Respondents

Caste	Agriculture		Agricultural labour		NGL Labour		Govt. employee		Private employee		Self-employed		Others		Total	
	No.	Per cent	No.	Per cent	No.	Per cent	No.	Per cent	No.	Per cent	No.	Per cent	No.	Per cent	No.	Per cent
OC	14	43.8	4	11.1	2	14.3	0	0.0	1	25.0	2	28.6	3	75.0	26	26.0
SC	3	9.4	13	36.1	6	42.9	1	50.0	1	25.0	1	14.3	0	0.0	25	25.0
ST	7	21.9	11	30.6	5	35.7	0	0.0	0	0.0	2	28.6	0	0.0	25	25.0
OBC	8	25.0	8	22.2	1	7.1	1	50.0	2	50.0	3	28.6	1	25.0	24	24.0
Total	32	100.0	36	100.0	14	100.0	2	100.0	4	100.0	8	100.0	4	100.0	100	100.0
Total	32	32.0	36	36.0	14	14.0	2	2.0	4	4.0	8	8.0	4	4.0	100	100.0

Table 5.11: Distribution of Land of the Respondents (Caste-wise) (in acres)

Caste	Landless		Marginal Farmer		Small Farmer		Medium Farmer		Large Farmer		Total	
	No.	Per cent	No.	Per cent	No.	Per cent	No.	Per cent	No.	Per cent	No.	Per cent
OC	2	10.0	2	5.9	14	41.2	5	62.5	3	75.0	26	25.0
SC	3	15.0	12	35.3	8	23.5	2	25.0	0	0.0	25	25.0
ST	9	45.0	10	29.4	6	17.6	0	0.0	0	0.0	25	25.0
OBC	6	30.0	10	29.4	6	17.6	1	12.5	1	25.0	24	24.0
Total	20	100.0	34	100.0	34	100.0	8	100.0	4	100.0	100	100.0
Total	20	20.0	34	34.0	34	34.0	8	8.0	4	4.0	100	100.0

Particulars of family members of the respondents

Table 5.12: No of Working Male Members in the Respondents' Household

Caste/ Members	*Less than 3*		*3 to 5*		*Above 5*		*Total*	
OC	3	60.0	21	24.7	2	20.0	26	26.0
SC	0	0.0	21	24.7	4	40.0	25	25.0
ST	1	20.0	23	27.1	1	10.0	25	25.0
OBC	1	20.0	20	23.5	3	30.0	24	24.0
Total	5	100.0	85	100.0	10	100.0	100	100.0
Total	5	5.0	85	85.0	10	10.0	100	100.0

Table 5. 13: Age Particulars of the Family Members of the Respondents (Age in Years)

	Lessthan 15		*15-20*		*21-30*		*31-40*		*41-55*		*Above55*		*Total*	
Caste	*No.*	*Per cent*	*No.*	*Per cent*	*No.*	*Per cent*	*No.*	*Per cent*	*No.*	*Per cent*	*No.*	*Per cent*	*No.*	*Per cent*
OC	19	26.8	12	28.6	21	21.6	14	31.1	14	27.5	9	40.9	89	27.1
SC	15	21.1	11	26.2	31	32.0	11	24.4	10	19.6	3	13.6	81	24.7
ST	19	26.8	11	26.2	21	21.6	9	20.0	12	23.5	6	27.3	78	23.8
OBC	18	25.4	8	19.0	24	24.7	11	24.4	15	29.4	4	18.2	80	24.4
Total	71	100.0	42	100.0	97	100.0	45	100.0	51	100.0	22	100.0	328	100.0
Total	71	21.6	42	12.8	97	29.6	45	13.7	51	15.5	22	6.7	328	100.0

communities. The caste wise analysis reveals that the monthly expenditure of the forward castes is slightly more (Rs 7076) than the average expenditure of the total respondents.

The outstanding debt of the respondents reveals that 79 per cent of them have less than one lakh, while the remaining 21 per cent have above one lakh loan. The average outstanding debt of the respondents is Rs 68,947 as on the date of field survey. The caste-wise analysis reveals that the average outstanding debt of the forward caste is Rs 1,10,000. The outstanding debt of the SCs, STs and OBC households is Rs 36,875 to Rs 50,208. Thus, forward castes have more access to credit /financial institutions or moneylenders than the other castes in the district (field notes).

The gender particulars of the household members of the respondents indicate that more than half of the members (52.7 per cent) are female, while the remaining 47.3 per cent of them are male members. This indicates that there is imbalance in the sex ratio of the family and it is relatively more among the forward castes and scheduled tribes compared to other communities. The average age of the household members of the respondents is 26 years and nearly two-thirds of household members (64 per cent) belong to the young age group i.e., below 30 years. Among these a little one-fifth of them are very young i.e., below 15 years that are dependent on the household. The members, whose age between 31-40 years and 41-55 years account for 13.7 per cent, 15.5 per cent respectively, contribute income to the family. A negligible percentage of members of the households (6.7 per cent) represent the age group 55 years and above, who are mostly depends on the respondents. The analysis reveals that about one-third of the HH members are earning and nearly three-fourths of members are dependent on the HH (See Table 5.13).

The educational levels of the household members indicate that one-fourth of them are illiterate. About 13.7 per cent, 11.9 per cent and 11.9 per cent of the members have completed primary, upper primary and high school education, respectively. Considerable percentage of the household members (40 per cent) has completed higher education i.e., Intermediate (11.9 per cent), Graduation (14.3 per cent), Diploma and Post-Graduation. A negligible percentage of the members (7.0 per cent) are under pre-school age group.

Thus, the analysis reveals that nearly three-fourths of the household members are educated (Table 5.14). This progress is a welcome trend in the coming years.

The occupational background of the household members of the respondents reveals that there is occupational shift from their parental occupation. This is evident from the fact that while one-third of the respondents depend on agriculture, only 17 per cent of their children depend on it. Similar trend exists even in the case of agricultural and non-agricultural labour professions. Hardly anybody in the HH opted for traditional/rural artisan (0.3 per cent) and government employment occupations. Some of the family members are working as self-employed (10.1 per cent), homemaker (8.5 per cent) and private employees (4.3 per cent). Considerable percentage of the members (30.8 per cent) is pursuing their education. Only 9.5 per cent of the members are old age or physically challenged and dependent on the respondents. Thus, the analysis reveals that family members are giving priority to the education, self-employment or private employment than the traditional agricultural, non-agricultural, and rural artisan occupation, which were the main occupations of their parents. These trends indicate that there is occupational transformation is taking place in the rural areas. There is hardly anybody in the HH working as government employee (see Table 5.15).

Of the total students (101), the respondent's families, and 43 are school going age group. Unlike in the past, there is not much discrimination between the male and female in sending them to the school. Of 43 students, 22 are male and 21 are female members. However, the mid-day meal scheme is not equally accessible to both male and female members. Among the children, who are availing mid-day-meal scheme, more than half of them (55.8 per cent) are male, and the remaining (44.2 per cent) are female (see Table 5.15). The caste-wise analysis reveals that more number of members of children belonging to backward classes, SCs, STs are availing the scheme compared to the forward castes. This indicates the forward caste children perhaps are not willing to take food along with the other communities or not availing the food supplied under MDM scheme is not in good quality or sending to the private schools where MDM scheme is not in operation.

Table 5.14: Education Particulars of the Family Members of the Respondents

Caste	Illiterate		Primary		Upper		SSC		Inter		Graduate		Diploma		PG		Total	
	No.	Per cent	No.	Per cent	No.	Per cent	No.	Per cent	No.	Per cent	No.	Per cent	No.	Per cent	No.	Per cent	No.	Per cent
OC	21	25.9	14	31.1	12	30.8	9	23.1	15	31.9	11	27.5	1	11.1	1	25.0	89	27.1
SC	14	17.3	12	26.7	10	25.6	12	30.8	10	21.3	14	35.0	3	33.3	1	25.0	81	24.7
ST	26	32.1	11	24.4	7	17.9	8	20.5	11	23.4	8	20.0	3	33.3	0	0.0	78	23.8
OBC	20	24.7	8	17.8	10	25.6	10	25.6	11	23.4	8	20.0	2	22.2	2	50.0	80	24.4
Total	81	100	45	100	39	100	39	100	47	100	40	100	9	100.0	4	100	328	100.0
Total	81	24.7	45		13.7		39	11.9	39	11.9	47	14.3	40	12.2	4	1.2	328	100.0

Table 5.15: Occupation Particulars of the Family Members of the Respondents

Caste	Agriculture		Agri labour		Non Agri labour		Traditional Occupation		Govt Employees		Private employees	
	No.	Per cent	No.	Per cent	No.	Per cent	No.	Per cent	No.	Per cent	No.	Per cent
OC	26	46.4	0	0.0	0	0.0	1	100.0	0	0.0	1	7.1
SC	11	19.6	9	30.0	10	40.0	0	0.0	0	0.0	8	57.1
ST	9	16.1	13	43.3	8	32.0	0	0.0	1	100.0	2	14.3
OBC	10	17.9	8	26.7	7	28.0	0	0.0	0	0.0	3	21.4
Total	56	100.0	30	100.0	25	100.0	1	100.0	1	100.0	14	10C.0
Total	56	17.1	30	9.1	25	7.6	1	0.3	1	0.3	14	4.3

Continued

Caste	Self Employed		House wife		Student		Dependant		Others		Total	
	No.	Per cent	No.	Per cent	No.	Per cent	No.	Per cent	No.	Per cent	No.	Per cent
OC	11	33.3	12	42.9	25	24.8	9	29.0	4	50.0	89	27.1
SC	7	21.2	5	17.9	26	25.7	4	12.9	1	12.5	81	24.7
ST	7	21.2	3	10.7	29	28.7	6	19.4	0	0.0	78	23.8
OBC	8	24.2	8	28.6	21	20.8	12	38.7	3	37.5	80	24.4
Total	33	100.0	28	100.0	101	100.0	31	100.0	8	100.0	328	100.0
Total	33	10.1	28	8.5	101	30.8	31	9.5	8	2.4	328	100.0

Table 5.16: Average Consumption of Commodities by Different Social Groups (PDS and Open market) in the Selected Villages during 2014 (Quantity in kgs and price in Rs)

Commodities (quantity in Kg/liters/and price in Rs)		*OC*	*SC*	*ST*	*OBC*	*Total*
Rice	FPS	17.15	16.76	18.32	17.83	17.51
	Open Market	20.71	24	21.47	21.43	22.27
Sugar	FPS	0.5	0.54	0.5	0.5	0.51
	Open Market	1.76	1.38	1.37	1.19	1.43
Wheat	FPS	0.98	1	1	1	0.99
	Open Market	2.2	1	0	0	2
Redgram	FPS	1	1	1	1	1
	Open Market	0.72	0.51	0.32	0.2	0.47
Oil	FPS	1	1	1	1	1
	Open Market	2.48	2.14	2.16	2.46	2.31
Tea powder	Tea Open Market	0.3	4.96	4.54	13.24	5.66
Soap	Soaps Open Market	5.68	5.16	4.87	4.96	5.17
Dish bar	Dish bar Open Market	1.32	1.02	1.07	1.44	1.23
Surf packet	Surf Open Market	1.26	20.84	8.83	8.85	10.04
Salt	FPS	1	1	1	1	1
	Open Market	1	0	1	1	1
Chilly	Chilly Open Market	0.56	0.52	0.49	0.51	0.52
Agarbathi	Agarbathi Open Market	1.9	1.47	1.63	1.75	1.71
Kerosene	Kerosene FPS	2	2.34	2.04	2.12	2.12
Tamarind	Tamarind Open Market	21.24	71.15	14.45	6.11	28.46

Table 5.17: Average Consumption of Commodities by Different Social Groups per month (PDS and Open market) in the Selected Villages during 2014 (Quantity in kgs and Price in Rs))

Variables	*OC*	*SC*	*ST*	*OBC*	*Total*
1. Rice					
Purchased under FPS (Quantity)	17.15	16.76	18.32	17.83	17.51
Purchased Price per kg under FPS	1.25	1.00	1.00	1.00	1.06
Purchased in Open Market (Quantity)	20.71	24.00	21.47	21.43	22.27
Purchased Price per kg Open Market	37.00	33.48	32.69	36.00	34.29
2. Sugar					
Purchased under FPS (Quantity)	0.50	0.54	0.50	0.50	0.51
Purchased Price per kg under FPS	7.00	6.97	7.00	7.00	6.99
Purchased in Open Market (Quantity)	1.76	1.38	1.37	1.19	1.43
Purchased Price per kg Open Market	26.68	25.38	26.22	27.65	26.51

3. Wheat					
Purchased under FPS (Quantity)	0.98	1.00	1.00	1.00	0.99
Purchased Price per kg under FPS	8.25	7.00	7.00	8.30	7.65
Purchased in Open Market (Quantity)	2.20	1.00	0.00	0.00	2.00
Purchased Price per kg Open Market	25.40	28.00	0.00	0.00	25.83
Redgram					
Purchased under FPS (Quantity)	1.00	1.00	1.00	1.00	1.00
Purchased Price per kg under FPS	50.00	50.00	50.00	50.00	50.00
Purchased in Open Market (Quantity)	0.72	0.51	0.32	0.20	0.47
Purchased Price per kg Open Market	54.60	39.00	25.29	20.00	36.53
Oil					
Purchased under FPS (Quantity)	1.00	1.00	1.00	1.00	1.00
Purchased Price per kg under FPS	40.38	40.00	40.00	40.00	40.10
Purchased in Open Market (Quantity)	2.48	2.14	2.16	2.46	2.31
Purchased Price per kg Open Market	81.65	79.16	77.80	79.83	79.63
Tea					
Purchased in Open Market (Quantity)	0.30	4.96	4.54	13.24	5.66
Purchased Price Open Market	32.00	30.52	23.09	23.09	27.25
Soaps					
Purchased in Open Market (nos)	5.68	5.16	4.87	4.96	5.17
Purchased Price Open Market (nos)	16.16	15.28	13.79	14.92	15.05
Dishbar					
Purchased in Open Market (nos)	1.32	1.02	1.07	1.44	1.23
Purchased Price Open Market (nos)	12.53	13.38	11.29	11.67	12.24
Surf					
Purchased under FPS (Quantity)	7.50	0.00	0.00	0.00	7.50
Purchased Price per kg under FPS	1.26	20.84	8.83	8.85	10.04
Purchased in Open Market (Quantity)	37.50	27.60	27.00	27.33	29.81
Purchased Price per kg Open Market	1.00	1.00	1.00	1.00	1.00
Salt					
Salt Open Market quantity in kgs	1.00	0.00	1.00	1.00	1.00
Salt Open Market price per kg	38.75	0.00	20.00	25.00	30.63
Chilly					
Purchased Salt in Open Market (Quantity)	0.56	0.52	0.49	0.51	0.52
Purchased Price per kg Open Market	47.33	42.96	43.43	44.88	44.65
Agarbathi					
Purchased Salt Open in Market quantity in kgs	1.90	1.47	1.63	1.75	1.71
Purchased Price per kg Open Market	17.43	18.33	15.89	18.65	17.55

Kerosene					
Purchased Kerosene under FPS (in liters)	2.00	2.34	2.04	2.12	2.12
Purchased price per litre	15.00	16.12	15.00	14.50	15.16
Tamarind					
Purchased Salt in Open in Market (Quantity)	21.24	71.15	14.45	6.11	28.46
Purchased Price per kg in Open Market	13.84	15.16	13.86	16.88	14.86

Section-IV

Awareness of the Respondents on the Availability of Foodgrains

An understanding and assessment of opinions of the respondents on government price policy for crops, availability of foodgrains at the village and measures for increasing agricultural production etc., would provide a clue to understand the process of procurement of foodgrains in the district. The field data analysis reveals that almost all the respondents, except four belonging to scheduled tribe and scheduled caste, are aware of the government policy of procuring the foodgrains and MSP more than two thirds of them (69 per cent) have maintained that the government/corporation is purchasing the paddy at MSP. More than three-fourths of the respondents opined that the paddy production in their respective villages is adequate to meet their food requirement and therefore supported the decentralised procurement of foodgrain policy of the government and the recent programme i.e., Mana Biyyam Manakosam (our rice for our purpose). With regard to the availability of pulses and its adequacy to the villagers and MSP, only a negligible percentage of respondents (seven per cent) responded positively. The respondents argued that the government should encourage the farmers to raise the pulse crops by declaring MSP for each crop. In the case of heavy nutritious food i.e., Milk, nearly half of the respondents (45 per cent) have argued that they have their own milch animals. Among these respondents, majority of them are selling the milk to the milk centres situated in their respective villages for using the money for other household activities. Though they are aware that the milk is a nutrients food for keeping good health, their socio-economic necessities are compelling them to sell it, they remarked. During the field study, some of the old generation people commented that, prior to dairy technology, the family members used to consume the milk or supply the milk, curd, buttermilk to the neighbours when they are in need of them. In turn, the later used to give agricultural inputs as and when former is in need of them. In the process the social bondage among the families/villagers were strengthened and improved the economic conditions. The dairy technology not only disturbed the social bondage but also reduced the consumption of nutritious food of the household members, they commented.

When asked to suggest measures for increasing the agricultural production especially foodgrains and its availability in their respective villages, majority of them expressed the government should declare MSP policy for all the crops, especially pulses and enhance the price keeping in view of the food inflation in the State. Further, more credit from the public banks for investment in agriculture, regular power supply, improving the irrigation facilities, supply of agricultural inputs, controlling the malpractices in the agricultural markets, especially commission agents, establishment market yards in cluster villages, etc., are the important factors for enhancing the foodgrains production and making its availability at the door steps of the farmers/villagers. This would also reduce the burden of the government in terms of procurement of foodgrains, transport, storage and distribution of foodgrains to the target group. It also addresses the issue of black marketing of essential commodities by the traders, and control of food inflation in the State, they maintained.

Thus, the analysis reveals that lack of availability of proper storage facilities, economic bondage of the farmers to the moneylenders/ commission agents collectively contributing for inaccessibility of food-grains at the village level. However, the government policy is to provide loans to the farmers for construction of godowns at the field level or cold storage facilities at market yards, many a times it is on paper. The financial institutions are not coming forward to advance the loans to the farmers for the said purpose. The agricultural marketing committees, though collect marketing fee from storage facilities at the market yard, do not take interest in providing basic infrastructural facilities. If these issues are tackled, perhaps the availability of foodgrains at the local level is possible and reduce burden to some extent, on the PDS in the district/state.

Distribution of Foodgrains to the Households

The Government of Andhra Pradesh has been taking measures to distribute the essential commodities to the targeted groups or supply the foodgrains through Rythu Bazar at lower than the market price. These measures aimed at not only enhancing the well-being of the targeted group (as welfare measure) but also control the price of essential commodities in the open market and control blackmarketing of foodgrains. As a part of the welfare, measure the Andhra Pradesh Government has been distributing the foodgrains at subsidised rate to the BPL families, physically challenged and others, since 1983. The perceptions of the respondents on these and others issues are presented below. All the respondents are aware of the supply of rice at subsidised rate to the BPL households, AAY families and Annapurna households. However, nearly three-fourths (73 per cent), especially forward castes and scheduled tribes, are not aware of the distribution of foodgrains to the physically challenged/infirm and crippled weavers.

With regard to the welfare policy of wheat distribution to the urban people, who are poor, two-thirds of the respondents (68 per cent) are not aware of the policy, while the remaining of them (32 per cent) have expressed that they are aware of it. On the policy of 'our rice for our purpose', more than half of the respondents (56 per cent) mentioned that they are aware of the policy. Almost all the respondents expressed that they are aware of the recent policy of the government 'Amma Hastam', under which the target group members are expected to get nine essential commodities at the subsidised rate i.e., Rs 178.

Almost all the respondents, except one, are BPL/white cardholders, who come from forward caste. These trends indicate that all the households possess BPL/white cards, irrespective of castes and classes in the rural areas. Further, it is also confirming the general view of the government and public that a majority of ineligible households have acquired the BPL cards either bribing or influencing the officials. The lenient approach of the State Government during 2009 and later period for political support 'vote security' etc., the officials issued BPL ration cards indiscriminately to the households. In every Rachha Banda – a programme organised by the government for every three months to get the feedback on the government programmes and solving the problems on the sport – under the pressure of political leaders the officials granted BPL cards/coupons to the households. In the process in certain villages, the BPL cards arc more than the total number of households in the village. During the field survey, it is reported that the non-poor household members obtained the BPL cards for availing other benefits such as medical relief under Arogyasree, fee reimbursement to the children. This has given scope for the relatively better-off people and FPS dealers to claim the foodgrains under PDS and dispose in the open market for higher price. The lenient approach of the government and lack of clarity in the welfare policies, malpractice of the dealer or cardholders, etc, are causing heavy burden on the government exchequer.

The Government norm for granting ration cards is based on both income and landholding particulars of the households. An overwhelming percentage of the respondents (89 per cent) mentioned that they got the ration cards based on the household income of Rs 65,000 per year. A negligible percentage of the respondents (10 per cent) said that they submitted both income and land particulars of the household for getting ration cards. Only one respondent expressed that he got it based on the land particulars. During the informal discussion, some of the villagers and FPS dealers acknowledge that the medium and large farmers and higher income household members obtained income certificate below the Rs 65,000 per year per household. The income particulars of the respondents also confirm the fact that majority of them are earning more than Rs 1 lakh per year. The average income of the respondents is Rs 1,33,380 per year. The certificate is useful not only for obtaining BPL cards but also for availing medical relief under Arogya Sree Programme and fee reimbursement scheme. Due to these reasons, 91 per cent of the respondents supported the income criteria for issuing ration cards. An insignificant percentage of the respondents (four per cent) suggested that land should be criteria. When asked to indicate the competent authority for granting ration card, 80 per cent of the respondents replied that it is the Mandal Revenue Officer (MRO) and the remaining one fifth of them (20 per cent) said village Revenue Officer (VRO).

With regard to the number of years having ration cards, more than three-fourths of the respondents (77 per cent) mentioned that they possess them for the past 10 to 15 years and above. About one-fourth of them (23 per cent) mentioned that they possess them from the past 5 to 10 years. The trends indicate that more number of cardholders are availing the benefits for more than one decade under PDS. In fact, the officials are expected to revise the status of the ration cardholders if necessary issue a new card based on the norms prescribed by the government. The ration cardholders can also apply for revision of their cards depending on their income. For instance, in the beginning the household income may be more than the prescribed norm fixed for White cards and latter due to separation of family or selling of property to meet the social and economic needs of the household etc., the income sources are reduced and living under BPL. In such case, the households are eligible to get White cards. It is also other way round i.e., while card holders may cross the poverty line due to the improvement in the income levels of the households. In such case, they are not eligible to claim benefits under TPDS. In both the cases, the officials have to act appropriately and issue fresh cards as and when required. The field data indicates that three-fourths of the respondents have not converted their ration cards i.e., white to pink or pink to white. Some of the respondents have maintained that the officials have not visited their village for verification or revalidation of the cards. The officials even if they attempt to do so the political parties, especially ruling party will not allow the former to act on this matter, they commented. Any change in the process affect the voting pattern in the rural areas. However, nearly one-fourth of the respondents (23 per cent) have converted from pink to white cards. In 2009, the Government of Andhra Pradesh increased the income levels i.e., from Rs 65, 000 to one lakh for per year for granting white ration cards to a household. In addition to this, some of the relatively better off households also converted the pink card to white card. The reasons for converting the ration card are mostly to avail the benefits from the government and sudden demise of the head of the family and changes in income levels of the households. Thus, the above trends indicate that rationalisation of the process of granting ration cards is the major challenge in the district. The regular monitoring by the authorities concerned and revising the status of cardholders and issuing the cards to the genuine household, to some extent, solve the problems in the implementation of the PDS in the state.

Section – V

Availability and Supply of Quantity of Foodgrains at FPS

As mentioned earlier, the FPS dealer is expected to display the commodities available, time, date of distribution of foodgrains to the ration cardholders. Nearly three-fourths of the respondents (71 per cent) expressed that the commodities are not supplied on the due dates. However, the remaining of them mentioned that they are available. With regard to the time taken for collecting the foodgrains from the FPs, more than half of the respondents (53 per cent) said that it has taken one hour and a little over one-fourth (27 per cent) of them expressed that it look more than hour. One-fifth of the respondents expressed the time taken was less than half an hour.

The respondents have maintained that the FPs dealers offered several reasons for non-availability of foodgrains at FPs on the due date and time. The reasons are shortage of workers, overcrowd with cardholders on the first and second day of the issuing ration, issuing sale bills, etc., caused inconvenient to the respondents. On the rationality of the supply of foodgrains at subsidised rates, nearly 80 per cent of the respondents argued that it is the responsibility of the government to protect the rights of the people, especially right to live, right to employment, right to food. Further, they have maintained that in an unequal socio-economic system the formulation of social security policies for inclusive growth in the society are inevitable more so in the era of globalisation, where the poor cannot compete on par with the upper class.

However, about one-fifth of the respondents, who are relatively better off, have expressed that the government should focus more on the creation of infrastructure, supply of inputs, support price for the product, control of food inflation and enhancement of production etc., than launching the food subsidised policies. But the experience with Indian agricultural production, during the post-Independence period, indicates that agricultural production is not only linked with the factors mentioned above but also related to monsoon, climate change, international trade policies, which are not totally under the control of government. In this context the continuation of social security, policies are inevitable.

Average Monthly Consumption of Commodities Consumed (PDS and open market) by the Respondents

The data on the consumption pattern of respondents unfolds that they are purchasing the commodities such as rice, wheat, sugar, red-gram, oil, salt, both from PDS and open market. The chilly is purchased only in the open market, while the kerosene is purchased in FPS and not in the open market. The foodgrains supplied under PDS are not adequate to meet their monthly requirements and compelled to depend on the open market, where the price is very high. The respondents households, on an average, are consuming 39.78 kgs , 1.94 kgs, 2.09 kgs, 1.47 kgs, 3.31 kgs, 2 kgs, 0.52 kgs of rice, sugar, wheat, red-gram dal, oil, salt, chilly, respectively. Except red-gram, more than half of the requirement is purchased in the open market. With specific to each commodity monthly requirement, rice i.e. 22.27 (54 per cent), sugar 1.43 kgs (74 per cent), wheat 2 kgs, (66.8 per cent), red-gram dal 0.47 (40 per cent), oil 2.31 liters (70 per cent), and salt 1 kg. (50 per cent), and chilli 0.52 kgs (100 per cent) is purchased in the open market. These trends indicate that the target group members are left to the market forces in procuring their monthly requirement. Therefore, there is need for expand the purview/quota of the allotment under PDS or control the prices of the foodgrains in the open market.

In order to gain deeper insights on the phenomenon, here an attempt is made to present the disaggregate analysis on each of the above commodities. With regard to the rice, an overwhelming percentage of the respondents (89 per cent) have opined that they received 11-20 kgs from FPS during the last month. A negligible per cent (5 per cent), mostly representing forward castes received less than 10 kgs from PDS. However, the data reveals that more than half of the respondents (54 per cent) have purchased 30 kgs rice or more at the rate of Rs 40-45 per kg. from the open market to meet the monthly consumption of the family. This indicates that the quantity of rice supplied under PDS is not adequate to meet their demand. It is important to note that the mostly the SCs, STs and who belong to marginal and small farmers, purchased the rice from open market. In the case of the forward castes, which belong to the medium farmers and higher income groups, only a negligible percentage (11.1 per cent), purchased rice from the open market.

All the respondents, except six, have purchased three kgs of wheat from the FPS at the subsidised rate. While the six respondents, who belong to forward castes, purchased wheat from open market. These respondents feel that the wheat supplied under PDS is not in good quality. Thus, there is not much demand for the wheat in the open market as the rice is the staple food of the respondents/people of the region.

With regard to the sugar, almost all the respondents are availing the sugar 1 to 2 kgs under PDS, but the quantity is not adequate to meet their monthly consumption. They are compelled to purchase about 1 to 2 kgs sugar, in addition to what they are getting from PDS, from the open market to meet their monthly requirement. The caste-wise analysis reveals that the more number of forward castes are purchasing sugar in the open market compared to other communities. Thus, the consumption of sugar is more among the forward castes.

The field data reveals that more than one-fourth of the respondents (28 per cent) are not availing the dal (red-gram) supplied under PDS as the quality (taste is not suitable to the people) is not good. It is imported from other states, which is of low quality. However, remaining of them (72 per cent) are availing it. A few of the respondents (10 per cent) are purchasing less than 2 kgs dal, per month, in the open market. The analysis unfolds that a great majority of respondents are not purchasing the palm oil under PDS and are purchasing the refinery oil of branded company in the open market ranging between two to 3 kgs per month. During the field study some of the respondents reported that the palm oil is imported from other countries and not tasty and healthy like groundnut oil and other refined oil. In this context, it is important to note the observation made by the officer of the Civil Supplies Corporation. The oil traders/ middlemen distributed the pamphlets on the positive aspects of refinery oil and negative effects of the palm oil. This has sent wrong signals to the public on the utility of the palm oil. The Civil Supplies Department/ Corporation neither condemn the activities of the traders nor initiated measures to educate the public on the intentions of the traders. On the other hand, the people are consciousness about health opting for edible oil of branded companies over the palm oil supplied under PDS. This has become more convenient for the FPS dealers to divert it to the open market, especially to the hotels. However, some of the poor HHs is purchasing palmoil from FPS for cooking purpose. While relatively better off HHs are availing it for preparing tiffins during the festival period.

The supply of the other essential commodities such as chilly, tamarind, salt and agarbathi under PDS is not uniform quantity in all the districts and FPS and not supplied every month. The most of respondents are not opting the chilly and tamarind, as they do not have faith in the quality of the products. They prefer the products, which are locally produced in either their own land and others. In the case of Agarbathi, only the middle class use it and majority of them are not habituated to use it, as it is not the part of their culture. With regard to the kerosene, almost all the respondents, except seven are availing it under FPS. During the field survey, it is observed that the respondents purchase the kerosene at Rs 15 per liter and sell it to the blackmarket at Rs 25 per litre. The respondents either they make use it as a substitute to the wood fuel or gas for cooking purposes.

The overall analysis unfolds that an overwhelming percentage of respondents (86 per cent) expressed that the ration supplied under PDS is not adequate to meet their monthly consumption of the HH members. In the case of Annapurna and AAY, schemes and small size households are in a position to meet their monthly consumption, especially rice. For other commodities, the respondents are depending on the open market. The respondents, who said that the quantity of foodgrains was not sufficient, were asked to indicate the quantity of foodgrains required for each member/household, majority of them opined that the present supply of rice and red-gram dal and other items should be enhanced to almost double the quantity or supply of 8 kgs rice per individual per month and 3 kgs and 2 kgs red-gram dal and oil packets, respectively, per month per household. It is to be noted that recently (November 8th, 2014) the Telangana State government has enhanced the quantity of rice from 4 kgs to 6 kgs irrespective of number of members of the white card holder HH.

With regard to the weight of the quantity of foodgrains supplied to the cardholders, the respondents opined that there is under weight ranging between 250 grams to 500 grams of the total ration supplied to each family. This situation, according to the FPS dealers, is due to the leakages in the transportation of foodgrains from MLS point to FPS. In fact, the problem begin in the first stage i.e., levy of rice-by-rice traders to the FCI and from FCI to MLS point. During the course of informal discussion some the officials admitted this fact. In order to reduce its losses that occur during storage and the transportation of rice and other expenditure, the FCI try to reduce half/one kg rice while packing the rice in gunny bags. Similar trend continues even in the second stage i.e. from State Warehousing Corporation to MLS point and from MLS to FPS. As per the rule at every stage, the weighment of rice bags has to be done, especially using electronic weighing machine, but in practice, this is not being done properly. There are no weighing machines, which can weigh the 50/100 kgs bag at MLS point. That apart, it is not an easy task to weigh every bag by unloading and loading at every stage, as there is no adequate staff and infrastructure facilities- place, power supply for it. The government also do not allow extra amount for this. They admitted that it has become common practice to accept whatever is recorded in the weighing bill/receipt issued at the stage of transportation by FCI. One officer admitted that sometimes they hesitate to inspect about the stock and its net weight at the MLS points and try to escape from the problem. Sometimes they simply endorse on the bills. The officials do not find fault with the dealers even if they supply less quantity of foodgrains to the target group, as the problem is originated at the top level. Ultimately, the loss is passed on to the target group.

The quality of the foodgrains

The respondents have expressed opinion on the quality of the foodgrains supplied under PDS is mixed opinion. The respondents, who expressed satisfaction, have maintained that the rice quality is good mainly due to the constant pressure from the public on the authorities concerned and FPS dealer to supply the quantity grains. They gave several instances, where the target group members protested against the dealer/s for not supplying quality foodgrains. The authorities concerned also responded to the reaction from the public and warned the dealers not to indulge in malpractices. However, considerable percentage of the respondents mentioned that the poor quality of rice– broken rice, insects in the rice, discoloured rice (change in the rice colour) tasteless rice – is supplied to the target group. The rice imported from other states like Punjab, Haryana are preserved for years to together and in the process, it is prone to insects and become tasteless. The majority of the respondents have maintained that the red gram dal is imported from other states/countries. Unlike the imported, the local variety is better in terms of time taken for cooking and taste and the government should encourage the farmers to grow the red-gram in each district, they opined.

With regard to the duration of opening ration shops, almost all the respondents expressed that the shop is opened only for three to four days in a month and with short duration i.e., three to four hours. Many a times they make visits to the shop for verifying the arrival of the ration to the village. Sometimes all the items such as rice, wheat, oil, sugar, kerosene, are not supplied on the same date and they have to make several trips to the shop, as its arrival to the shop from MLS is not scheduled properly. The non-remittance of money for lifting the foodgrain and delay in furnishing the details of the disbursement of the foodgrains of the previous month/s and available stock at the FPS/ MLS etc., by the FPS dealer to the higher authorities for taking appropriate measures for supply them on time etc., are causing inconvenience to the respondents in getting the ration from the FPS. The respondents suggested that the information about the foodgrains availability and the opening timings of the shop need to be updated every day and displayed it on the notice board and, if necessary, to send SMS to mobile phone. The FPS need to be opened for weekdays both in the morning and evening as the poor are engaged in their livelihood activities during 10 A.M. to 5 P.M.

During the field survey, it is observed that the circulation of ration cards among villagers has become a common phenomenon. Many households are availing/lifting the ration by collecting ration cards from their relatives, neighbours, friends, who are not interested to claim it or migrated to the cities in search of livelihood. There are also instances, where they paid some amount to the person, who gave ration cards for lifting the ration. It is interesting to note that some of the rich peasants give the ration cards to their servants for claiming the ration from the FPS and the latter, in turn 'obliged to serve the master' with more loyalty. In a way circulation of cards is contributing for 'strengthening of bonded labour system' in the rural areas.

Cash Transfer to the Beneficiary

In Andhra Pradesh some of the political parties, during the election period propagated that it would transfer the money directly to the bank accounts of the beneficiaries, who are availing various social security benefits such as old-age pensions, scholarships, including PDS beneficiaries. The media also gave priority for discussion on the subject, especially the media controlled/supported by the political parties and tried to legitimise it on the alleged reason that the benefits are misused and costing more money in governance or delivery of the service to the people. However, a great majority of the respondents have rejected the idea of cash transfer, especially in PDS, as it would affect their food security and cause for conflicts among the family members. The respondents opined that there is a possibility of diverting the amount for spending on liquor consumption and other socio-cultural needs of the beneficiaries. Instances are not lacking in the State where the families are ruined due to the excess consumption of alcohol. These trends indicates that the government instead of taking stringent measures against the corrupt people/authorities/respondents, who are indulging in malpractices in supply of foodgrains or receiving the foodgrains, it is resorting to innovative practice of cash transfer to the target group.

Display of Information on the Notice Board

The FPS dealer, as per the norms of the government, is obligated to display the information on the notice board and update it every day to ensure accountability and transparency in the delivery of foodgrains/ services to the beneficiaries. The details include: number of ration cards (BPL/APL) allotted, entitlement of various commodities by the card holders, allotted foodgrains (commodity-wise), prices of commodities, working hours of FPS, the complaints/suggestions made by the villagers/card holders, toll-free number (18004252977), duties and obligations of FPS dealer, etc.

The data analysis on the above items indicates that nearly three-fourths of the respondents expressed that the dealer/s is/are displaying the required information, except the toll number, details of complaints or suggestions made by the respondents. During the field, survey some of the respondents reported that they made complaints about the poor quality of foodgrains, but dealer/s did not care to register it or display on the notice board or forwarded it to the higher authorities for necessary action. The higher officials are not showing interest on the redressal of the complaints made by the consumers. In the process, the poor householders are helpless to check the activities of the functionaries of FPS. The FPS dealer, apart from the display of information, is obligated to place the records/accounts to the cardholders, who demand for it for verification. The respondents, who demanded for records/accounts, expressed that there are variations in the information furnished on the notice board and recorded in the official books. This is mostly due to the bogus cards on which the dealer is claiming more ration from the government. These trends indicate that there is no transparency and accountability in the functioning of FPSs in the district.

Awareness on the Guidelines for Sanctioning of FPS

The majority of the respondents are aware of the norms/guidelines issued by the government for establishing FPS, reservation for appointment of dealers, eligible criteria for making application for the post of dealer, etc. However, they commented that there is heavy competition for the post as it is most profitable in the present scenario. Many people compete for this position and political parties show keen interest on this matter. Sometimes the political leaders' kith and kin and relatives or supporters are appointed as dealers. Instances are not lacking where the dealers control the Gram Panchayat and higher-level institutions. They maintain close rapport with the local elite, Sarpanch, political parties, seek their support in public/social auditing systems, and protect themselves. The dealers also keep good relationship with the media and pay the amount or supply the foodgrains for organising social functions at their residence. Some of the respondents commented that these are the qualities one needs to posses, if he/she is aspiring the dealership and the least is the norms prescribed by the government.

Viability of Fair Price Shops

The Government (the Commissioner of Civil Supplies) prescribes the amount of commission to be paid to FPS dealers specifying the rate for each commodity keeping in view the interest of target group and viability of the FPS. Nevertheless, the dealers' complaint is that the rate fixed by the government is not viable for running the shop. The average income per shop covering 500 to 600 cardholders is about Rs 4500 to Rs 6000. This amount is not viable to run the shop, as the dealer has to incur expenditure on items like rent for shop, electricity charges, salary to assistant and hamalies, stationary and sometimes interest on the loan, license fee, seals for weighment of foodgrains, etc. The expenditure on these items accounts for about Rs 3500 to Rs 4000. Though government permitted dealer to trade non-PDS items such as tea, salt, grocery items, garments, electronic goods or opening general/kirana shop to make the profession more profitable, the latter is not showing interest in it. On the other hand, the dealers association is demanding higher rate of commission for managing FPS. This situation makes the dealer for indulging in unlawful activities. Even after the GoI guidelines, the PDS Control Order and Supreme Court directions, the FPS dealers are not obeying the guidelines/orders given by the government. There are instances where the dealers association challenged the government orders in fixing the commission rate.

The existing system requiring the FPS to submit their closing stock and requiring the deposit of the demand draft for the next month by the 18th of every month has resulted in a situation where ration is not distributed after the 18th of every month. There are instances where FPS owners open shop for two to six days. Due to this some of the target group members could not avail the ration as they were away from the village and also lack the money to purchase the ration, especially red-gram dal, sugar, palm-oil and kerosene. The beneficiary is expected to lift the quota for the entire month at one time. There is no provision for collecting a commodity in more than one instalment. The FPS owners do not deposit the amount to the higher authorities for all the ration items at one time and hence not all commodities are available at the Shop. Sometimes the consumer has to make several visits to the FPS to get rice, kerosene, sugar, red gram dal and palm oil. Recently, the State government has allowed dealer for paying the deposit amount through online to reduce the delay. However, the dealers are not showing interest to do so as they are not well versed with the new method.

Social Audit

In terms of the provisions of the Control Order 2001, the Government of Andhra Pradesh provided for the Social Audit of the FPS shops. Social Audits of FPS is to be conducted every month at Villages by Praja Committee or Food Advisory Committees (vide Memo No.1242 dated 7.5.2008). The Praja Committee consists of 10 per cent of the total cardholders in the FPS. One-third of the FPSs in a Mandal are to be covered every month. The issues to be covered in the social audits are: (a) scrutiny of the appointment letter of the FPS; (b) number of cards (category-wise) allotted ; (c) checking the date of stamping done by weights and measures department; (d) quantity of stocks received during the month; (e) checking the registers of the FPS; (f) scrutinising the aspects relating to quantity, quality, scale of distribution, price and timings of operation; (g) complaints/suggestions books. During the social audit if any dealer is found indulging in unethical practices the Tahasildhar is competent authority to take necessary action against the dealer.

In many instances FACs are not meeting regularly and even if they meet, not registering cases/ complaints against the FPS dealers or any other malpractices cropping up in the implementation of PDS. Instances are not lacking about the forgery of the signatures of members of FAC or Sarpanch of the Gram Panchyat to fulfil the legal formality and there is no proper verification of it. The FPS dealers maintain close contracts with the political leaders, media, youth associations, village elite, and any other pressure groups at the village level and see that no complaint is registered against them. They are also backed by MLA/MP and, if necessary, Chief Minister of the State. The Justice Wadwa Committee observed that the CM's Office intervened in the revocation of license of FPS dealer, who was allegedly indulged in black-marketing of the PDS grain. The only penalty imposed was forfeiture of his trade deposit.

The basic problems with the FACs members are lack of knowledge about their duties and responsibilities; lack of interest and enthusiasm; interested in personal incentives for attending the meetings, etc. The elected Gram Panchayat is not playing much role in scrutinising and verifying the actual position at the ground level. The system of social auditing is actually not functional and the concerned officials are not showing interest in conduct of social audit. Thus, the social audit mechanism is only a formality and symbolising FW Riggs' 'formalism', the character of underdeveloped country.

Inspections

The Andhra Pradesh PDS (Control) Order, 2008, prescribes for detailed provisions with regard to penalties on FPS dealers and any other persons indulging in activities that hamper the PDS. This includes imposition of penalties on dealers diverting any essential commodities into blackmarket, prohibition on applying for Duplicate Supply (Ration) Cards, empowering officials and members of Food Advisory Committees to inspect, search and seize stocks at the FPS and furnish reports on which disciplinary enquiries are to be initiated. Clause 23 of the order provides for regular inspections of the FPS by the Joint Collectors, District Supply Officers / Revenue Divisional Officer, Tehsildar / Assistant Supply Officer, Deputy Tehsildar (CS) (Enforcement), Revenue Inspector and team of Food Advisory Committee. This Clause also provides that the Senior Revenue Inspector / Civil Supplies Inspector shall ensure opening of the FPS on time and running of the shop in distributing the commodities as per scheduled timings. The inspection of FPS by the higher authorities, especially Revenue Divisional officer (5 FPS shops in a month) and Tehsildhar is not being done properly. However, they fulfil the formality and send the inspection reports to the higher authorities. The 'formalism' as characterised by F W Riggs, famous thinker of Public Administration, is prevailing in Indian Administration even after six and a half decades of Independence India.

Vigilance System

State Government is responsible to ensure regular inspections of FPSs, not less than once in six months by the designated authority. The meetings of the Vigilance Committees on the PDS at the State, District, Block and FPS level will be held on a regular basis at such dates and periodicity as notified by State Government and every unit of is responsible to send the information to the immediate higher authority. The sequence of flow of information is (i) FPSs to the District Authorities by the 7th of every month (ii) the district authorities to State Government by the 15th of the month; (iii) the State Government to the Central Government by the end of the month. Based on the reports allocation of foodgrains is made to the respective bodies for distribution.

The Issues at MLS point in the Field

Justice Wadwa Committee (2009) highlighted several issues/ constraints, which are hampering the progress of the PDS in the State. They are: non-receipt of sample from FCI by the Godown in-charges; negligence of Route Officer to accompany the truck carrying their stock; carrying the Truck Chits without the signature of authority concerned; non-availability of electronic weigh bridge at mandal level or incapacity of the available machine to weigh the stock received from the FCI; transporting the stock directly positioned in the godown without weighment; a variation of 40-50 kg per 20 MT in weighment between FCI weighbridge and at Private weighbridge; non-receipt of samples of grain from FCI by MLS points; no display of stock on the notice board and distinction of stock- BPL rice, AAY rice, or Annapurna foodgrain, ICDS or MDM; the stacking of entire stock of grain together irrespective of the date of arrival; long distance between godown and FPS (40 kms); possessing about 50-60 bogus/ghost ration cards by each FPS dealer, etc. All these are the challenges of governance of food security policies in the State.

Awareness of Respondents on Institutions Involved in Delivery of Foodgrains

The knowledge of the respondents on the process of procurement, storage, transport and delivery of foodgrains are as important to that of collecting the foodgrains from FPS. The data analysis reveals that the respondents are aware only about role of State Government (Civil Supplies Corporation Limited) in procuring the foodgrains. They are not aware of the institutions such as warehousing corporation, agricultural marketing Committees, private godowns, etc, responsible for store and transportation of the grains/ration items. Many of the respondents (80 per cent) are not aware about the process of storage and transportation of foodgrains i.e. electronic bridge for weighment of grains, location of the godowns, computerisation of all transactions, application of modern machine for identification of the finger prints of the card holder, surprise check/inspection of trucks carrying foodgrains by metrology department, the responsibility of the corporation in arresting the malpractices in delivery of foodgrains to the ration card holders. The awareness on these aspects and others would dispel the misunderstandings, if any, and provide conducive environment between the civil supplies department/FPS dealer and the villagers/card holders. This would also enable the respondents to know the difficulties involved in the process of ensuring food security to the people and fight for their rights. Hence, the awareness campaign through all the methods- media, wall posters, display on the notice board at the FPS – is most important for proper governance of the food security programmes.

Innovative Practices

The Government of Andhra Pradesh, for the last two or three years, making efforts to introduce innovative measures such as computerisation of records and transactions at all levels; global position system; on taking finger prints for issuing ration; cash transfer in place of distribution of foodgrains; linking Aadhar card to the PDS etc., for arresting the leakages/administrative dysfunctionalities and ultimately for improving the effectiveness government of the programme. The responses of the respondents on these items reveals that though majority of them are not aware of them, they welcomed the above measures especially the giving computer code to each FPS, the details of each commodity allotted to each FPS, number of ration cards allotted to each FPS, the quantity distributed to each ration card holder along with time, introduction GPS. However, they opposed the introduction of cash transfer system in lieu of the distribution of the foodgrains, as it give scope for the family members to divert the cash for other than the food items. This would further accentuate the problems of the people. They also did not welcome the linking of Aadhar card to the PDS.

With regard to the taking fingerprints, especially arranging machine at each FPS, considerable percentage the respondents expressed that at present the dealer is taking the signature of the card holder/recipient of the ration. This method would enable the higher officials to verify the signature and make the cardholders responsible, if they indulge in any wrongful claim of the benefit. However, in the case of fingerprints, the cardholder only should come to the FPS and undergo the test for collecting the ration and other family members are not allowed to collect it. It is not always possible for the cardholder to visit the FPS, especially on the specified dates of distribution of ration items. However, more than half of the respondents have welcomed the idea of taking fingerprints of the cardholders. They also expressed the doubts on this method, as it is dependent on the availability of electricity at FPS for operating the machine and its linkage with the main server.

Respondent's Perception of the Impact of PDS on the Living Conditions of the Poor

More than half of the respondents (55 per cent) have expressed that they are getting good quality of foodgrains, especially rice, and able to meet one-third of the monthly ration. Unlike in the past, the government in the recent past, especially past two years, is supplying local variety of rice suitable to our conditions. With regard to the reduction of poverty about one-fourth of the respondents mentioned that the scheme has reduced their expenditure on the food and to that extent it has reduced the indebtedness. A few of them (less than 10 per cent) have opined that they are able to meet the amount spent on the health and educational needs of the household. Some of the respondents have mentioned that each household, an average, is getting 17 kgs and enabling them to save Rs 400 to 500 per month, (the market rate for the same rice is about Rs 30 per kg). This amount is almost equal to the expenditure incurred on the health and education of a household per month. They agreed that this is a positive aspect of the food security policies.

Considerable percentage of the respondents have argued that the non-poor category households are misusing the programme by selling the rice in the open market or middlemen/dealer at Rs 15-20 per kg, who in turn supplying the same to the rice traders/millers or the poultry merchants collecting their margin amount from the latter. The rice traders/millers are polishing the rice and recycling it in the open market or supply to the civil supplies corporation under levy system. The later again supply it to the poor households. The authorities concerned know this entire process. They are becoming part of it by getting benefits or helpless, as they are unable to arrest this vicious circle. These trends are weakening the intensions of the policies, they commented. In spite of the above problems, almost all the respondents have expressed the TPDS scheme should be continued. In this context, the enactment of National Food Security Act, 2013 is a positive direction in ensuring food security to the poor. However, the success of this Act, to a large extent depend on the arresting the above mentioned vicious circle and it is one of major challenges of the governance of food security, the respondents remarked.

All the respondents were asked to suggest measures for improvement of the working of the TPDS in the State. The suggestions include – (i) improvement in the quality of rice and other foodgrains; increase allotment for each member from 4 kgs to 8 kgs rice per month or minimum of 35-40 kgs of rice per household per month, expansion of the ration items such as vegetables, milk, egg; supply of local variety of foodgrains ensuring food sovereignty of the people; opening the FPS for more than a week days both morning and evening in a month; elimination of bogus cards and issue of cards to the genuine households; continuous monitoring of the process of procurement of foodgrains, transport, storage and distribution; organising awareness campaign on the role of food committees in the delivery of foodgrains, especially at the village level; arresting the corrupt practices of FPS dealer. Considerable percentage of the respondents opined that the social security schemes – food security policies are incremental in nature, as they would give temporary relief to the poor to overcome their problems. Thus, TPDS will serve the purpose of postponing the issues of food insecurity and inequalities in the society. Therefore, while formulating the public policies the priority should be given to both on the incremental and long-term benefits to the poor. Further democratisation of governance of food security policies is all the more important.

Summing Up

The field study unfolds that most of the sample beneficiaries of PDS belong to all the castes and communities, especially Hindu and belong to middle and young age groups: are illiterate and/or have completed primary and upper primary education. The demographic features of the respondents' reveal that the average size of the family is five and the percentage of male population is more than the female. The analysis indicates that people of all castes have access to PDS in the district. However, the civil supplies department has issued ration cards in the name of male members. This indicates that the patriarchy system is still dominant in granting ration cards to the HHs. This is also true in other poverty alleviation programmes. In this context, the Telangana State's recent decision to issue ration cards in the name of female members of the households is a positive measure towards the process of empowerment of women.

Most of the respondents belong to the marginal and small farmers' categories; lower and middle-income groups and their primary occupations are agriculture, agricultural labour and non-agricultural labour. The average number of workers in the family is three members, especially male as wage/income earners. The outstanding debt of the respondents is less than one lakh. Further, the analysis reveals that considerable percentages of the respondents, who are ineligible on the criteria of income/land, have acquired the ration cards and access to foodgrains under PDS in the district. The caste-wise analysis reveals that the upper caste respondents have better economic conditions in terms of primary occupation, land ownership, income generation etc., compared to other communities. The public policies have not contributed much for change in the occupations of lower castes. They still dependent on the agricultural labour and non-agricultural labour for their livelihood.

The socio-economic background of the household members of the respondents reveals that the sex ratio is favourable especially among the forward castes and scheduled tribes. Among these communities, female members are more than the male. There is also shift in the occupational status of the household members from their parental occupation or traditional rural artisan occupation. The household members' dependency on agriculture is declined (only 17 per cent are dependent on agriculture). However, the analysis reveals that the households are giving priority to human resources development, as two-thirds of the members are pursuing education and working as self-employed. The members are giving priority to the education and self-employment. The analysis reveals that though the respondents got ration cards and have access to PDS the family members especially the school children are not availing the MDM, partly because the children are pursuing education in private schools since the parents believe that private English medium schools are better than the Government Telugu medium schools where no such facility exists. The non-availment of MDM scheme by the students is also due to the supply of poor quality of food supplied at public schools.

The field study reveals that improving irrigation facilities, supply of agricultural inputs, uninterrupted and quality power supply, access to credit institutions, enhancing MSP and more public expenditure in agricultural sector, arresting malpractices in market yards and commission agents/traders, providing proper storage facilities at the village level or cluster of villages, etc, would not only promote agricultural production, but also make people to get access to the foodgrains and, to some extent, reduce burden on the PDS in the district. The analysis reveals that the government is operating PDS and rythubazzars (where the foodgrains are supplied at less than the market rate) to ensure availability of essential commodities at the village level. However, the later is mostly accessible to the urban and middle class, while the former is to the rural people.

The study reveals that in the era of globalisation, food security policies are more relevant to protect the rights, particularly right to live, right to food of people and reduce inequalities in the society. But food security policies have contributed to a saving of about Rs 400 to Rs 500 per month to each HH, as each HH, received about 18 kgs rice per month under PDS at Re one per kg, which is normally priced Rs 25-30 in the open market. The saving is almost equivalent to the expenditure incurred on health and education of the HH in a month.

The quantity of foodgrains consumed by the respondents procured both from PDS and open market, unfolds that the quantity supplied under PDS, especially rice, sugar are not adequate to meet the monthly consumption demand of the family. Many respondents, especially the poor respondents are compelled to purchase equal quantity or more from the open market at higher price. The other commodities supplied under PDS are not in demand. Respondents opt for local products/self produced products suitable to their taste and choice. These trends suggest that it is better to supply the commodities, which are produced at local level similar to Mana Biyyam – Mana Kosam policy – through the FPS. This would not only ensure the supply of good quality foodgrains at cheaper rate to the target group, but also control food inflation in the State. Further, the analysis unfolds that doubling/ enhancing the quantity of foodgrains from 4 kgs to 8 kgs rice per person per month and other essential commodities under PDS would enable the BPL HHs to meet their monthly demand.

There is a need to control disgraceful marketing strategies of private companies- posters and displaying the information comparing advantages and disadvantages of their products with that of palm-oil and attracting the consumers to the products. The relatively better-off people are purchasing oil from the branded companies by paying higher price. The field study reveals that majority of non-poor, especially medium and large farmers obtained White ration cards with the support of politicians and bureaucracy. They are availing the pensions, medical relief and foodgrains for more than one decade. The government is not reviewing the status of cardholders and not taking measures to correct the irregularities. On the other hand, it is issuing new ration cards or temporary cards at the Rachhabanda, conducted by government three times in a year. All these trends are contributing to increase number of ration cards, sometimes more than the total HHs in the village, indicating the ineffectiveness of the governance at the grass-roots level.

The major challenges in the implementation of food security policies are: evolving norms for rationalising the issue of ration cards; leakages in the distribution of foodgrains; unethical practices of traders/ millers, dealers; recycling of rice; off-take of red gram dal and palm-oil; emancipation of poor from the economic bondage; transparency and accountability of field functionaries and institutions; political intervention/corruption in granting FPSs and appointment of dealers; viability of running the FPS; formalism in the functioning of food advisory committees and conducting social audit; lack of monitoring by the higher officials over the field functionaries; non-compliance of rules by higher bodies (in issuing samples of foodgrains and electronic weigh bill), etc, are hampering the food security policies at the grass-roots level in the State.

Chapter- VI

Conclusion

Ensuring food security to the people engross several dimensions, i.e. food as nutritional commodity, as an economic commodity and as political commodity. People starve when their energy and protein intake is not sufficient over a period. Food is also a source of profit in exchange. Traders, brokers, commission agents and/or other intermediaries in trade are less concerned with the nutritional content and function of food for human well-being than with price. For them, food is primarily a source of profit, to be purchased as cheaply as possible and sold for a much higher price. The result of this profit orientation can be speculation, impoverishment of the producers, artificial scarcity, and inadequate access to food by some who lack sufficient purchasing power and famines even when food is available in the market. Food is also a political commodity and it is a means of power. Those who have command over food can exercise power or influence political relations while others (food insecure) are vulnerable and the former exercise control on the later. This characterises the fundamental inequality (Mooji, Jos, 1999). These factors affect the governance of food security policies and programmes.

Public policies to alleviate hunger, poverty, unemployment etc, and ensuring nutrious food to the poor have come to assume vital importance in post-Independent India. The Millennium Development Goals (MDG) 2000-15 and the proposed MDG 2015-30 also emphasise the elimination of hunger and poverty. The policies relating to self-employment, wage employment, social security, and food security are aimed at direct attack on hunger, malnutrition and poverty and are considered the important programmes for providing employment, income and foodgrains to the poor. An examination of policies reveals that the Indian State is giving priority to the incremental policies neglecting structural change oriented policies. Further, the policies are formulated and implemented mostly to tide over the unrest among the poor; get the support of the poor in the elections; take on technological innovations; expand the market of MNC; oblige the Judiciary directions; guard the ruling class power structure from the threat of the unrest of masses; vote security in the elections, etc. Today, the public policies and the related concepts, norms and institutions, technology, capital, resources are globalised. The Indian State has little freedom to modify the norms of the policies/projects as most of them are financially and technically supported by the IGOs. In a way, it amounts to 'globalisation of democratic power', which ought to rest with the people and their representatives. Globalisation has changed the context, focus and the very notion of the Constitutional mandate, nation state and the public policies and institutions. The analysis shows that the present globalised model is the new face of development where the State either with private sector or with voluntary organisations / civil society organisation work in collaboration and cooperate with each other to further common goals of market-driven, growth oriented agenda and adopt PPP mode for governance of programmes. Given the unequal socio-economic structure of India, this approach to development further accentuates the inequalities.

An examination of food security programmes, during the pre-Independence period, especially during World War periods reveals that they were meant to cater to the needs of armed forces and urban people of certain cities. In order to overcome the serious shortage of foodgrains, the then Governments initiated measures to regulate prices and procure and distribute foodgrains on a centralised basis. However, there were a large number of complaints about foodgrains delivery system. They include low coverage of households (HHs) and exclusion of large number of HHs, inadequate supply of ration items, variation in the entitlements from state to state and area to area, and also variation in the prices of the ration items and poor off-take of ration by the HHs due to poor quality of foodgrains.

The State intervention to ensure food security, during the post-Independent period, can be broadly categorised into seven phases. The first phase from 1945 to 1960, the focus then was on achieving self-sufficiency in agricultural production especially in foodgrain production and stabilising prices. Public distribution system was expanded to selected cities and it was generally dependent on imports of foodgrains. The second phase, from 1960 to 1978, was one, which saw major organisational changes. Specifically, in response to the food crisis of the mid-1960s, the Government of India took a holistic approach to food security, and set up the Agricultural Prices Commission and the Food Corporation of India in order to strengthen domestic procurement, storage, and supply of foodgrains. The third phase, from 1979 to 1996, was marked by large-scale expansion of the PDS, supported by domestic procurement and stocks. The fourth phase, from 1997 to 2005, is one in which the policy of universal food security has been replaced by a targeted policy in line with the directions of World Bank and objectives of economic liberalisation. The fifth phase, from 2006 to 2014, is making food security a fundamental right and adopting life cycle approach to a large majority people. The seventh phase from 2015 is likely to undermining the role of FCI, and reduces the coverage of PDS and a gradual transition to cash transfers and downsizing NFSA. Thus, over the period, the food security grew from a rationing scheme in selected cities to a national programme of food distribution; to a policy of supplying foodgrains to the target group and; to ensuring fundamental rights to vast majority of the people and now a gradual transition to cash transfers and downsizing NFSA.

State Regulative Measures

A close examination of government policies, particularly in the economic reforms period reveals that the government focused on four important aspects i.e. decontrol of foodgrain distribution; regulation of foodgrain distribution; special provisions for the benefit of marginalised sections; and organisational reforms. First the decontrol of foodgrain production and distribution includes: promoting growth of production; limiting State intervention in the food market; elimination of state's sales tax benefiting the traders, scaling down the buffer stock and encouraging more exports/imports; liberalising internal trade of foodgrains; stabilising the prices of the commodities by releasing more foodgrains to open market; reduction in distribution of basket items and confining to homogeneous goods; cutting down the subsidies on food items and targeted PDS and dropping the sizeable subsidy on the public exchequer; dual price policy for the BPL and APL card holders; reduction in number of FPSs and encourage private limited shops for distribution by introducing a system of food stamps, food credit cards, etc.

Second, the measures to regulate foodgrain production and distribution include: maintaining adequate foodgrains reserve at all times; opening of FPSs and supply of foodgrains; issuing foodgrains licensing and procurement order 1952; enacting Essential Commodities Act, 1955 to have control over the production, supply and distribution and trade and commerce in certain essential commodities and directing the State governments to adhere to the Act; State government restrictions on foodgrains movements; price control and stock holding limits of foodgrains; nationalisation of wholesale trade in foodgrains and fixing maximum selling price for rice and wheat; correction of seasonal and regional variations; strengthening of cooperative network for procurement and distribution of foodgrains.

The Central Government, recently, has communicated its decision to procure only 25 per cent of the requirement of the foodgrains for distribution to the target groups and institutions and the remaining 75 per cent has to be procured by the respective State governments. This amounts to shifting its financial burden to the State governments, which would cost heavily to the State exchequer. Though the Andhra Pradesh government has the autonomy to undertake food security policies or modify the norms, they do not have the adequate infrastructure- such as market yards, storage facilities, transportation facilities, power to maintain cold storages- and adequate number of skilled personnel to cope with the procurement and distribution of foodgrains. Added to these, the deficit budget of State government makes it to depend on the Central Government and adhere to its norms set for implementation of food security programmes. Nevertheless, the State government is bringing pressure on the Central Government to procure 75 per cent of the requirement.

Third, the Central and State governments have initiated special programmes to improve the nutritional and health status of the children and women and developing human capital; increase in the budget allocation for food subsidies; strategies for integrating the food security with other PAPs; organising Village Grain Banks for the benefit of the poor; food and cash component supply to the poor; priority to the poorest of the poor in the distribution of foodgrains; encourage the farmers to raise the horticultural crops for assuring variety of nutrient foods; etc.

Fourth, the government measures for organisational reforms include establishment of FCI and separate government Agencies/ Corporations and involving Multipurpose Cooperative Societies; the NGOs, SHGs, PACs, AMSs, SERP and PRIs Societies, promoting PPP in procurement and its storage, transportation and distribution to targeted group and social welfare institutions and application of e-governance for implementation of the food security policies in the State.

Fifth, enacting NFSA, 2013, to ensure right to food to the people and adopting life cycle approach in providing foodgrains to the people. The NFSA is hailed as an important step towards eradication of hunger, malnutrition and resultant poverty and towards ensuring right to food and fulfilment of basic needs such as protection of health, education and other risks of the people thereby investment in human capital. The main features of the Act are laudable, especially adoption of life cycle approach, provision of safe drinking water, proper sanitation and hygienic toilets, primary healthcare, special schemes for those who are economically vulnerable and the physically challenged and reforms in PDS and involvement of local governments in the implementation of the Act.

Organisational Pattern

The Central and State government are responsible for implementation of food security policies in India. Nevertheless, the decision-making on the formulation and implementation of policies is centralised, as the Central Government determines the extent of procurement and allocation of foodgrains and the norms for its distribution to different categories of target groups or social groups and institutions, including criterion for identification of target groups. It also exercises control on inter-state trade and commerce, quality control and specifications of foodgrains, fixation of price of levy of sugar and other commodities, granting funds to the State governments for construction of godowns, etc.

An examination of the organisational pattern at the State level shows that the Andhra Pradesh government has a separate Ministry for Agriculture for production and Ministry for Consumer Affairs Food and Civil Supplies and autonomous Civil Supplies Corporation for procurement and distribution of essential commodities to the people. Though the Corporation has the autonomy in its day-to-day operations, for all practical purposes it is working as per the directions of the State government. The analysis reveals that, during the four decades of its existence, the Corporation has been undertaking several activities such as opening foodgrains purchasing centres; purchasing damaged paddy; opening retail counters; distribution of essential commodities such as rice, wheat, sugar, dal at subsidised rate/ free of cost, cement distribution (as and when the situation demand due to the shortage or hoarding by traders); opening LPG centres and retail counters, etc. It is also implementing the special schemes – Mana Biyyam- Manakosam and Amma Ahstam, as per the directions of the State government. Today the Corporation is overburdened with multiple activities.

The effectiveness of the Civil Supplies Department/Corporation, to a large extent, depends on the cooperation of Central Government, State Warehousing Corporations, GCC, ITDA, district administration units/wings– revenue, agriculture, agriculture marketing committees-PRIs, SHGs, and the private agencies i.e., traders/ millers, transporters, NGOs, etc. The Civil Supplies Department/Corporation is encountering several problems in the implementation of food security policies at the district and below levels. They are: illegitimate interference of politicians in the administrative matters; legal loopholes in the provisions of government orders/circulars; lack of coordination between government departments/agencies at all levels; cumbersome official procedures in procurement and distribution of foodgrains; lack of autonomy to the field functionaries; fear of allegation for overlooking the procedures in the interest of public; malpractices of traders/millers in levy of commodities are the major concerns of the district authorities. Lack of clarity on the criterion of identification of target groups; lack of monitoring by the higher authorities on the implementation of activities at the grass-roots level; non-availability of instrument to read Irish-based ration cards at FPSs; lack of infrastructural facilities and skilled personnel for making end to end computerisation of the operational details of the programme; non-existence or non-functioning of food advisory committees; involvement of middleman in the implementation of activities; availing foodgrains by non-poor; circulation of bogus ration cards; recycling of ration rice/wheat; diversion of foodgrains to the blackmarket; importing foodgrain-red gram dal from other States /countries; cardholders' reluctance to avail the ration items owing to its poor quality, etc, are the concerns of field level functionaries. All these factors are collectively affecting the functioning of the Civil Supplies department/ Corporation in the State.

The analysis also reveals that the State government has initiated several measures to arrest the malpractices in the implementation of the programmes. They include: application of global positioning system and monitoring the movement of foodgrains transportation vehicle; third party verification of quality of foodgrains; instalment of modern machine (point of Service), application of e-PDS and acquiring finger prints of the cardholder/person collecting the ration while distributing the foodgrains; linking the Aadhar card for identification of the beneficiary and distribution of foodgrains; weeding out bogus ration cards and issuing new cards through Mee-seva centres; conducting Integrated kutumba survey for identification of the real beneficiaries; sending SMS to the cardholder about the arrival/availability of foodgrains at FPS; activating the vigilance and enforcement to file legal case against the culprits or hoarder or diversion of foodgrains to the black market, etc. Not all these initiatives could deter the illegal activities of traders/millers, corrupt bureaucrats, FPSs dealers and politicians. However, the effectiveness of the food security policies and its governance has to be understood in the context of the area under foodgrain cultivation, output of foodgrains, procurement and distribution of foodgrains, which are main components of food security, especially at the State level. Unlike other studies, the present study focuses on these areas.

Area under Foodgrains in Andhra Pradesh

The analysis indicates that the regional imbalances in terms of area under foodgrain continue to exist and this would seriously affect the availability of foodgrains to the people in the State. The economic reforms and diversion of agricultural land for non-agricultural purposes, etc have resulted in declining the area under foodgrain production, an average of over eight million hectares, during the past five decades in the State. This trend is more or less similar across all the three regions and districts of the State. However, the deceleration in area is observed more in the backward regions i.e. Rayalaseema region, followed by Telangana. The Rayalaseema region exhibited a continual decline right from the beginning observing a double digit declining all through the decades. However, in Rayalaseema, during the last decade, there is considerable improvement in the area, which grew by 17.8 per cent. While in Telangana region the trend decline is observed from 1981 onwards and it continued even to date. The district-wise analysis discloses that area under foodgrain crops is declining in many districts; during the past, one and a half decades especially from 2001-2010 onwards.

Output of Foodgrains in the State

In spite of declining trend in the area under foodgrain production, the output of foodgrains increased during all past five decades in Andhra Pradesh as it grew from an annual average of 5.8 million tonnes recorded during the decade prior to 1960 to over 16.1 million tonnes in the decade of 2001-2010. The growth rate has been positive and around 20.0 per cent during all the times. The average agricultural production, during 1955-56 to 2008-09, is 104.07 lakh tonnes in the State. However, the data on the foodgrain production indicates that there is four-fold increase in the production i.e. from 55.33 lakh tonnes in 1955-56 to 204.21 lakh tonnes in 2008-09 in the State. The increase is mostly from 1988-89 onwards. This is mostly due to the adoption of modern technology in the agriculture sector.

When it comes to regional perspective, while Andhra and Telangana regions recorded growth during all the periods, Rayalaseema continued to exhibit deceleration in foodgrain output as it recorded negative growth in most of the periods, except during 1971-80 (22.3 per cent) and 2001-2010 (32.8 per cent). However, during the last decade (2001-2010) the output is more in the Rayalaseema and Telangana compared to the Andhra region. The production of foodgrains and its availability is not uniform across the districts. Certain districts like West Godavari, East Godavari, Krishna, Guntur, Karimnagar, Warangal, and Nizamabad have surplus paddy, while other drought prone districts like Chittur, Cuddapha, Anantapur, Adilabad, and Nalgonda have deficit in paddy production.

Per capita Availability of Foodgrains

An examination of the per capita availability of foodgrains to the population in different decades (from 1961 to 2011, except 2011) reveals that it is less than 200 kgs per HH per year in the State. This works out to be less than 20 kgs per month per household in the state (average is 16.6 kgs), indicating that there is shortage of foodgrains in the State. It is lowest during the decades of 1971 and 1991.

The Procurement of Paddy/ Rice under Levy System in the State

Several players (Central and State governments, autonomous agencies, private traders/ millers/ workers) are involved in procurement, transportation and storage of paddy and rice in the State. An analysis of the data on the procurement of rice, during 1996-97 to 2011-12, reveals that on an average the state government is procuring about 63,98,798 Metric tonnes of rice through different sources for distribution to the target group members and also other welfare programmes. However, there are variations in different years ranging from 2622678 Mts (in 2002-03) to 17363626 Mts (in 2011-12). The procurement of rice is more from 2002-03 onwards. It is important to note that there is also unprecedented increase in the number of ration cards i.e. 1981100 in 2005-06 to 2516900 in 2011-12. The then government and the political leaders with a view to gain support of the people for the party encouraged the villagers to take the ration cards, especially White cards. There were informal instructions from the political executive to the officials to be liberal in granting the ration cards. This has given the opportunity to the non-poor to take White Cards and issue of bogus ration cards by the local authorities to the FPS dealers in the State, some of the officials maintained.

The analysis also reveals that the average procurement of rice per card /HH per year and per month is 254 kgs and 21 kgs, respectively. This works out to be 5 kgs of rice per person in the HH (assuming that the average size of the family is four) and it is hardly sufficient to meet the 10 days requirement and the remaining days (20) the individual/ family has to depend on the open market, where the price of the rice is beyond the reach of common man.

The district and decade-wise analysis indicate that the Civil Supplies Corporation, during the past three decades (1983-84 to 2013-14), on an average has been procuring 31568454 Metric tonnes (all the districts) of rice for distribution to the ration cardholders and other target groups/ institutions, in the State. However, there are variations in the procurement of rice among the regions and districts. The analysis unfolds that the procurement of rice is more in Andhra region i.e. the average of all the districts of the region is 18926028 Metric tonnes, followed by Telangana region i.e. 12230206 Metric tonnes. It is very less in Rayalaseema region i.e. 412220 Metric tonnes. The procurement of rice in the districts (average of all the decades) is ranging between 23412 Metric tonnes to 5798714 Metric tonnes indicating the wide disparities among the districts. The highest procurement of rice is more in the developed districts like East Godavari and West Godavari in Andhra region, followed by Nalgonda, Karimnagar and Nizamabad in Telangana region. In Rayalaseema region, the highest procurement of rice is more in Kurnool and Cuddapah.

Distribution of Fair Price Shops and Ration Cards in 2001 and 2011 in the State

As we scrutinise the decadal progress in the distribution of FPSs and ration cards, it is observed that each FPS was catering 424 HHs/ ration cards in 2001 and it has increased to 470 in 2011 in the State. With regard to the distribution of ration cards, all the HHs (99 per cent) obtained ration cards, in 2001. The BPL HHs and APL HHs account for 69.57 per cent and 30.43 per cent, respectively, of the total ration cards in the State. However, there are insignificant variations in the distribution of ration cards among the regions and districts. In Andhra region, more than 100 per cent HHs have obtained ration cards, followed by Telengana (98 per cent) and Rayalaseema (96 per cent). Similarly, there are variations among the districts. The highest is in Hyderabad (118 per cent HHs) and the lowest is Khammam, Chittoor and Rangareddy (92 per cent HHs).

With regard to the distribution of ration cards to the BPL HHs, Andhra and Rayalaseema regions account for seventy per cent of the total cards distributed in the State. While Telangana region account for nearly two-thirds of (63 per cent) of the total cardholders. There are also variations among the districts ranging 32 per cent to 81 per cent of the HHs received the ration cards. The highest number of BPL cards distribution is in Vizianagaram (81 per cent) and Srikakulam (80 per cent) and the lowest number is in Hyderabad (32 per cent), Rangareddy (57 per cent) and Nizamabad (61 per cent).

In 2011, of the total number of HHs, more than hundred per cent (119 per cent) obtained the ration cards, indicating that the ration cards are more than the HHs in the State. The number of HHs obtained white cards and APL/pink cards are accounting for 106 per cent and 14 per cent of the total HHS, respectively, in the State. Recognising this fact in 2010, the government has directed the officials to eliminate the bogus cards by conducting Gram Sabha's throughout the State. Despite this, the number of ration cards has increased in the subsequent years. The region-wise analysis reveals that it is almost reflecting the State average in all the regions.

During the past one and a half decades (1998-99 to 2012-13), on an average the government granted 8,99,887 ration cards to the BPL and APL HHs in the State. Of this, nearly 80 per cent are white cardholders. However, there are variations in the distribution of ration cards in different years and among regions and districts. There is a gradual increase in granting the cards from 1998-99 to 2005-06 and it is very high from 2006-07 onwards. The districts, which has more than the State average number of cards are East Godavari, Guntur, Krishna, West Godavari and Visakhapatnam in Andhra region; while it is Warangal, Hyderabad, Rangareddy and Karimnagar districts in Telangana region. In Rayalaseema, region Chittoor and Ananatapur districts received the highest number of ration cards. This is mostly due to the 'vote security' approach of the then government. Similar trend prevailed in all the regions and districts. The administrative machinery has succumbed to pressure of the ruling class and failed to arrest the malpractices.

Distribution of Foodgrains to the Cardholders

The analysis shows that ensuring food security to the poor through public policies appears to be gigantic task in the State. The State government, in 2011-12, has distributed 3168969 tonnes (3168969000 kgs) of foodgrains (rice and wheat) to the cardholders in the state. If we distribute it to the total population, it works out to be 37.45 kgs and 3.12 kgs per person per year and per month, respectively. The distribution of foodgrains per hh per year and per month works out to be 150.72 kgs per year and 12.56 kgs per month, respectively, in the State. The average foodgrain distribution to the BPL cardholders was less than the above i.e. 142.33 kgs per year 11.86 kgs per month. It is pertinent to mention here that the computation is on the assumption that (a) PDS foodgrains are distributed equally among the whole hhs/ population in the state, and (b) that no diversion of foodgrains from PDS to the open market.

If the foodgrain requirement were taken as 450gms per person per day, the foodgrains supplied under PDS would make available for six days and seven days in a month to the total cardholders and white cardholders, respectively, in the State. In other words, PDS contributed to about 20 per cent of the total foodgrain requirement of the HHs. For the remaining 24/23 days (80 per cent) he/she has to depend on the open market or foodgrains produced in their own fields.

While we analyse distribution of rice (subsidised and non-subsidised), during one and a half decades (1998-99 to 2012-13), it discloses that the government, on an average, distributed 1,77,972 quintals (qls) of rice to the BPL and APL HHs and the social welfare institutions. The analysis unfolds that overwhelming percentage (91.4 per cent) rice is distributed to White cardholders, including AAY and Annapurna. The remaining of it (7.5 per cent) is distributed to APL cardholders. However, the official document of these categories is doubtful, as considerable percentage of APL HHs have obtained the BPL ration cards. There are variations in the distribution of rice in different years and among regions and districts. There is enormous increase in the allotment of rice to the districts, during the years 2004-05 and 2009-10, in which State Assembly elections were held. This indicates that the ruling party considered the PDS as 'vote security programme'.

Region-wise analysis reveals that rice distribution is more in Andhra region followed by Rayalaseema higher than State average. The districts, which received highest number of qtls of rice i.e. more than the State average, are East Godavari, Guntur, West Godavari and Visakhapatnam, Krishna in Andhra region; while it is Warangal, Mahabubnagar, Rangareddy and Karimnagar districts in Telangana region. In Rayalaseema, region Chittoor and Ananatapur districts received the highest quantity of rice. The districts which received lowest quantity of rice (less than the State average) are Vizianagaram and Srikakulam, Nellore and Prakasam districts in Andhra region; Cuddapah and Kurnool in Rayalaseema region; Nizamabad, Khammam, Adilabad, Hyderabad, Medak and Nalgonda districts in Telangana region.

Distribution of Wheat

An examination of the distribution of wheat, during 1998-99 to 2012-13, reveals that on an average, 1,797 tonnes per year is distributed to the cardholders in the State. If we share this to the total White cardholders/hhs (22264634), it works out to be eight kgs and 0.66 kgs per cardholder per year and per month. There are variations in the distribution of wheat in different years and among regions and districts. This is mostly due to the policy change in the allotment of foodgrains to different categories/ groups/ institutions. Prior to 1997 the State government used to procure wheat from Central government for distribution to APL/BPL cardholders, but the Government subsequently gave priority to the Subsidised Rice Scheme (SRS) to the target group and social welfare institutions.

Distribution of Sugar

With regard to the distribution of sugar, during 1998-99 to 2012-13 the data reveals that on an average, 6,578 tonnes is distributed to the cardholders in the State. If we compute this to the total White cardholders/hhs in the State, it works out to be 29.54 kgs and 2.5 kgs per cardholder per year and per month. There are variations in the distribution of Sugar in different years and among regions and districts.

Governance Challenges

Despite government's initiatives for ensuring food security to the people, reports of hunger and malnutrition have been pouring in from different parts of the country. An assessment of the governance of food security policies reveals that there is a wide gap between promise and performance, mostly due to the failure of governance of food security programmes. Firstly, there is no democratic governance. The real beneficiaries are not involved in core components of democratic governance- the formulation, implementation, monitoring and supervision and evaluation of policies. These are prerequisites for effective governance of any policy, including FS policy. Secondly, most of the provisions of the FS projects/policies are suggested/ determined by the donor agencies or IGOs, as the latter extend financial and technical support for the projects. With the result the policies have not taken into account the cultural habits or food habits/practices, food sovereignty, regional and seasonal variations, family size, age group, gender, and adequate quantity and quality of foodgrains. Thirdly, at the state and below levels, the decision-making on the issues like, procurement and distribution of foodgrains, minimum support price is mostly influenced by multiple actors like agricultural commission agents, rice millers, FPS dealers, transport agents for their benefits, which affect the proper implementation of programmes. In fact, they determine 'what a Food Security policy should accomplish'. Fourthly, the lack of integrated administrative structure is causing for ineffectiveness of the policies. Multiple Ministries/Departments are associated with the decision-making on the issues related to the FS policies. Ensuring coordination from various departments is a formidable task to the authorities concerned at all levels of government. Fifthly, ensuring availability, accessibility of nutritious food in adequate quantity and food sovereignty to all the people and on a consistent basis are the formidable challenges of the governance, especially at the grassroot level. Sixthly, the foodgrain items like red-gram dal, Palm oil (edible oil) etc, distributed under PDS are imported from other countries, which are not tasty or normal/ habitual food of local people. Lastly, privatisation of agriculture sector, and priority to commercial crops, allowing Foreign Direct Investment (FDI) in food and agriculture related segments would not only undermine India's sovereignty, but also make the country to depend on the food crops industry, located within or outside the country. The genetically engineered crops are major invaders on the food crop area. For instance, 30 per cent of food production area had been occupied by Bt cotton in the past decade and this situation is threatening the food security and food sovereignty of communities in several states, especially the Telangana region of AP.

All the above factors collectively and individually are weakening the food security policies and its governance. Even the 'so called NPM model'–efficiency, effectiveness, economy, transparent, responsive and accountability have not succeeded in managing the Food Security policies in India. Therefore, the potential of these policies, largely depend, on the community participation in evolving the policies based on the ground realities; ensuring food sovereignty to the beneficiaries; regulating the private traders in procurement, storage and distribution of foodgrains; allocation of more budgets to agriculture and taking necessary measures to increase the production. These factors in fact, would ensure democratic governance of FS policies - legitimacy; accountability; competency; participatory; consensus; equitable and inclusive: respect for law and protection of human rights, etc. Democratic governance is recognised as one of the important strategies of FS policies to identify the eligible target groups; make the target group/s access to adequate quantity and quality of food; and ensure food sovereignty of the people; etc., rather than mere receivers of foodgrains supplied by government agencies. Thus, people-centred governance in the design, implementation, monitoring and evaluation are prerequisites for the success of the programme.

In this context, the democratic governance, with emphasis on involvement of community (all the social groups) in the management of FS policies, appears to be better model, compared to State-centred model (bureaucratic) and NPM model (more incentives to the individual or private agencies) to overcome the obstacles of FS policies. The Deccan Development Society (DDS) an NGO based in Medak District (now Telangana State) of Andhra Pradesh has developed an alternative strategy for PDS on the lines of democratic governance. It is an innovative programme. It has evolved local solutions for local problems, where foodgrain production, procurement, storage and distribution are done at community/village level and are entirely managed by the women sangham members. The programme integrates sustainable agricultural goals such as bio-diversity and soil fertility with community goals of rural livelihoods, food security and socio-economic empowerment of dalits and women based on plural values, local customs and practices and indigenous knowledge. The strategy of DDS is based on the principles: evolving strategy/ planning with community participation; taking decisions based on the ideas that originate in the village; local community and their traditional knowledge, community spirit are the main resources; flexibility in framing the rules suitable to the local conditions; mutual learning and sharing experience; continuous monitoring of the programme by the community; and, the main goal is to think systemic, holistic that integrates bio-diversity, natural resource management with rural livelihoods and empowerment of community (DDS, 2004).

The field study unfolds that most of the sample beneficiaries of PDS belong to all the castes and communities, especially Hindu and belong to middle and young age groups; are illiterate and/or have completed primary and upper primary education. The demographic features of the respondents' reveal that the average size of the family is five and the percentage of male population is more than the female. The analysis indicates that people of all castes have access to PDS in the district. However, the civil supplies department has issued ration cards in the name of male members. This indicates that the patriarchy system is still dominant in granting ration cards to the HHs. This is also true in other poverty alleviation programmes. In this context, the Telangana State's recent decision to issue ration cards in the name of female members of the households is a positive measure towards the process of empowerment of women.

Most of the respondents belong to the marginal and small farmers' categories; lower and middle-income groups and their primary occupations are agriculture, agricultural labour and non-agricultural labour. The average number of workers in the family is three, especially male as wage/income earners. The outstanding debt of the respondents is less than one lakh. Further, the analysis reveals that considerable numbers of respondents, who are ineligible on the criteria of income/ land, have acquired the ration cards and access to foodgrains under PDS in the district. The caste-wise analysis reveals that the upper caste respondents have better economic conditions in terms of primary occupation, land ownership, income generation etc., compared to other communities. The public policies have not contributed much for change in the occupations of lower castes. They are still dependent on the agricultural labour and non-agricultural labour.

However, there is a shift in the occupational status of the household members, especially younger generation, from their parental occupation or traditional rural artisan occupation. The household members' dependency on agriculture has declined (only 17 per cent are dependent on agriculture). However, the analysis reveals that the households are giving priority to human resources development, as two-thirds of the members are pursuing education and working as self-employed. The members are giving priority to the education and self-employment. It is pertinent to note that though the respondents got ration cards and have access to PDS, their children are not availing the MDM partly because the children are pursuing education in private schools since the parents believe that private English medium schools are better than the Government Telugu medium schools, where no such facility exists. The non-availment of MDM scheme by the students is also due to the supply of poor quality of food supplied at public schools.

The field study reveals that improving irrigation facilities, supply of agricultural inputs, uninterrupted and quality power supply, access to credit institutions, enhancing MSP and more public expenditure in agricultural sector, arresting malpractices in market yards and commission agents/traders, providing proper storage facilities at the village level or cluster of villages, etc, would not only promote agricultural production, but also make people to get access to the foodgrains and to some extent reduce burden on the TPDS in the district. The analysis reveals that the government is operating PDS and rythubazzars (where the foodgrains are supplied at less than the market rate) to ensure availability of essential commodities at the village level. However, the later is mostly accessible to the urban and middle class, while the former is to the rural people. Further, the analysis reveals that there is a need to control disgraceful marketing strategies of private companies- posters and displacing the information comparing advantages and disadvantages of their products with that of palm-oil and attracting the consumers to the products. The relatively better-off people are purchasing oil from the branded companies by paying higher price.

The study reveals that majority of non-poor, especially medium and large farmers obtained white ration cards with the support of politicians and bureaucracy. They are availing the pensions, medical relief and foodgrains for more than one decade. The government is not reviewing the status of cardholders and not taking measures to correct the irregularities. On the other hand, it is issuing new ration cards or temporary cards at the Rachhabanda, conducted by government three times in a year. All these trends are contributing to increase number of ration cards, sometimes more than the total HHs in the village, indicating the ineffectiveness of the governance at the grass-roots level.

These trends indicate that the governance of food security policies is symbolising F.W. Riggs' 'Prismatic Society'- 'Formalism', 'Overlapping' and 'Heterogeneity',- (proposed in 1960s), the characteristies of underdeveloped countries. In spite of six and a half decades or more, the governance system has not reformed its organisational structures to meet the challenges in the formulation and implementation of policies and programmes effectively. This is not only unique in the implementation of food security policies, but also exists in almost all poverty alleviation programmes in the State.

The quantity of foodgrains consumed by the respondents procured both from PDS and open market, unfolds that the quantity supplied under PDS, especially rice, sugar are not adequate to meet the monthly consumption demand of the family. Many respondents, especially the poor respondents are compelled to purchase equal quantity or more from the open market at higher price. The other commodities supplied under PDS are not in demand. The field analysis reveals that TPDS has contributed to a saving about Rs 400 to Rs 500 per month to each HH, as each HH received about 18 kgs rice per month under PDS at Re one per kg, which is normally priced Rs 25-30 in the open market. The saving is almost equivalent to the expenditure incurred on health and education of the HH in a month.

Respondents opt for local products/self-produced products suitable to their taste and choice. These trends suggest that it is better to supply the commodities, which are produced at local level similar to Mana Biyyam – Mana Kosam policy – through the FPS. This would not only ensure the supply of good quality foodgrains at cheaper rate to the target group, but also control food inflation in the State. Further, the analysis unfolds that doubling/enhancing the quantity of foodgrains from 4 kgs to 8 kgs rice per person per month and other essential commodities under PDS would enable the BPL HHs to meet their monthly demand.

While framing the food security policies the major concerns of the government need to be on giving priority to food sovereignty of people and democratisation of governance; decentralised decision-making; coordination between the Centre and State governments; initiating measures to increase the agricultural growth across all regions; restricting the indiscriminate/wholesale transfer of productive natural resources-land and water- to non-agricultural purposes and the commercialisation of agriculture; supply of agricultural inputs at subsidised rates to the farmers; control of food inflation and control over food markets; giving autonomy to the states in evolving the norms for identification of target groups; nutritional security suitable to cultural/traditions of a particular region; supply of millets, pulses and egg and milk under PDS; arresting the leakages in the distribution of foodgrains; introduction of cash transfers in place of distribution of foodgrains, etc. These measures are important for addressing the issues related to food security, as an immediate concern. Nevertheless, the elimination of hunger, malnutrition, poverty, inequalities, and ensuring inclusive growth in the society are the long-term concern of the State, which require a multi-prolonged strategy involving policies and programmes that bring about both the incremental and structural changes.

Thus, Food security policies are incremental in nature, as they would give temporary relief to poor to overcome their problems. The TPDS will serve the purpose of postponing the issues of food insecurity and inequalities in the society. The better-endowed regions and traders/ millers, bureaucracy and non-poor have a built-in gravitational pull to avail the benefits of the policy. The policy has a propensity to respond to better-off people/conditions rather than create those conditions for effective implementation of food security programmes. This indicates that the failure of the policy and its governance, both in terms of their capacity to intervene and transform the existing conditions in which poor people have been trapped for centuries. Above all, lack of political will to ensure food security to poor is the major concern of the governance. Every political party/ government viewed the food security initiatives as an instrument to get 'vote security' system and remain in power.

Index